ABOUT THIS PUBLICATION

FOR SERVICE ASSISTANCE

Customer Service
1.704.898.0770

North Carolina General Statues is published by The Muliti-Media Group of Greater Charlotte in Charlotte, North Carolina. Copyright 2015 by the Multi-Media Group of Greater Charlotte. This book or parts thereof may not be reproduced in any form, stored in a retrieval system, or transmitted in any form by any means—electronic, mechanical, photocopy, recording or otherwise—without prior written permission of the publisher, except as provided by United States of America copyright law.

The records required by U.S. Code 2257(a) through (c) and the pertinent regulations 28 C.F.R. Cli. 1, Part 75 with respect to this publication and all materials associated with such records are maintained by The Multi-Media Group of Greater Charlotte, Publisher and available for review by Attorney General.

www.visionbooks.org

Copyright © 2015 by MMGGC
All rights reserved!

TID: 4989448
ISBN (10) digit: 1502305798
ISBN (13) digit: 978-1502305794

123-4-56789-01239-Paperback
123-4-56789-01239-Hardback

First Edition

090520140547

Printed in the United States of America

2015 EDITION

North Carolina Criminal Law And Procedure-Pamphlet # 39

Printed In conjunction with the Administration of the Courts

North Carolina Criminal Law and Procedure
Pamphlet Reference Guide

Chapters	Pamphlet
Chapter 1 Civil Procedure	1
Chapter 1 Civil Procedure (Continue)	2
Chapter 1A Rules of Civil Procedure	2
Chapter 1B Contribution.	2
Chapter 1C Enforcement of Judgments.	2
Chapter 1D Punitive Damages.	2
Chapter 1E Eastern Band of Cherokee Indians.	2
Chapter 1F North Carolina Uniform Interstate Depositions and Discovery Act.	2
Chapter 2 - Clerk of Superior Court [Repealed and Transferred.]	3
Chapter 3 - Commissioners of Affidavits and Deeds [Repealed.]	3
Chapter 4 - Common Law	3
Chapter 5 - Contempt [Repealed.]	3
Chapter 5A - Contempt	3
Chapter 6 - Liability for Court Costs	3
Chapter 7 - Courts [Repealed and Transferred.]	3
Chapter 7A – Judicial Department	3
Chapter 7A – Continuation (Judicial Department)	4
Chapter 7A – Continuation (Judicial Department)	5
Chapter 7B - Juvenile Code	5
Chapter 8 - Evidence	6
Chapter 8A - Interpreters for Deaf Persons [Recodified.]	6
Chapter 8B - Interpreters for Deaf Persons	6
Chapter 8C - Evidence Code	6
Chapter 9 - Jurors	6
Chapter 10 - Notaries [Repealed.]	6
Chapter 10A - Notaries [Recodified.]	6
Chapter 10B - Notaries	6
Chapter 11 - Oaths	6
Chapter 12 - Statutory Construction	6
Chapter 13 - Citizenship Restored	6
Chapter 14 - Criminal Law	7
Chapter 14 –Criminal Law (Continuation)	8
Chapter 15 - Criminal Procedure	9
Chapter 15A - Criminal Procedure Act (Continuation)	10
Chapter 15A - Criminal Procedure Act (Continuation)	11
Chapter 15B - Victims Compensation	11
Chapter 15C - Address Confidentiality Program	11
Chapter 16 - Gaming Contracts and Futures	11
Chapter 17 - Habeas Corpus	11

Chapter 17A - Law-Enforcement Officers [Recodified.]	11
Chapter 17B - North Carolina Criminal Justice Education and Training System [Recodified.] Chapter 17C - North Carolina Criminal Justice Education and Training Standards Commission	11 11
Chapter 17D - North Carolina Justice Academy	11
Chapter 17E - North Carolina Sheriffs' Education and Training Standards Commission	11
Chapter 18 - Regulation of Intoxicating Liquors [Repealed.]	12
Chapter 18A - Regulation of Intoxicating Liquors [Repealed.]	12
Chapter 18B - Regulation of Alcoholic Beverages	12
Chapter 18C - North Carolina State Lottery	12
Chapter 19 - Offenses against Public Morals	12
Chapter 19A - Protection of Animals	12
Chapter 20 - Motor Vehicles	13
Chapter 20 - Motor Vehicles (Continuation)	14
Chapter 20 - Motor Vehicles (Continuation)	15
Chapter 20 - Motor Vehicles (Continuation)	16
Chapter 21 - Bills of Lading	17
Chapter 22 - Contracts Requiring Writing	17
Chapter 22A - Signatures	17
Chapter 22B - Contracts Against Public Policy	17
Chapter 22C - Payments to Subcontractors	17
Chapter 23 - Debtor and Creditor.	17
Chapter 24 – Interest	17
Chapter 25 – Uniform Commercial Code	18
Chapter 25 – Uniform Commercial Code (Continuation)	19
Chapter 25A – Retail Installment Sales Act	20
Chapter 25B - Credit	20
Chapter 25C - Sales of Artwork	20
Chapter 26 - Suretyship	20
Chapter 27 - Warehouse Receipts [Repealed.]	20
Chapter 28 - Administration [Repealed.]	20
Chapter 28A - Administration of Decedents' Estates	20
Chapter 28B - Estates of Absentees in Military Service	20
Chapter 28C - Estates of Missing Persons	20
Chapter 29 - Intestate Succession	21
Chapter 30 - Surviving Spouses	21
Chapter 31 - Wills	21
Chapter 31A - Acts Barring Property Rights	21
Chapter 31B - Renunciation of Property and Renunciation of Fiduciary Powers Act	21
Chapter 31C - Uniform Disposition of Community Property Rights at Death Act	21
Chapter 32 - Fiduciaries	21
Chapter 32A - Powers of Attorney	21
Chapter 33 - Guardian and Ward [Repealed and Recodified.]	21

Chapter 33A - North Carolina Uniform Transfers to Minors Act	21
Chapter 33B - North Carolina Uniform Custodial Trust Act	21
Chapter 34 - Veterans' Guardianship Act	22
Chapter 35 - Sterilization Procedures	22
Chapter 35A - Incompetency and Guardianship	22
Chapter 36 - Trusts and Trustees [Repealed.]	22
Chapter 36A - Trusts and Trustees	22
Chapter 36B - Uniform Management of Institutional Funds Act [Repealed.]	22
Chapter 36C - North Carolina Uniform Trust Code	22
Chapter 36D - North Carolina Community Third Party Trusts, Pooled Trusts	23
Chapter 36E - Uniform Prudent Management of Institutional Funds Act	23
Chapter 37 - Allocation of Principal and Income [Repealed.]	23
Chapter 37A - Uniform Principal and Income Act	23
Chapter 38 - Boundaries	23
Chapter 38A - Landowner Liability	23
Chapter 39 - Conveyances	23
Chapter 39A - Transfer Fee Covenants Prohibited	23
Chapter 40 - Eminent Domain [Repealed.]	23
Chapter 40A - Eminent Domain	23
Chapter 41 - Estates	23
Chapter 41A - State Fair Housing Act	23
Chapter 42 - Landlord and Tenant	23
Chapter 42A - Vacation Rental Act	23
Chapter 43 - Land Registration	23
Chapter 44 - Liens	24
Chapter 44A - Statutory Liens and Charges	24
Chapter 45 - Mortgages and Deeds of Trust	24
Chapter 45A - Good Funds Settlement Act	24
Chapter 46 - Partition	24
Chapter 47 - Probate and Registration	25
Chapter 47A - Unit Ownership	25
Chapter 47B - Real Property Marketable Title Act	25
Chapter 47C - North Carolina Condominium Act	25
Chapter 47D - Notice of Settlement Act [Expired.]	25
Chapter 47E - Residential Property Disclosure Act	25
Chapter 47F - North Carolina Planned Community Act	25
Chapter 47G - Option to Purchase Contracts	25
Chapter 47H - Contracts for Deed	25
Chapter 48 - Adoptions +	26
Chapter 48A - Minors	26
Chapter 49 - Bastardy	26
Chapter 49A - Rights of Children	26
Chapter 50 - Divorce and Alimony	26
Chapter 50A - Uniform Child-Custody Jurisdiction and	

Enforcement Act	26
Chapter 50B - Domestic Violence	26
Chapter 50C - Civil No-Contact Orders	26
Chapter 51 - Marriage	26
Chapter 52 - Powers and Liabilities of Married Persons	27
Chapter 52A - Uniform Reciprocal Enforcement of Support Act [Repealed.]	27
Chapter 52B - Uniform Premarital Agreement Act	27
Chapter 52C - Uniform Interstate Family Support Act	27
Chapter 53 - Banks	27
Chapter 53A - Business Development Corporations and North Carolina Capital Resource Corporations	28
Chapter 53B - Financial Privacy Act	28
Chapter 54 - Cooperative Organizations	28
Chapter 54A - Capital Stock Savings and Loan Associations [Repealed.]	28
Chapter 54B - Savings and Loan Associations	29
Chapter 54C - Savings Banks	29
Chapter 55 - North Carolina Business Corporation Act	30
Chapter 55A - North Carolina Nonprofit Corporation Act	31
Chapter 55B - Professional Corporation Act	31
Chapter 55C - Foreign Trade Zones	31
Chapter 55D - Filings, Names, and Registered Agents for Corporations, Nonprofit Corporations, and Partnerships	31
Chapter 56 - Electric, Telegraph and Power Companies [Repealed.]	31
Chapter 57 - Hospital, Medical and Dental Service Corporations [Recodified.]	31
Chapter 57A - Health Maintenance Organization Act [Recodified.]	31
Chapter 57B - Health Maintenance Organization Act [Recodified.]	31
Chapter 57C - North Carolina Limited Liability Company Act.	31
Chapter 58 - Insurance.	32
Chapter 58 - Insurance (Continuation)	33
Chapter 58 - Insurance (Continuation)	34
Chapter 58 - Insurance (Continuation)	35
Chapter 58 - Insurance (Continuation)	36
Chapter 58 - Insurance (Continuation)	37
Chapter 58 - Insurance (Continuation)	38
Chapter 58A - North Carolina Health Insurance Trust Commission [Recodified.]	38
Chapter 59 - Partnership.	39
Chapter 59B - Uniform Unincorporated Nonprofit Association Act.	39
Chapter 60 - Railroads and Other Carriers [Repealed and Transferred.]	39
Chapter 61 - Religious Societies	39
Chapter 62 - Public Utilities	39

Chapter 62 - Public Utilities (Continuation)	40
Chapter 62A - Public Safety Telephone Service And Wireless Telephone Service	40
Chapter 63 - Aeronautics	40
Chapter 63A - North Carolina Global TransPark Authority	40
Chapter 64 - Aliens	40
Chapter 65 – Cemeteries	40
Chapter 66 - Commerce and Business	41
Chapter 67 - Dogs	41
Chapter 68 - Fences and Stock Law	41
Chapter 69 - Fire Protection	41
Chapter 70 - Indian Antiquities, Archaeological Resources and Unmarked Human Skeletal Remains Protection	42
Chapter 71 - Indians [Repealed.]	42
Chapter 71A - Indians	42
Chapter 72 - Inns, Hotels and Restaurants	42
Chapter 73 - Mills	42
Chapter 74 - Mines and Quarries	42
Chapter 74A - Company Police [Repealed.]	42
Chapter 74B - Private Protective Services Act [Repealed.]	42
Chapter 74C - Private Protective Services	42
Chapter 74D - Alarm Systems	42
Chapter 74E - Company Police Act	42
Chapter 74F - Locksmith Licensing Act	42
Chapter 74G - Campus Police Act	42
Chapter 75 - Monopolies, Trusts and Consumer Protection	42
Chapter 75A - Boating and Water Safety	43
Chapter 75B - Discrimination in Business	43
Chapter 75C - Motion Picture Fair Competition Act	43
Chapter 75D - Racketeer Influenced and Corrupt Organizations	43
Chapter 75E - Unlawful Activities in Connection With Certain Corporate Transactions	43
Chapter 76 - Navigation	43
Chapter 76A - Navigation and Pilotage Commissions	43
Chapter 77 - Rivers, Creeks, and Coastal Waters	43
Chapter 78 - Securities Law [Repealed.]	43
Chapter 78A - North Carolina Securities Act	43
Chapter 78B - Tender Offer Disclosure Act [Repealed.]	43
Chapter 78C - Investment Advisers	43
Chapter 78D - Commodities Act	43
Chapter 79 - Strays [Repealed.]	43
Chapter 80 - Trademarks, Brands, etc.	44
Chapter 81 - Weights and Measures [Recodified.]	44
Chapter 81A - Weights and Measures Act of 1975.	44
Chapter 82 - Wrecks [Repealed.]	44
Chapter 83 - Architects [Recodified.]	44

Chapter 83A - Architects	44
Chapter 84 - Attorneys-at-Law	44
Chapter 84A - Foreign Legal Consultants	44
Chapter 85 - Auctions and Auctioneers [Repealed.]	44
Chapter 85A - Bail Bondsmen and Runners [Recodified.]	44
Chapter 85B - Auctions and Auctioneers	44
Chapter 85C - Bail Bondsmen and Runners [Recodified.]	44
Chapter 86 - Barbers [Recodified.]	44
Chapter 86A - Barbers	44
Chapter 87 - Contractors	44
Chapter 88 - Cosmetic Art [Repealed.]	44
Chapter 88A - Electrolysis Practice Act	44
Chapter 88B - Cosmetic Art	45
Chapter 89 - Engineering and Land Surveying [Recodified.]	45
Chapter 89A - Landscape Architects	45
Chapter 89B - Foresters	45
Chapter 89C - Engineering and Land Surveying	45
Chapter 89D - Landscape Contractors	45
Chapter 89E - Geologists Licensing Act	45
Chapter 89F - North Carolina Soil Scientist Licensing Act	45
Chapter 89G - Irrigation Contractors	45
Chapter 90 - Medicine and Allied Occupations	45
Chapter 90 - Medicine and Allied Occupations (Continuation)	46
Chapter 90 - Medicine and Allied Occupations (Continuation)	47
Chapter 90 - Medicine and Allied Occupations (Continuation)	48
Chapter 90A - Sanitarians and Water and Wastewater Treatment Facility Operators	48
Chapter 90B - Social Worker Certification and Licensure Act	48
Chapter 90C - North Carolina Recreational Therapy Licensure Act	48
Chapter 90D - Interpreters and Transliterators	48
Chapter 91 - Pawnbrokers [Repealed.]	48
Chapter 91A - Pawnbrokers Modernization Act of 1989	48
Chapter 92 - Photographers [Deleted.]	48
Chapter 93 - Certified Public Accountants	48
Chapter 93A - Real Estate License Law	49
Chapter 93B - Occupational Licensing Boards	49
Chapter 93C - Watchmakers [Repealed.]	49
Chapter 93D - North Carolina State Hearing Aid Dealers and Fitters Board.	49
Chapter 93E - North Carolina Appraisers Act	49
Chapter 94 - Apprenticeship	49
Chapter 95 - Department of Labor and Labor Regulations	49
Chapter 95 - Department of Labor and Labor Regulations (Continuation)	50
Chapter 96 - Employment Security	50
Chapter 97 - Workers' Compensation Act	50
Chapter 97 - Workers' Compensation Act (Continuation)	51

Chapter 98 - Burnt and Lost Records	51
Chapter 99 - Libel and Slander	51
Chapter 99A - Civil Remedies for Criminal Actions	51
Chapter 99B - Products Liability	51
Chapter 99C - Actions Relating to Winter Sports Safety and Accidents	51
Chapter 99D - Civil Rights	51
Chapter 99E - Special Liability Provisions	51
Chapter 100 - Monuments, Memorials and Parks	51
Chapter 101 - Names of Persons	51
Chapter 102 - Official Survey Base	51
Chapter 103 - Sundays, Holidays and Special Days	51
Chapter 104 - United States Lands	51
Chapter 104A - Degrees of Kinship	51
Chapter 104B - Hurricanes or Other Acts of Nature	51
Chapter 104C - Atomic Energy, Radioactivity and Ionizing Radiation [Repealed and Recodified.]	51
Chapter 104D - Southern States Energy Compact	51
Chapter 104E - North Carolina Radiation Protection Act	51
Chapter 104F - Southeast Interstate Low-Level Radioactive Waste Management Compact [Repealed]	51
Chapter 104G - North Carolina Low-Level Radioactive Waste Management Authority Act of 1987 [Repealed]	51
Chapter 105 - Taxation	51
Chapter 105 - Taxation (Continuation)	52
Chapter 105 - Taxation (Continuation)	53
Chapter 105 - Taxation (Continuation)	54
Chapter 105A - Setoff Debt Collection Act	55
Chapter 105B - Defaulted Student Loan Recovery Act	55
Chapter 106 - Agriculture	55
Chapter 106 - Agriculture (Continue)	56
Chapter 106 - Agriculture (Continue)	57
Chapter 107 - Agricultural Development Districts [Repealed.]	57
Chapter 108 - Social Services [Repealed and Recodified.]	57
Chapter 108A - Social Services	57
Chapter 108B - Community Action Programs	58
Chapter 108C Medicaid and Health Choice Provider Requirements.	58
Chapter 108D Medicaid Managed Care for Behavioral Health Services.	58
Chapter 109 - Bonds [Recodified.]	58
Chapter 110 - Child Welfare	58
Chapter 111 - Aid to the Blind	58
Chapter 112 - Confederate Homes and Pensions [Repealed.]	58
Chapter 113 - Conservation and Development	58
Chapter 113 - Conservation and Development (Continuation)	59

Chapter 113A - Pollution Control and Environment	59
Chapter 113A - Pollution Control and Environment (Continuation)	60
Chapter 113B - North Carolina Energy Policy Act of 1975	60
Chapter 114 - Department of Justice	60
Chapter 115 - Elementary and Secondary Education [Repealed.]	60
Chapter 115A - Community Colleges, Technical Institutes, and Industrial Education Centers [Repealed.]	60
Chapter 115B - Tuition and Fee Waivers	60
Chapter 115C - Elementary and Secondary Education	60
Chapter 115C - Elementary and Secondary Education (Continuation)	61
Chapter 115C - Elementary and Secondary Education (Continuation)	62
Chapter 115C - Elementary and Secondary Education (Continuation)	63
Chapter 115D - Community Colleges	63
Chapter 115E - Private Educational Facilities Finance Act [Recodified]	63
Chapter 116 - Higher Education	63
Chapter 116 - Higher Education (Continuation)	63
Chapter 116A - Escheats and Abandoned Property [Repealed.]	64
Chapter 116B - Escheats and Abandoned Property	64
Chapter 116C - Continuum of Education Programs	64
Chapter 116D - Higher Education Bonds	64
Chapter 117 - Electrification	64
Chapter 118 - Firemen's and Rescue Squad Workers' Relief and Pension Funds [Recodified.]	64
Chapter 118A - Firemen's Death Benefit Act [Repealed.]	64
Chapter 118B - Members of a Rescue Squad Death Benefit Act [Repealed.]	64
Chapter 119 - Gasoline and Oil Inspection and Regulation	64
Chapter 120 - General Assembly	65
Chapter 120 - General Assembly (Continuation)	66
Chapter 120 - General Assembly (Continuation)	67
Chapter 120C - Lobbying	67
Chapter 121 - Archives and History	67
Chapter 122 - Hospitals for the Mentally Disordered [Repealed.]	67
Chapter 122A - North Carolina Housing Finance Agency	67
Chapter 122B - North Carolina Agricultural Facilities Finance Act [Repealed.]	67
Chapter 122C - Mental Health, Developmental Disabilities, and Substance Abuse Act of 1985	67
Chapter 122C - Mental Health, Developmental Disabilities, and Substance Abuse Act of 1985 (Continuation)	68
Chapter 122D - North Carolina Agricultural Finance Act	68

Chapter 122E - North Carolina Housing Trust and Oil Overcharge Act	68
Chapter 123 - Impeachment	69
Chapter 123A - Industrial Development [Repealed.]	69
Chapter 124 - Internal Improvements	69
Chapter 125 - Libraries	69
Chapter 126 - State Personnel System	69
Chapter 127 - Militia [Repealed.]	69
Chapter 127A - Militia	69
Chapter 127B - Military Affairs	69
Chapter 127C - Advisory Commission on Military Affairs	69
Chapter 128 - Offices and Public Officers	69
Chapter 128 - Offices and Public Officers (Continuation)	70
Chapter 129 - Public Buildings and Grounds	70
Chapter 130 - Public Health [Repealed.]	70
Chapter 130A - Public Health	70
Chapter 130A - Public Health (Continuation)	71
Chapter 130A - Public Health (Continuation)	72
Chapter 130B - Hazardous Waste Management Commission [Repealed.]	72
Chapter 131 - Public Hospitals [Repealed.]	72
Chapter 131A - Health Care Facilities Finance Act	72
Chapter 131B - Licensing of Ambulatory Surgical Facilities [Repealed.]	72
Chapter 131C - Charitable Solicitation Licensure Act [Repealed.]	72
Chapter 131D - Inspection and Licensing of Facilities	72
Chapter 131E - Health Care Facilities and Services	72
Chapter 131E - Health Care Facilities and Services (Continuation)	73
Chapter 131F - Solicitation of Contributions	73
Chapter 132 - Public Records	73
Chapter 133 - Public Works	74
Chapter 134 - Youth Development [Recodified.]	74
Chapter 134A - Youth Services [Repealed.]	74
Chapter 135 - Retirement System for Teachers and State Employees; Social Security; Health Insurance Program for Children	74
Chapter 135 - Retirement System for Teachers and State Employees; Social Security; Health Insurance Program for Children	75
Chapter 136 - Transportation	75
Chapter 136 - Transportation (Continuation)	76
Chapter 137 - Rural Rehabilitation [Repealed.]	76
Chapter 138 - Salaries, Fees and Allowances	76
Chapter 138A - State Government Ethics Act	76
Chapter 139 - Soil and Water Conservation Districts	76

Chapter 140 - State Art Museum; Symphony and Art Societies	76
Chapter 140A - State Awards System	76
Chapter 141 - State Boundaries	76
Chapter 142 - State Debt	76
Chapter 143 - State Departments, Institutions, and Commissions	77
Chapter 143 - State Departments, Institutions, and Commissions (Continuation)	78
Chapter 143 - State Departments, Institutions, and Commissions (Continuation)	79
Chapter 143 - State Departments, Institutions, and Commissions (Continuation)	80
Chapter 143A - State Government Reorganization	80
Chapter 143B - Executive Organization Act of 1973	80
Chapter 143B - Executive Organization Act of 1973 (Continuation)	81
Chapter 143B - Executive Organization Act of 1973 (Continuation)	82
Chapter 143C - State Budget Act	83
Chapter 143D - The State Governmental Accountability and Internal Control Act	83
Chapter 144 - State Flag, Official Governmental Flags, Motto, and Colors	83
Chapter 145 - State Symbols and Other Official Adoptions.	83
Chapter 146 - State Lands	83
Chapter 147 - State Officers	83
Chapter 148 - State Prison System	84
Chapter 149 - State Song and Toast	84
Chapter 150 - Uniform Revocation of Licenses [Repealed.]	84
Chapter 150A - Administrative Procedure Act [Recodified.]	84
Chapter 150B - Administrative Procedure Act	84
Chapter 151 - Constables [Repealed.]	84
Chapter 152 - Coroners	84
Chapter 152A - County Medical Examiner [Repealed.]	84
Chapter 152A - County Medical Examiner [Repealed.] (Continuation)	85
Chapter 153 - Counties and County Commissioners [Repealed.]	85
Chapter 153A - Counties	85
Chapter 153B - Mountain Resources Planning Act	85
Chapter 153C - Uwharrie Regional Resources Act	85
Chapter 154 - County Surveyor [Repealed.]	85
Chapter 155 - County Treasurer [Repealed.]	85
Chapter 156 - Drainage	85
Chapter 156 – Drainage (Continuation)	86

Chapter 157 - Housing Authorities and Projects	86
Chapter 157A - Historic Properties Commissions [Transferred.]	86
Chapter 158 - Local Development	86
Chapter 159 - Local Government Finance	86
Chapter 159 - Local Government Finance (Continuation)	87
Chapter 159A - Pollution Abatement and Industrial Facilities Financing Act [Unconstitutional.]	87
Chapter 159B - Joint Municipal Electric Power and Energy Act	87
Chapter 159C - Industrial and Pollution Control Facilities Financing Act	87
Chapter 159D - The North Carolina Capital Facilities Financing Act	87
Chapter 159E - Registered Public Obligations Act	87
Chapter 159F - North Carolina Energy Development Authority [Repealed.]	87
Chapter 159G - Water Infrastructure	87
Chapter 159H - [Reserved.]	87
Chapter 159I - Solid Waste Management Loan Program and Local Government Special Obligation Bonds	87
Chapter 160 - Municipal Corporations [Repealed And Transferred.]	87
Chapter 160A - Cities and Towns	88
Chapter 160A - Cities and Towns (Continuation)	89
Chapter 160B - Consolidated City-County Act	89
Chapter 160C - Baseball Park Districts [Repealed.]	90
Chapter 161 - Register of Deeds	90
Chapter 162 - Sheriff	90
Chapter 162A - Water and Sewer Systems	90
Chapter 162B Continuity of Local Government in Emergency.	90
Chapter 163 Elections and Election Laws.	90
Chapter 163 Elections and Election Laws. (Continuation)	91
Chapter 164 Concerning the General Statutes of North Carolina.	92
Chapter 165 Veterans.	92
Chapter 166 Civil Preparedness Agencies [Repealed.]	92
Chapter 166A North Carolina Emergency Management Act.	92
Chapter 167 State Civil Air Patrol [Repealed.]	92
Chapter 168 Persons with Disabilities.	92
Chapter 168A Persons With Disabilities Protection Act.	92

Chapter 58A

North Carolina Health Insurance Trust Commission.

§§ 58A-1 through 58A-5: Recodified as Article 68 of Chapter 58.

Chapter 59.

Partnership.

ARTICLE 1.

Uniform Limited Partnership Act.

§§ 59-1 through 59-30.1: Repealed by Session Laws 1985 (Regular Session, 1986), c. 989, s. 2.

Article 2.

Uniform Partnership Act.

Part 1. Preliminary Provisions.

§ 59-31. North Carolina Uniform Partnership Act.

Articles 2 through 4A, inclusive, of this Chapter shall be known and may be cited as the North Carolina Uniform Partnership Act. (1941, c. 374, s. 1; 2000-140, s. 101(j); 2001-487, s. 20.)

§ 59-32. Definition of terms.

As used in this Chapter, except as otherwise defined in Article 5 of this Chapter for purposes of that Article, unless the context otherwise requires:

(01) "Act" means the North Carolina Uniform Partnership Act and refers to all provisions therein.

(1) "Bankrupt" means bankrupt under the Federal Bankruptcy Act or insolvent under any State insolvent act.

(2) "Business" means every trade, occupation, or profession.

(3) "Conveyance" means every assignment, lease, mortgage, or encumbrance.

(4) "Court" means every court and judge having jurisdiction in the case.

(4a) "Domestic corporation" has the same meaning as in G.S. 55-1-40.

(4b) "Domestic limited liability company" has the same meaning as the term "LLC" in G.S. 57D-1-03.

(4c) "Domestic limited partnership" has the same meaning as in G.S. 59-102.

(4d) "Domestic nonprofit corporation" means a corporation as defined in G.S. 55A-1-40.

(4e) "Foreign corporation" has the same meaning as in G.S. 55-1-40.

(4f) "Foreign limited liability company" has the same meaning as the term "foreign LLC" in G.S. 57D-1-03.

(4g) "Foreign limited liability partnership" means a partnership that (i) is formed under laws other than the laws of this State, and has the status of a limited liability partnership or registered limited liability partnership under those laws.

(4h) "Foreign limited partnership" has the same meaning as in G.S. 59-102.

(4i) "Foreign nonprofit corporation" means a foreign corporation as defined in G.S. 55A-1- 40.

(5) "Person" means individuals, partnerships, corporations, limited liability companies, and other associations.

(5a) "Principal office" means the office (in or out of this State) where the principal executive offices of a registered limited liability partnership or a foreign limited liability partnership are located, as designated in its most recent annual report filed with the Secretary of State or, if no annual report has yet been filed, in its application for registration as a registered limited liability partnership or foreign limited liability partnership.

(6) "Real property" means land and any interest or estate in land.

(7) "Registered limited liability partnership" means a partnership that is registered under G.S. 59-84.2 and complies with G.S. 59-84.3. (1941, c. 374, s. 2; 1993, c. 354, s. 3; 1999-362, s. 4; 2000-140, s. 101(k); 2001-387, s. 103; 2013-157, s. 15.)

§ 59-33. Interpretation of knowledge and notice.

(a) A person has "knowledge" of a fact within the meaning of this Act not only when he has actual knowledge thereof, but also when he has knowledge of such other facts as in the circumstances show bad faith.

(b) A person has "notice" of a fact within the meaning of this Act when the person who claims the benefit of the notice:

(1) States the fact to such person, or

(2) Delivers through the mail, or by other means of communication a written statement of the fact to such person or to a proper person at his place of business or residence. (1941, c. 374, s. 3; 2000-140, s. 101(n).)

§ 59-34. Rules of construction.

(a) The rule that statutes in derogation of the common law are to be strictly construed shall have no application to this Act.

(b) The law of estoppel shall apply under this Act.

(c) The law of agency shall apply under this Act.

(d) This Article shall be so interpreted and construed as to effect its general purpose to make uniform the law of those states which enact it.

(e) This Article and the other provisions of this Act shall not be construed so as to impair the obligations of any contract existing when the Article or any other provision of this Act, as applicable, goes into effect, nor to affect any action or proceedings begun or right accrued before this Article or any other provision of this Act, as applicable, takes effect. (1941, c. 374, s. 4; 2000-140, s. 101(l).)

§ 59-35. Rules for cases not provided for in this Act.

In any case not provided for in this Act, the rules of law and equity, including the law merchant, shall govern. (1941, c. 374, s. 5; 2000-140, s. 101(m).)

§ 59-35.1. Filing of documents.

(a) A document required or permitted by this Act to be filed by the Secretary of State must be filed under Chapter 55D of the General Statutes.

(b) A document submitted for filing by the Secretary of State on behalf of a general partnership must be executed by a general partner of the partnership.

(c) The Secretary of State may adopt and furnish on request forms for:

(1) An application for registration as a registered limited liability partnership;

(2) Cancellation of registration as a registered limited liability partnership;

(3) Application for registration as a foreign limited liability partnership; and

(4) Cancellation of registration as a foreign limited liability partnership.

If the Secretary of State so requires, use of these forms is mandatory.

(d) The Secretary of State may adopt and furnish on request forms for other documents required or permitted to be filed by this Act, but their use is not mandatory. (1999-369, s. 4.1; 2001-358, ss. 9, 38, 51(c); 2001-387, ss. 104, 105(c), 155, 170(a), 173, 175(a); 2001-413, s. 6; 2002-58, s. 4.)

§ 59-35.2. Filing, service, and copying fees.

(a)   The Secretary of State shall collect the following fees when the documents described in this subsection are submitted by a partnership to the Secretary of State for filing:

Document
Fee

(1)   Application for reserved name $10.00

(2)   Notice of transfer of reserved name 10.00

(3)   Application for registered name 10.00

(4)   Application for renewal of registered name 10.00

(5)   Registered limited liability partnership's or foreign limited liability partnership's statement of change of registered agent or registered office or both 5.00

(6)   Agent's statement of change of registered office for each affected registered limited liability partnership or foreign limited liability partnership 5.00

(7)   Agent's statement of resignation .... No Fee

(8)   Designation of registered agent or registered office or both............... 5.00

(9)   Articles of conversion (other than articles of conversion included as part of another document).. 50.00

19

(10) Articles of merger 50.00

(11) Application for registration as a registered limited liability partnership 125.00

(12) Certificate of amendment of registration as a registered limited liability partnership 25.00

(13) Cancellation of registration as a registered limited liability partnership 25.00

(14) Application for registration as a foreign limited liability partnership .. 125.00

(15) Certificate of amendment of registration as a foreign limited liability partnership 25.00

(16) Cancellation of registration as a foreign limited liability partnership .. 25.00

(17) Application for certificate of withdrawal by reason of merger, consolidation, or conversion 10.00

(18) Annual report 200.00

(19) Articles of correction 10.00

(20) Any other document required or permitted to be filed pursuant to this Act 10.00

(b) Whenever the Secretary of State is deemed appointed as a registered agent under this Act or under Chapter 55D of the General Statutes, the Secretary of State shall collect a fee of ten dollars ($10.00) each time process is served on the Secretary of State under this Act. The party to the proceeding causing service of process is entitled to recover this fee as costs if the party prevails in the proceeding.

(c) The Secretary of State shall collect the following fees for copying, comparing, and certifying a copy of a filed partnership document:

(1) One dollar ($1.00) a page for copying or comparing a copy to the original.

(2) Fifteen dollars ($15.00) for a paper certificate.

(3) Ten dollars ($10.00) for an electronic certificate. (2001-387, s. 170(b); 2001-487, s. 62(q); 2005-435, s. 46.)

Part 2. Nature of a Partnership.

§ 59-36. Partnership defined.

(a) A partnership is an association of two or more persons to carry on as co-owners a business for profit.

(b) But any association formed under any other statute of this State, or any statute adopted by authority, other than the authority of this State, is not a partnership under this Article, unless such association would have been a partnership in this State prior to the adoption of this Article; but this Article shall apply to limited partnerships except insofar as the statutes relating to such partnerships are inconsistent herewith. (1941, c. 374, s. 6.)

§ 59-37. Rules for determining the existence of a partnership.

In determining whether a partnership exists, these rules shall apply:

(1) Except as provided by G.S. 59-46 persons who are not partners as to each other are not partners as to third persons.

(2) Joint tenancy, tenancy in common, tenancy by the entireties, joint property, common property, or part ownership does not of itself establish a

partnership, whether such co-owners do or do not share any profits made by the use of the property.

(3) The sharing of gross returns does not of itself establish a partnership, whether or not the persons sharing them have a joint or common right or interest in any property from which the returns are derived.

(4) The receipt by a person of a share of the profits of a business is prima facie evidence that he is a partner in the business, but no such inference shall be drawn if such profits were received in payment:

a. As a debt by installments or otherwise,

b. As wages of an employee or rent to a landlord,

c. As an annuity to a widow or representative of a deceased partner,

d. As interest on a loan, though the amount of payment vary with the profits of the business,

e. As the consideration for the sale of a goodwill of a business or other property by installments or otherwise. (1941, c. 374, s. 7.)

§ 59-38. Partnership property.

(a) All property originally brought into the partnership stock or subsequently acquired by purchase or otherwise, on account of the partnership, is partnership property.

(b) Unless the contrary intention appears, property acquired with partnership funds is partnership property.

(c) Any estate in real property may be acquired in the partnership name. Title so acquired can be conveyed only in the partnership name.

(d) A conveyance to a partnership in the partnership name, though without words of inheritance, passes the entire estate of the grantor unless a contrary intent appears. (1941, c. 374, s. 8.)

Part 3. Relations of Partners to Persons Dealing with the Partnership.

§ 59-39. Partner agent of partnership as to partnership business.

(a)   Every partner is an agent of the partnership for the purpose of its business, and the act of every partner, including the execution in the partnership name of any instrument, for apparently carrying on in the usual way the business of the partnership of which he is a member binds the partnership, unless the partner so acting has in fact no authority to act for the partnership in the particular matter, and the person with whom he is dealing has knowledge of the fact that he has no such authority.

(b)   An act of a partner which is not apparently for the carrying on of the business of the partnership in the usual way does not bind the partnership unless authorized by the other partners.

(c)   Unless authorized by the other partners or unless they have abandoned the business, one or more but less than all the partners have no authority to:

(1)   Assign the partnership property in trust for creditors, or on the assignee's promise to pay the debts of the partnership,

(2)   Dispose of the goodwill of the business,

(3)   Do any other act which would make it impossible to carry on the ordinary business of a partnership,

(4)   Confess a judgment,

(5)   Submit a partnership claim or liability to arbitration or reference.

(d)   No act of a partner in contravention of a restriction on authority shall bind the partnership to persons having knowledge of the restriction. (1941, c. 374, s. 9.)

§ 59-39.1. Act, admission or acknowledgment by partner.

After a cause of action has accrued on any obligation of a partnership, any act, admission or acknowledgment by any partner acting in the ordinary course of the business of the partnership or with the authority of his copartners which removes the bar of the statute of limitations or causes the statutes to begin running anew with respect to the partner doing such act or making such admission or acknowledgment has a like effect with respect to all of the partners and with respect to partnership liability, but when any partner is not so acting and does not have the authority of his copartners, any act, admission or acknowledgment by such partner which removes the bar of the statute of limitations or causes the statute to begin running anew has such effect only as to the partner doing such act or making such admission or acknowledgment, and shall not renew, extend or in any manner impose liability of any kind against any partner who has not authorized or ratified the same nor against the partnership. (1953, c. 1076, s. 2.)

§ 59-40. Conveyance of real property of the partnership.

(a) Where title to real property is in the partnership name, any partner may convey title to such property by a conveyance executed in the partnership name; but the partnership may recover such property unless the partner's act binds the partnership under the provisions of subsection (a) of G.S. 59-39, or unless such property has been conveyed by the grantee or a person claiming through such grantee to holder for value without knowledge that the partner, in making the conveyance, has exceeded his authority.

(b) Where title to real property is in the name of the partnership, a conveyance executed by a partner, in his own name, passes the equitable interest of the partnership, provided the act is one within the authority of the partner under the provisions of subsection (a) of G.S. 59-39.

(c) Where title to real property is in the name of one or more, but not all the partners, and the record does not disclose the right of the partnership, the partners in whose name the title stands may convey title to such property, but the partnership may recover such property if the partners' act does not bind the partnership under the provisions of subsection (a) of G.S. 59-39, unless the purchaser or his assignee, is a holder for value, without knowledge.

(d) Where the title to real property is in the name of one or more or all the partners, or in a third person in trust for the partnership, a conveyance executed by a partner in the partnership name, or in his own name, passes the equitable interest of the partnership, provided the act is one within the authority of the partner under the provisions of subsection (a) of G.S. 59-39.

(e)   Where the title to real property is in the names of all the partners a conveyance executed by all the partners passes all their rights in such property. (1941, c. 374, s. 10; 1959, c. 1161, s. 3.)

§ 59-41. Partnership bound by admission of partner.

An admission or representation made by any partner concerning partnership affairs within the scope of his authority as conferred by this Act is evidence against the partnership. (1941, c. 374, s. 11; 2000-140, s. 101(n).)

§ 59-42. Partnership charged with knowledge of or notice to partner.

Notice to any partner of any matter relating to partnership affairs, and the knowledge of the partner acting in the particular matter, acquired while a partner or then present to his mind, and the knowledge of any other partner who reasonably could and should have communicated it to the acting partner, operate as notice to or knowledge of the partnership, except in the case of a fraud on the partnership committed by or with the consent of that partner. (1941, c. 374, s. 12.)

§ 59-43. Partnership bound by partner's wrongful act.

Where, by any wrongful act or omission of any partner acting in the ordinary course of the business of the partnership or with the authority of his copartners, loss or injury is caused to any person, not being a partner in the partnership, or any penalty is incurred, the partnership is liable therefor to the same extent as the partner so acting or omitting to act. (1941, c. 374, s. 13.)

§ 59-44. Partnership bound by partner's breach of trust.

The partnership is bound to make good the loss:

(1)   Where one partner acting within the scope of his apparent authority receives money or property of a third person and misapplies it; and

(2)   Where the partnership in the course of its business receives money or property of a third person and the money or property so received is misapplied by any partner while it is in the custody of the partnership. (1941, c. 374, s. 14.)

§ 59-45. Nature of partner's liability in ordinary partnerships and in registered limited liability partnerships.

(a)   Except as provided by subsections (a1) and (b) of this section, all partners are jointly and severally liable for the acts and obligations of the partnership.

(a1)   Except as provided in subsection (b) of this section, a partner in a registered limited liability partnership is not individually liable for debts and obligations of the partnership incurred while it is a registered limited liability partnership solely by reason of being a partner and does not become liable by participating, in whatever capacity, in the management or control of the business of the partnership.

(b)   Nothing in this Chapter shall be interpreted to abolish, modify, restrict, limit, or alter the law in this State applicable to the professional relationship and liabilities between the individual furnishing the professional services and the person receiving the professional services, the standards of professional conduct applicable to the rendering of the services, or any responsibilities, obligations, or sanctions imposed under applicable licensing statutes. A partner in a registered limited liability partnership is not individually liable, directly or indirectly, including by indemnification, contribution, assessment, or otherwise, for the debts, obligations, and liabilities of, or chargeable to, the registered limited liability partnership that arise from errors, omissions, negligence, malpractice, incompetence, or malfeasance committed by another partner or by an employee, agent, or other representative of the partnership; provided, however, nothing in this Chapter shall affect the liability of a partner of a professional registered limited liability partnership for his or her own errors, omissions, negligence, malpractice, incompetence, or malfeasance committed in the rendering of professional services.

(c) Repealed by Session Laws 1999-362, s. 5.

(d) A partner in a registered limited liability partnership is not a proper party to proceedings by or against a limited liability partnership, except where the object of the proceeding is to enforce a partner's right against or liability to the limited liability partnership.

(e) The liability of partners of a registered limited liability partnership formed and existing under this Chapter shall at all times be determined solely and exclusively by this Chapter and the laws of this State.

(f) If a conflict arises between the laws of this State and the laws of any other jurisdiction with regard to the liability of a partner of a registered limited liability partnership formed and existing under this Chapter for the debts, obligations, and liabilities of the registered limited liability partnership, this Chapter and the laws of this State shall govern in determining the liability. (1941, c. 374, s. 15; 1953, c. 881; 1993, c. 354, s. 4; 1999-362, s. 5.)

§ 59-46. Partner by estoppel.

(a) When a person, by words spoken or written, by conduct, or by contract, represents himself, or consents to another representing him to anyone, as a partner in an existing partnership or with one or more persons not actual partners, he is liable to any such person to whom such representation has been made, who has, on the faith of such representation, given credit to the actual or apparent partnership, and if he has made such representation or consented to its being made in a public manner, he is liable to such person, whether the representation has or has not been made or communicated to such person so giving credit by or with the knowledge of the apparent partner making the representation or consenting to its being made.

(1) When a partnership liability results, he is liable as though he were an actual member of the partnership.

(2) When no partnership liability results, he is liable jointly with the other persons, if any, so consenting to the contract or representation as to incur liability, otherwise separately.

(b) When a person has been thus represented to be a partner in an existing partnership, or with one or more persons not actual partners, he is an agent of the persons consenting to such representation to bind them to the same extent and in the same manner as though he were a partner in fact, with respect to persons who rely upon the representation. Where all the members of the existing partnership consent to the representation, a partnership act or obligation results; but in all other cases it is the joint act or obligation of the person acting and the persons consenting to the representation. (1941, c. 374, s. 16; 1975, c. 732.)

§ 59-47. Liability of incoming partner.

A person admitted as a partner into an existing partnership is liable for all the obligations of the partnership arising before his admission as though he had been a partner when such obligations were incurred, except that this liability shall be satisfied only out of partnership property. (1941, c. 374, s. 17.)

Part 4. Relations of Partners to One Another.

§ 59-48. Rules determining rights and duties of partners.

The rights and duties of the partners in relation to the partnership shall be determined, subject to any agreement between them, by the following rules:

(1) Each partner shall be repaid his contributions, whether by way of capital or advances to the partnership property and share equally in the profits and surplus remaining after all liabilities, including those to partners, are satisfied; and must contribute towards the losses, whether of capital or otherwise, sustained by the partnership according to his share in the profits.

(2) The partnership must indemnify every partner in respect of payments made and personal liabilities reasonably incurred by him in the ordinary and

proper conduct of its business, or for the preservation of its business or property.

(3)   A partner, who in aid of the partnership makes any payment or advance beyond the amount of capital which he agreed to contribute, shall be paid interest from the date of the payment or advance.

(4)   A partner shall receive interest on the capital contributed by him only from the date when repayment should be made.

(5)   All partners have equal rights in the management and conduct of the partnership business.

(6)   No partner is entitled to remuneration for acting in the partnership business, except that a surviving partner is entitled to reasonable compensation for his services in winding up the partnership affairs.

(7)   No person can become a member of a partnership without the consent of all the partners.

(8)   Any difference arising as to ordinary matters connected with the partnership business may be decided by a majority of the partners; but no act in contravention of any agreement between the partners may be done rightfully without the consent of all the partners. (1941, c. 374, s. 18.)

§ 59-49. Partnership books.

The partnership books shall be kept, subject to any agreement between the partners, at the principal place of business of the partnership, and every partner shall at all times have access to and may inspect and copy any of them. (1941, c. 374, s. 19.)

§ 59-50. Duty of partners to render information.

Partners shall render on demand true and full information of all things affecting the partnership to any partner or the legal representative of any deceased partner or partner under legal disability. (1941, c. 374, s. 20.)

§ 59-51. Partner accountable as a fiduciary.

(a) Every partner must account to the partnership for any benefit, and hold as trustee for it any profits derived by him without the consent of the other partners from any transaction connected with the formation, conduct or liquidation of the partnership or from any use by him of its property.

(b) This section applies also to the representatives of a deceased partner engaged in the liquidation of the affairs of the partnership as the personal representatives of the last surviving partner. (1941, c. 374, s. 21.)

§ 59-52. Right to an account.

Any partner shall have the right to a formal account as to partnership affairs:

(1) If he is wrongfully excluded from the partnership business or possession of its property by his copartners,

(2) If the right exists under the terms of any agreement,

(3) As provided by G.S. 59-51,

(4) Whenever other circumstances render it just and reasonable. (1941, c. 374, s. 22.)

§ 59-53. Continuation of partnership beyond fixed term.

(a) When a partnership for a fixed term or particular undertaking is continued after the termination of such term or particular undertaking without any express agreement, the rights and duties of the partners remain the same as they were at such termination, so far as is consistent with a partnership at will.

(b) A continuation of the business by the partners or such of them as habitually acted therein during the term, without any settlement or liquidation of the partnership affairs, is prima facie evidence of a continuation of the partnership. (1941, c. 374, s. 23.)

Part 5. Property Rights of a Partner.

§ 59-54. Extent of property rights of a partner.

The property rights of a partner are:

(1) His right in specific partnership property,

(2) His interest in the partnership, and

(3) His right to participate in the management. (1941, c. 374, s. 24.)

§ 59-55. Nature of a partner's right in specific partnership property.

(a) A partner is co-owner with his partners of specific partnership property holding as a tenant in partnership.

(b) The incidents of this tenancy are such that:

(1) A partner, subject to the provisions of this Act and to any agreement between the partners, has an equal right with his partners to possess specific partnership property for partnership purposes; but he has no right to possess such property for any other purpose without the consent of his partners.

(2) A partner's right in specific partnership property is not assignable except in connection with the assignment of rights of all the partners in the same property.

(3) A partner's right in specific partnership property is not subject to attachment or execution, except on a claim against the partnership. When partnership property is attached for a partnership debt the partners, or any of

them, or the representatives of a deceased partner, cannot claim any right under the homestead or exemption laws.

(4)   On the death of a partner his right in specific partnership property vests in the surviving partner or partners, except where the deceased was the last surviving partner, when his right in such property vests in his legal representative. Such surviving partner, or partners, or the legal representative of the last surviving partner, has no right to possess the partnership property for any but a partnership purpose.

(5)   A partner's right in specific partnership property is not subject to dower, curtesy, or allowances to widows, heirs, or next of kin. (1941, c. 374, s. 25; 2000-140, s. 101(n).)

§ 59-56. Nature of partner's interest in the partnership.

A partner's interest in the partnership is his share of the profits and surplus, and the same is personal property. (1941, c. 374, s. 26.)

§ 59-57. Assignment of partner's interest.

(a)   A conveyance by a partner of his interest in the partnership does not of itself dissolve the partnership, nor, as against the other partners in the absence of agreement, entitle the assignee, during the continuance of the partnership, to interfere in the management or administration of the partnership business or affairs, or to require any information or account of partnership transactions, or to inspect the partnership books; but it merely entitles the assignee to receive in accordance with his contract the profits to which the assigning partner would otherwise be entitled.

(b)   In case of a dissolution of the partnership, the assignee is entitled to receive his assignor's interest and may require an account from the date only of the last account agreed to by all the partners. (1941, c. 374, s. 27.)

§ 59-58. Partner's interest subject to charging order.

(a) On due application to a competent court by any judgment creditor of a partner, the court which entered the judgment, order or decree, or any other court, may charge the interest of the debtor partner with payment of the unsatisfied amount of such judgment debt with interest thereon; and may then or later appoint a receiver of his share of the profits, and of any other money due or to fall due to him in respect of the partnership, and make all other orders, directions, accounts and inquiries which the debtor partner might have made, or which the circumstances of the case may require.

(b) The interest charged may be redeemed at any time before foreclosure, or in case of a sale being directed by the court may be purchased without thereby causing a dissolution:

(1) With separate property, by any one or more of the partners, or

(2) With partnership property, by any one or more of the partners with the consent of all the partners whose interests are not so charged or sold.

(c) Nothing in this Act shall be held to deprive a partner of his right, if any, under the exemption laws, as regards his interest in the partnership. (1941, c. 374, s. 28; 2000-140, s. 101(n).)

Part 6. Dissolution and Winding Up.

§ 59-59. Dissolution defined.

The dissolution of a partnership is the change in the relation of the partners caused by any partner ceasing to be associated in the carrying on as distinguished from the winding up of the business. (1941, c. 374, s. 29.)

§ 59-60. Partnership not terminated by dissolution.

On dissolution the partnership is not terminated, but continues until the winding up of partnership affairs is completed. (1941, c. 374, s. 30.)

§ 59-61. Causes of dissolution.

Dissolution is caused:

(1)　Without violation of the agreement between the partners,

a.　By the termination of the definite term or particular undertaking specified in the agreement,

b.　By the express will of any partner when no definite term or particular undertaking is specified,

c.　By the express will of all partners who have not assigned their interests or suffered them to be charged for their separate debts, either before or after the termination of any specific term or particular undertaking,

d.　By the expulsion of any partner from the business bona fide in accordance with such a power conferred by the agreement between the partners;

(2)　In contravention of the agreement between the partners, where the circumstances do not permit a dissolution under any other provision of this section, by the express will of any partner at any time;

(3)　By any event which makes it unlawful for the business of the partnership to be carried on or for the members to carry it on in partnership;

(4)　By the death of any partner, unless the partnership agreement provides otherwise;

(5)　By the bankruptcy of any partner or the partnership;

(6)　By decree of court under G.S. 59-62. (1941, c. 374, s. 31; 1943, c. 384.)

§ 59-62. Dissolution by decree of court.

(a)　On application by or for a partner the court shall decree a dissolution whenever:

(1) A partner has been adjudicated incompetent or is shown to be of unsound mind,

(2) A partner becomes in any other way incapable of performing his part of the partnership contract,

(3) A partner has been guilty of such conduct as tends to affect prejudicially the carrying on of the business,

(4) A partner wilfully or persistently commits a breach of the partnership agreement, or otherwise so conducts himself in matters relating to the partnership business that it is not reasonably practicable to carry on the business in partnership with him,

(5) The business of the partnership can only be carried on at a loss,

(6) Other circumstances render a dissolution equitable.

(b) On the application of the purchaser of a partner's interest under G.S. 59-57 and 59-58:

(1) After the termination of the specified term or particular undertaking,

(2) At any time if the partnership was a partnership at will when the interest was assigned or when the charging order was issued.

(c) The name of a registered limited liability partnership becomes available for use by another entity as provided in G.S. 55D-21. (1941, c. 374, s. 32; 1985, c. 589, s. 29; 2001-358, s. 41; 2001-387, ss. 173, 175(a); 2001-413, s. 6; 2001-487, s. 107(b).)

§ 59-63. General effect of dissolution on authority of partner.

Except so far as may be necessary to wind up partnership affairs or to complete transactions begun but not then finished, dissolution terminates all authority of any partner to act for the partnership,

(1) With respect to the partners,

a. When the dissolution is not by the act, bankruptcy or death of a partner; or

b. When the dissolution is by such act, bankruptcy or death of a partner, in cases where G.S. 59-64 so requires,

(2) With respect to persons not partners, as declared in G.S. 59-65. (1941, c. 374, s. 33.)

§ 59-64. Right of partner to contribution from copartners after dissolution.

Where the dissolution is caused by the act, death or bankruptcy of a partner, each partner is liable to his copartners for his share of any liability created by any partner acting for the partnership as if the partnership had not been dissolved unless

(1) The dissolution being by act of any partner, the partner acting for the partnership had knowledge of the dissolution, or

(2) The dissolution being by the death or bankruptcy of a partner, the partner acting for the partnership had knowledge or notice of the death or bankruptcy. (1941, c. 374, s. 34.)

§ 59-65. Power of partner to bind partnership to third persons after dissolution; publication of notice of dissolution.

(a) After dissolution a partner can bind the partnership except as provided in subsection (c)

(1) By any act appropriate for winding up partnership affairs or completing transactions unfinished at dissolution;

(2) By any transaction which would bind the partnership if dissolution had not taken place, provided the other party to the transaction

a. Had extended credit to the partnership prior to dissolution and had no knowledge or notice of the dissolution; or

b. Though he had not so extended credit, had nevertheless known of the partnership prior to dissolution, and, having no knowledge or notice of dissolution, the fact of dissolution had not been published at least once a week for four successive weeks in some newspaper qualified for legal advertising in each county in which the partnership business was regularly carried on, or if no such newspaper is published in the county, posted for 30 days at the courthouse and three other public places in the county.

(b) The liability of a partner under subdivision (a)(2) shall be satisfied out of partnership assets alone when such partner had been prior to dissolution

(1) Unknown as a partner to the person with whom the contract is made; and

(2) So far unknown and inactive in partnership affairs that the business reputation of the partnership could not be said to have been in any degree due to his connection with it.

(c) The partnership is in no case bound by any act of a partner after dissolution

(1) Where the partnership is dissolved because it is unlawful to carry on the business, unless the act is appropriate for winding up partnership affairs; or

(2) Where the partner has become bankrupt; or

(3) Where the partner has no authority to wind up partnership affairs; except by a transaction with one who

a. Had extended credit to the partnership prior to dissolution and had no knowledge or notice of his want of authority; or

b. Had not extended credit to the partnership prior to dissolution, and, having no knowledge or notice of his want of authority, the fact of his want of authority has not been advertised in the manner provided for advertising the fact of dissolution in subdivision (a)(2)b.

(d) Nothing in this section shall affect the liability under G.S. 59-46 of any person who after dissolution represents himself or consents to another representing him as a partner in a partnership engaged in carrying on business. (1941, c. 374, s. 35; 1951, c. 381, s. 1.)

§ 59-66. Effect of dissolution on partner's existing liability.

(a) The dissolution of the partnership does not of itself discharge the existing liability of any partner.

(b) A partner is discharged from any existing liability upon dissolution of the partnership by an agreement to that effect between himself, the partnership creditor and the person or partnership continuing the business; and such agreement may be inferred from the course of dealing between the creditor having knowledge of the dissolution and the person or partnership continuing the business.

(c) Where a person agrees to assume the existing obligations of a dissolved partnership, the partners whose obligations have been assumed shall be discharged from any liability to any creditor of the partnership who, knowing of the agreement, consents to a material alteration in the nature or time of payment of such obligations.

(d) The individual property of a deceased partner shall be liable for all obligations of the partnership incurred while he was a partner but subject to the prior payment of his separate debts. (1941, c. 374, s. 36.)

§ 59-67. Right to wind up.

Unless otherwise agreed the partners who have not wrongfully dissolved the partnership or the legal representative of the last surviving partner, not bankrupt, has the right to wind up the partnership affairs; provided, however, that any partner, his legal representative or his assignee, upon cause shown, may obtain winding up by the court. (1941, c. 374, s. 37.)

§ 59-68. Rights of partners to application of partnership property.

(a)   When dissolution is caused in any way, except in contravention of the partnership agreement, each partner, as against his copartners and all persons claiming through them in respect of their interest in the partnership, unless otherwise agreed, may have the partnership property applied to discharge its liabilities, and the surplus applied to pay in cash the net amount owing to the respective partners. But if dissolution is caused by expulsion of a partner, bona fide under the partnership agreement, and if the expelled partner is discharged from all partnership liabilities, either by payment or agreement under G.S. 59-66, subsection (b), he shall receive in cash only the net amount due him from the partnership.

(b)   When dissolution is caused in contravention of the partnership agreement the rights of the partners shall be as follows:

(1)   Each partner who has not caused dissolution wrongfully shall have:

a.   All the rights specified in subsection (a) of this section, and

b.   The right, as against each partner who has caused the dissolution wrongfully, to damages for breach of the agreement.

(2)   The partners who have not caused the dissolution wrongfully, if they all desire to continue the business in the same name, either by themselves or jointly with others, may do so, during the agreed term for the partnership and for that purpose may possess the partnership property, provided they secure the payment by bond approved by the court, or pay to any partner who has caused the dissolution wrongfully, the value of his interest in the partnership at the dissolution, less any damages recoverable under clause (b)(1)b of this section, and in like manner indemnify him against all present or future partnership liabilities.

(3)   A partner who has caused the dissolution wrongfully shall have:

a.   If the business is not continued under the provisions of subdivision (b)(2) all the rights of a partner under subsection (a), subject to clause (b)(1)b, of this section,

b.   If the business is continued under subdivision (b)(2) of this section, the right as against his copartners and all claiming through them in respect of their interests in the partnership, to have the value of his interest in the partnership, less any damages caused to his copartners by the dissolution, ascertained and paid to him in cash, or the payment secured by bond approved by the court, and to be released from all existing liabilities of the partnership; but in ascertaining the value of the partner's interest the value of the goodwill of the business shall not be considered. (1941, c. 374, s. 38.)

§ 59-69. Rights where partnership is dissolved for fraud or misrepresentation.

Where partnership contract is rescinded on the ground of the fraud or misrepresentation of one of the parties thereto, the party entitled to rescind is, without prejudice to any other right, entitled,

(1) To a lien on, or right of retention of, the surplus of the partnership property after satisfying the partnership liabilities to third persons for any sum of money by him for the purchase of an interest in the partnership and for any capital or advances contributed by him; and

(2) To stand, after all liabilities to third persons have been satisfied, in the place of the creditors of the partnership for any payments made by him in respect of the partnership liabilities; and

(3) To be indemnified by the person guilty of the fraud or making the representation against all debts and liabilities of the partnership. (1941, c. 374, s. 39.)

§ 59-70. Rules for distribution.

In settling accounts between the partners after dissolution, the following rules shall be observed, subject to any agreement to the contrary:

(1) The assets of the partnership are

a. The partnership property,

b. The contributions of the partners necessary for the payment of all the liabilities specified in subdivision (2) of this section.

(2) The liabilities of the partnership shall rank in order of payment, as follows:

a. Those owing to creditors other than partners,

b. Those owing to partners other than for capital and profits,

c. Those owing to partners in respect of capital,

d. Those owing to partners in respect of profits.

(3) The assets shall be applied in the order of their declaration in subdivision (1) of this section to the satisfaction of the liabilities.

(4) The partners shall contribute, as provided by G.S. 59-48, subdivision (1) the amount necessary to satisfy the liabilities; but if any, but not all, of the partners are insolvent, or, not being subject to process, refuse to contribute, the other partners shall contribute their share of the liabilities, and, in the relative proportions in which they share the profits, the additional amount necessary to pay the liabilities.

(5) An assignee for the benefit of creditors or any person appointed by the court shall have the right to enforce the contributions specified in subdivision (4) of this section.

(6) Any partner or his legal representative shall have the right to enforce the contributions specified in subdivision (4) of this section, to the extent of the amount which he has paid in excess of his share of the liability.

(7) The individual property of a deceased partner shall be liable for the contributions specified in subdivision (4) of this section.

(8) When partnership property and the individual properties of the partners are in possession of a court for distribution, partnership creditors shall have priority on partnership property and separate creditors on individual property, saving the rights of lien or secured creditors as heretofore.

(9) Where a partner has become bankrupt or his estate is insolvent the claims against the separate property shall rank in the following order:

a. Those owing to separate creditors,

b. Those owing to partnership creditors,

c. Those owing to partners by way of contribution. (1941, c. 374, s. 40.)

§ 59-71. Liability of persons continuing the business in certain cases.

(a) When any new partner is admitted into an existing partnership, or when any partner retires and assigns (or the representative of the deceased partner assigns) his rights in partnership property to two or more of the partners, or to one or more of the partners and one or more third persons, if the business is continued without liquidation of the partnership affairs, creditors of the first or dissolved partnership are also creditors of the partnership so continuing the business.

(b) When all but one partner retire and assign (or the representative of a deceased partner assigns) their rights in partnership property to the remaining partner, who continues the business without liquidation of partnership affairs, either alone or with others, creditors of the dissolved partnership are also creditors of the person or partnership so continuing the business.

(c) When any partner retires or dies and the business of the dissolved partnership is continued as set forth in subsections (a) and (b) of this section, with the consent of the retired partners or the representative of the deceased partner, but without any assignment of his right in partnership property, rights of creditors of the dissolved partnership and of the creditors of the person or partnership continuing the business shall be as if such assignment had been made.

(d) When all the partners or their representatives assign their rights in partnership property to one or more third persons who promise to pay the debts and who continue the business of the dissolved partnership, creditors of the dissolved partnership are also creditors of the person or partnership continuing the business.

(e) When any partner wrongfully causes a dissolution and the remaining partners continue the business under the provisions of G.S. 59-68, subdivision (b)(2), either alone or with others, and without liquidation of the partnership affairs, creditors of the dissolved partnership are also creditors of the person or partnership continuing the business.

(f)   When a partner is expelled and the remaining partners continue the business either alone or with others, without liquidation of the partnership affairs, creditors of the dissolved partnership are also creditors of the person or partnership continuing the business.

(g)   The liability of a third person becoming a partner in the partnership continuing the business, under this section, to the creditors of the dissolved partnership shall be satisfied out of the partnership property only.

(h)   When the business of a partnership after dissolution is continued under any conditions set forth in this section the creditors of the dissolved partnership, as against the separate creditors of the retiring or deceased partner or the representative of the deceased partner, have a prior right to any claim of the retired partner or the representative of the deceased partner against the person or partnership continuing the business on account of the retired or deceased partner's interest in the dissolved partnership or on account of any consideration promised for such interest or for his right in partnership property.

(i)   Nothing in this section shall be held to modify any right of creditors to set aside any assignment on the ground of fraud.

(j)   The use by the person or partnership continuing the business of the partnership name, or the name of a deceased partner as part thereof, shall not of itself make the individual property of the deceased partner liable for any debts contracted by such person or partnership. (1941, c. 374, s. 41.)

§ 59-72. Rights of retiring partner or estate of deceased partner when the business is continued.

When any partner retires or dies, and the business is continued under any of the conditions set forth in G.S. 59-71, subsections (a), (b), (c), (e), (f), or G.S. 59-68, subdivision (b)(2), without any settlement of accounts as between him or his estate and the person or partnership continuing the business, unless otherwise agreed, he or his legal representative as against such persons or partnership may have the value of his interest at the date of dissolution ascertained, and shall receive as an ordinary creditor an amount equal to the value of his interest in the dissolved partnership with interest, or, at his option or at the option of his legal representative, in lieu of interest, the profits attributable to the use of his right in the property of the dissolved partnership; provided that the creditors of the dissolved partnership as against the separate creditors, or the representative of the retired or deceased partner, shall have priority on any claim arising under this section, as provided by G.S. 59-71, subsection (h). (1941, c. 374, s. 42.)

§ 59-73. Accrual of actions.

The right to an account of his interest shall accrue to any partner, or his legal representative, as against the winding up partners or the surviving partners or the person or partnership continuing the business, at the date of dissolution, in the absence of any agreement to the contrary. (1941, c. 374, s. 43.)

Article 2A.

Conversion and Merger.

Part 1. General Provisions.

§ 59-73.1. Definitions.

As used in this Article:

(1)   "Business entity" means a domestic corporation (including a professional corporation as defined in G.S. 55B-2), a foreign corporation (including a foreign professional corporation as defined in G.S. 55B-16), a domestic or foreign nonprofit corporation, a domestic or foreign limited liability company, a domestic or foreign limited partnership, a domestic partnership, or any other partnership.

(2)   "Domestic partnership" means a partnership as defined in G.S. 59-36 that is formed under the laws of this State, including a registered limited liability partnership, but excluding a domestic limited partnership.

(3) "Partnership" means a partnership as defined in G.S. 59-36 whether or not formed under the laws of this State including a registered limited liability partnership and a foreign limited liability partnership, but excluding a domestic limited partnership and a foreign limited partnership. (1999-369, s. 4.1; 2001-387, ss. 106, 107.)

§ 59-73.2: Recodified as § 59-73.20 by Session Laws 2001-387, s. 105(b).

§ 59-73.3: Recodified as § 59-73.30 by Session Laws 2001-387, s. 105(b).

§ 59-73.4: Recodified as § 59-73.31 by Session Laws 2001-387, s. 105(b).

§ 59-73.5: Recodified as § 59-73.32 by Session Laws 2001-387, s. 105(b).

§ 59-73.6: Recodified as § 59-73.33 by Session Laws 2001-387, s. 105(b).

§ 59-73.7: Recodified as § 59-35.1 by Session Laws 2001-358, s. 9.

§ 59-73.8. Reserved for future codification purposes.

§ 59-73.9. Reserved for future codification purposes.

Part 2. Conversion to Domestic Partnership.

§ 59-73.10. Conversion.

A business entity other than a domestic partnership may convert to a domestic partnership if:

(1)   The conversion is permitted by the laws of the state or country governing the organization and internal affairs of the converting business entity; and

(2)   The converting business entity complies with the requirements of this Part and, to the extent applicable, the laws referred to in subdivision (1) of this section. (2001-387, s. 108.)

§ 59-73.11. Plan of conversion.

(a)   The converting business entity shall approve a written plan of conversion containing:

(1)   The name of the converting business entity, its type of business entity, and the state or country whose laws govern its organization and internal affairs;

(2)   The name of the resulting domestic partnership into which the converting business entity shall convert;

(3)   The terms and conditions of the conversion; and

(4)   The manner and basis for converting the interests in the converting business entity into interests, obligations, or securities of the resulting domestic partnership or into cash or other property in whole or in part.

(a1)   The plan of conversion may contain other provisions relating to the conversion.

(a2)   The provisions of the plan of conversion, other than the provisions required by subdivisions (1) and (2) of subsection (a) of this section, may be made dependent on facts objectively ascertainable outside the plan of conversion if the plan of conversion sets forth the manner in which the facts will operate upon the affected provisions. The facts may include any of the following:

(1)   Statistical or market indices, market prices of any security or group of securities, interest rates, currency exchange rates, or similar economic or financial data.

(2)   A determination or action by the converting business entity or by any other person, group.

(3)   The terms of, or actions taken under, an agreement to which the converting business entity is a party, or any other agreement or document.

(b)   The plan of conversion shall be approved in accordance with the laws of the state or country governing the organization and internal affairs of the converting business entity.

(c)   After a plan of conversion has been approved as provided in subsection (b) of this section but before the articles of conversion become effective, the plan of conversion may be amended or abandoned to the extent permitted by the laws that govern the organization and internal affairs of the converting business entity. (2001-387, s. 108; 2001-487, s. 62(r); 2005-268, s. 52.)

§ 59-73.12. Filing of articles of conversion by converting business entity.

(a)   After a plan of conversion has been approved by the converting business entity as provided in G.S. 59-73.11, the converting business entity shall deliver articles of conversion to the Secretary of State for filing. The articles of conversion shall state:

(1)   That the domestic partnership is being formed pursuant to a conversion of another business entity;

(2)   The name of the resulting domestic partnership, a designation of its mailing address, and a commitment to file with the Secretary of State a statement of any subsequent change in its mailing address;

(3) The name of the converting business entity, its type of business entity, and the state or country whose laws govern its organization and internal affairs; and

(4) That a plan of conversion has been approved by the converting business entity as required by law.

If the resulting domestic partnership is to be a registered limited liability partnership when the conversion takes effect, then instead of the converting business entity delivering the articles of conversion to the Secretary of State for filing, the articles of conversion shall be included as part of the application for registration filed pursuant to G.S. 59-84.2 in addition to the matters otherwise required or permitted by law.

If the plan of conversion is abandoned after the articles of conversion have been filed with the Secretary of State but before the articles of conversion become effective, an amendment to the articles of conversion withdrawing the articles of conversion shall be delivered to the Secretary of State for filing prior to the time the articles of conversion become effective.

(b) The conversion takes effect when the articles of conversion become effective.

(c) Certificates of conversion shall also be registered as provided in G.S. 47-18.1. (2001-387, s. 108; 2001-487, s. 62(s); 2002-159, s. 34(a).)

§ 59-73.13. Effects of conversion.

(a) When the conversion takes effect:

(1) The converting business entity ceases its prior form of organization and continues in existence as the resulting domestic partnership;

(2) The title to all real estate and other property owned by the converting business entity continues vested in the resulting domestic partnership without reversion or impairment;

(3) All liabilities of the converting business entity continue as liabilities of the resulting domestic partnership;

(4) A proceeding pending by or against the converting business entity may be continued as if the conversion did not occur; and

(5) The interests in the converting business entity that are to be converted into interests, obligations, or securities of the resulting domestic partnership or into the right to receive cash or other property are thereupon so converted, and the former holders of interests in the converting business entity are entitled only to the rights provided in the plan of conversion.

The conversion shall not affect the liability or absence of liability of any holder of an interest in the converting business entity for any acts, omissions, or obligations of the converting business entity made or incurred prior to the effectiveness of the conversion. The cessation of the existence of the converting business entity in its prior form of organization in the conversion shall not constitute a dissolution or termination of the converting business entity.

(b) When the conversion takes effect, the resulting domestic partnership is deemed:

(1) To agree that it may be served with process in this State for enforcement of (i) any obligation of the converting business entity and (ii) any obligation of the resulting domestic partnership arising from the conversion; and

(2) To have appointed the Secretary of State as its agent for service of process in any such proceeding. Service on the Secretary of State of any such process shall be made by delivering to and leaving with the Secretary of State, or with any clerk authorized by the Secretary of State to accept service of process, duplicate copies of the process and the fee required by G.S. 59-35.2. Upon receipt of service of process on behalf of a resulting domestic partnership in the manner provided for in this section, the Secretary of State shall immediately mail a copy of the process by registered or certified mail, return receipt requested, to the resulting domestic partnership. If the resulting domestic partnership is a registered limited liability partnership, the address for mailing shall be its principal office or, if there is no principal office on file, its registered office. If the resulting domestic partnership is not a registered limited liability partnership, the address for mailing shall be the mailing address designated pursuant to G.S. 59-73.12(a)(2). (2001-387, s. 108; 2001-387, s. 170(c).)

§§ 59-73.14 through 59-73.19. Reserved for future codification purposes.

Part 3. Conversion of Domestic Partnership.

§ 59-73.20. Conversion.

A domestic partnership may convert to a different business entity if:

(1)   The conversion is permitted by the laws of the state or country governing the organization and internal affairs of such other business entity; and

(2)   The converting domestic partnership complies with the requirements of this Part and, to the extent applicable, the laws referred to in subdivision (1) of this section. (1999-369, s. 4.1; 2001-387, ss. 105(b), 109, 110.)

§ 59-73.21. Plan of conversion.

(a)   The converting domestic partnership shall approve a written plan of conversion containing:

(1)   The name of the converting domestic partnership;

(2)   The name of the resulting business entity into which the domestic partnership shall convert, its type of business entity, and the state or country whose laws govern its organization and internal affairs;

(3)   The terms and conditions of the conversion; and

(4)   The manner and basis for converting the interests in the domestic partnership into interests, obligations, or securities of the resulting business entity or into cash or other property in whole or in part.

(a1)   The plan of conversion may contain other provisions relating to the conversion.

(a2)   The provisions of the plan of conversion, other than the provisions required by subdivisions (1) and (2) of subsection (a) of this section, may be made dependent on facts objectively ascertainable outside the plan of conversion if the plan of conversion sets forth the manner in which the facts will operate upon the affected provisions. The facts may include any of the following:

(1)   Statistical or market indices, market prices of any security or group of securities, interest rates, currency exchange rates, or similar economic or financial data.

(2)   A determination or action by the converting domestic partnership or by any other person, group, or body.

(3)   The terms of, or actions taken under, an agreement to which the converting domestic partnership is a party, or any other agreement or document.

(b)   The plan of conversion shall be approved by the domestic partnership in the manner provided for the approval of the conversion in a written partnership agreement or, if there is no such provision, by the unanimous consent of its partners. If any partner of the converting domestic partnership has or will have personal liability for any existing or future obligation of the resulting business entity solely as a result of holding an interest in the resulting business entity, then in addition to the requirements of the preceding sentence, approval of the plan of conversion by the domestic partnership shall require the consent of that partner. The converting domestic partnership shall provide a copy of the plan of conversion to each partner of the converting domestic partnership at the time provided in a written partnership agreement or, if there is no such provision, prior to its approval of the plan of conversion.

(c)   After a plan of conversion has been approved by a domestic partnership but before the articles of conversion become effective, the plan of conversion (i) may be amended as provided in the plan of conversion, or (ii) may be abandoned, subject to any contractual rights, as provided in the plan of conversion or written partnership agreement or, if not so provided, as determined in the manner necessary for approval of the plan of conversion. (2001-387, s. 111; 2001-487, s. 62(t); 2005-268, s. 53.)

§ 59-73.22. Articles of conversion.

(a) After a plan of conversion has been approved by the converting domestic partnership as provided in G.S. 59-73.21, the converting domestic partnership shall deliver articles of conversion to the Secretary of State for filing. The articles of conversion shall state:

(1) The name of the converting domestic partnership;

(2) The name of the resulting business entity, its type of business entity, the state or country whose laws govern its organization and internal affairs, and, if the resulting business entity is not authorized to transact business or conduct affairs in this State, a designation of its mailing address and a commitment to file with the Secretary of State a statement of any subsequent change in its mailing address; and

(3) That a plan of conversion has been approved by the domestic partnership as required by law.

(b) If the domestic partnership is converting to a business entity whose formation requires the filing of a document with the Secretary of State, then notwithstanding subsection (a) of this section the articles of conversion shall be included as part of that document and shall contain the information required by the laws governing the organization and internal affairs of the resulting business entity.

(c) If the plan of conversion is abandoned after the articles of conversion have been filed with the Secretary of State but before the articles of conversion become effective, the converting domestic partnership shall deliver to the Secretary of State for filing prior to the time the articles of conversion become effective an amendment of the articles of conversion withdrawing the articles of conversion.

(d) The conversion takes effect when the articles of conversion become effective.

(e) Certificates of conversion shall also be registered as provided in G.S. 47-18.1. (2001-387, s. 111; 2001-487, s. 62(u).)

§ 59-73.23. Effects of conversion.

(a) When the conversion takes effect;

(1) The converting domestic partnership ceases its prior form of organization and continues in existence as the resulting business entity;

(2) The title to all real estate and other property owned by the converting domestic partnership continues vested in the resulting business entity without reversion or impairment;

(3) All liabilities of the converting domestic partnership continue as liabilities of the resulting business entity;

(4) A proceeding pending by or against the converting domestic partnership may be continued as if the conversion did not occur; and

(5) The interests in the converting domestic partnership that are to be converted into interests, obligations, or securities of the resulting business entity or into the right to receive cash or other property are thereupon so converted, and the former holders of interests in the converting domestic partnership are entitled only to the rights provided in the plan of conversion.

The conversion shall not affect the liability or absence of liability of any holder of an interest in the converting domestic partnership for any acts, omissions, or obligations of the converting domestic partnership made or incurred prior to the effectiveness of the conversion. The cessation of the existence of the converting domestic partnership in its form of organization as a domestic partnership in the conversion shall not constitute a dissolution or termination of the converting domestic partnership.

(b) If the resulting business entity is not a domestic corporation, a domestic limited partnership, or a domestic limited liability company, when the conversion takes effect the resulting business entity is deemed:

(1) To agree that it may be served with process in this State for enforcement of (i) any obligation of the converting domestic partnership and (ii) any obligation of the resulting business entity arising from the conversion; and

(2) To have appointed the Secretary of State as its agent for service of process in any such proceeding. Service on the Secretary of State of any such process shall be made by delivering to and leaving with the Secretary of State, or with any clerk authorized by the Secretary of State to accept service of

process, duplicate copies of the process and the fee required by G.S. 59-35.2. Upon receipt of service of process on behalf of a resulting business entity in the manner provided for in this section, the Secretary of State shall immediately mail a copy of the process by registered or certified mail, return receipt requested, to the resulting business entity. If the resulting business entity is authorized to transact business or conduct affairs in this State, the address for mailing shall be its principal office designated in the latest document filed with the Secretary of State that is authorized by law to designate the principal office or, if there is no principal office on file, its registered office. If the resulting business entity is not authorized to transact business or conduct affairs in this State, the address for mailing shall be the mailing address designated pursuant to G.S. 59-73.22(a)(2). (2001-387, ss. 111, 170(c); 2001-487, s. 62(v).)

§§ 59-73.24 through 59-73.29. Reserved for future codification purposes.

Part 4. Merger.

§ 59-73.30. Merger.

A domestic partnership may merge with one or more other domestic partnerships or other business entities if:

(1)   The merger is permitted by laws of the state or country governing the organization and internal affairs of each other merging business entity; and

(2)   Each merging domestic partnership and each other merging business entity comply with the requirements of this Part and, to the extent applicable, the laws referred to in subdivision (1) of this section. (1999-369, s. 4.1; 2001-387, ss. 105(b), 112.)

§ 59-73.31. Plan of merger.

(a)   Each merging domestic partnership and each other merging business entity shall approve a written plan of merger containing:

(1) For each merging business entity, its name, type of business entity, and the state or country whose laws govern its organization and internal affairs;

(2) The name of the merging business entity that shall survive the merger;

(3) The terms and conditions of the merger; and

(4) The manner and basis for converting the interests in each merging business entity into interests, obligations, or securities of the surviving business entity or into cash or other property in whole or in part.

(a1) The plan of merger may contain other provisions relating to the merger.

(a2) The provisions of the plan of merger, other than the provisions referred to in subdivisions (1) and (2) of subsection (a) of this section, may be made dependent on facts objectively ascertainable outside the plan of merger if the plan of merger sets forth the manner in which the facts will operate upon the affected provisions. The facts may include any of the following:

(1) Statistical or market indices, market prices of any security or group of securities, interest rates, currency exchange rates, or similar economic or financial data.

(2) A determination or action by the domestic partnership or by any other person, group, or body.

(3) The terms of, or actions taken under, an agreement to which the domestic partnership is a party, or any other agreement or document.

(b) In the case of a merging domestic partnership, the plan of merger must be approved in the manner provided in a written partnership agreement that is binding on all the partners for approval of a merger with the type of business entity contemplated in the plan of merger or, if there is no provision, by the unanimous consent of its partners. If any partner of a merging domestic partnership has or will have personal liability for any existing or future obligation of the surviving business entity solely as a result of holding an interest in the surviving business entity, then in addition to the requirements of the preceding sentence, approval of the plan of merger by the domestic partnership shall require the consent of that partner. In the case of each other merging business entity, the plan of merger must be approved in accordance with the laws of the state or country governing the organization and internal affairs of such merging business entity.

(c) After a plan of merger has been approved by the domestic partnership but before the articles of merger become effective, the plan of merger (i) may be amended as provided in the plan of merger, or (ii) may be abandoned (subject to any contractual rights) as provided in the plan of merger or a written partnership agreement that is binding on all the partners or, if not so provided, as determined by the unanimous consent of the partners. (1999-369, s. 4.1; 2001-387, ss. 105(b), 112, 113; 2005-268, s. 54.)

§ 59-73.32. Articles of merger.

(a) After a plan of merger has been approved by each merging domestic partnership and each other merging business entity as provided in G.S. 59-73.31, the surviving business entity shall deliver articles of merger to the Secretary of State for filing. The articles of merger shall set forth:

(1) Repealed by Session Laws 2005-268, s. 55, effective October 1, 2005.

(2) For each merging business entity, its name, type of business entity, and the state or country whose laws govern its organization and internal affairs.

(3) The name of the merging business entity that will survive the merger and, if the surviving business entity is not authorized to transact business or conduct affairs in this State, a designation of its mailing address and a commitment to file with the Secretary of State a statement of any subsequent change in its mailing address.

(4) A statement that the plan of merger has been approved by each merging business entity in the manner required by law.

(5) Repealed by Session Laws 2005-268, s. 55, effective October 1, 2005.

If the plan of merger is amended after the articles of merger have been filed but before the articles of merger become effective, and any statement in the articles of merger becomes incorrect as a result of the amendment, the surviving business entity shall deliver to the Secretary of State for filing prior to the time the articles of merger become effective an amendment to the articles of merger correcting the incorrect statement. If the articles of merger are abandoned after the articles of merger are filed but before the articles of merger become effective, the surviving business entity shall deliver to the Secretary of State for filing prior to the time the articles of merger become effective an amendment reflecting the abandonment of the plan of merger.

(b) A merger takes effect when the articles of merger become effective.

(c) Certificates of merger shall also be registered as provided in G.S. 47-18.1. (1999-369, s. 4.1; 2001-387, ss. 105(b), 112, 114; 2005-268, s. 55.)

§ 59-73.33. Effects of merger.

(a) When a merger takes effect:

(1) Each other merging business entity merges into the surviving business entity, and the separate existence of each merging business entity except the surviving business entity ceases;

(2) The title to all real estate and other property owned by each merging business entity is vested in the surviving business entity without reversion or impairment;

(3) The surviving business entity has all liabilities of each merging business entity;

(4) A proceeding pending by or against any merging business entity may be continued as if the merger did not occur, or the surviving business entity may be substituted in the proceeding for a merging business entity whose separate existence ceases in the merger;

(5) The interests in each merging business entity that are to be converted into interests, obligations, or securities of the surviving business entity or into the right to receive cash or other property are thereupon so converted, and the former holders of the interests are entitled only to the rights provided to them in the plan of merger or, in the case of former holders of shares in a domestic corporation, as defined in G.S. 55-1-40, any rights they may have under Article 13 of Chapter 55 of the General Statutes; and

(6) If the surviving business entity is not a domestic corporation, the surviving business entity is deemed to agree that it will promptly pay to the

shareholders of any merging domestic corporation exercising appraisal rights the amount, if any, to which they are entitled under Article 13 of Chapter 55 of the General Statutes and otherwise to comply with the requirements of Article 13 as if it were a surviving domestic corporation in the merger.

The merger shall not affect the liability or absence of liability of any holder of an interest in a merging business entity for any acts, omissions, or obligations of any merging business entity made or incurred prior to the effectiveness of the merger. The cessation of separate existence of a merging business entity shall not constitute a dissolution or termination of the merging business entity.

(b) If the surviving business entity is not a domestic limited liability company, a domestic corporation, a domestic nonprofit corporation, or a domestic limited partnership, when the merger takes effect the surviving business entity is deemed:

(1) To agree that it may be served with process in this State in any proceeding for enforcement of (i) any obligation of any merging domestic limited liability company, domestic corporation, domestic nonprofit corporation, domestic limited partnership, or other partnership as defined in G.S. 59-36 that is formed under the laws of this State, (ii) the appraisal rights of shareholders of any merging domestic corporation under Article 13 of Chapter 55 of the General Statutes, and (iii) any obligation of the surviving business entity arising from the merger; and

(2) To have appointed the Secretary of State as its registered agent for service of process in any such proceeding. Service on the Secretary of State of any such process shall be made by delivering to and leaving with the Secretary of State, or with any clerk authorized by the Secretary of State to accept service of process, duplicate copies of such process and the fee required by G.S. 59-35.2. Upon receipt of service of process on behalf of a surviving business entity in the manner provided for in this section, the Secretary of State shall immediately mail a copy of the process by registered or certified mail, return receipt requested, to the surviving business entity. If the surviving business entity is authorized to transact business or conduct affairs in this State, the address for mailing shall be its principal office designated in the latest document filed with the Secretary of State that is authorized by law to designate the principal office or, if there is no principal office on file, its registered office. If the surviving business entity is not authorized to transact business or conduct affairs in this State, the address for mailing shall be the mailing address designated pursuant to G.S. 59-73.32(a)(3). (1999-369, s. 4.1; 2000-140, s. 52;

2001-358, s. 10(a); 2001-387, ss. 105(b), 112, 115, 170(c), 173, 175(a); 2002-159, s. 17; 2007-385, s. 5; 2011-347, ss. 17, 18.)

Article 3.

Surviving Partners.

§ 59-74. Surviving partner to give bond.

Upon the death of any member of a partnership, the surviving partner shall, within 30 days, execute before the clerk of the superior court of the county where the partnership business was conducted, a bond payable to the State of North Carolina, with sufficient surety conditioned upon the faithful performance of his duties in the settlement of the partnership affairs. The amount of such bond shall be fixed by the clerk of the court; and the settlement of the estate and the liability of the bond shall be the same as under the law governing administrators and their bonds. (1915, c. 227, ss. 1, 2, 3; C.S., s. 3277.)

§ 59-75. Effect of failure to give bond.

Upon the failure of the surviving partner to execute the bond provided for in G.S. 59-74, the clerk of the superior court shall, upon application of any person interested in the estate of the deceased partner, appoint a collector of the partnership, who shall be governed by the same law governing an administrator of a deceased person. (1915, c. 227, s. 4; C.S., s. 3278.)

§ 59-76. Surviving partner and personal representative to make inventory.

When a member of any partnership dies the surviving partner, within 60 days after the death of the deceased partner, together with the personal representative of the deceased partner, shall make out a full and complete inventory of the assets of the partnership, including real estate, if there be any, together with a schedule of the debts and liabilities thereof, a copy of which inventory and schedule shall be retained by the surviving partner, and a copy thereof shall be furnished to the personal representative of the deceased partner. (1901, c. 640; Rev., s. 2540; C.S., s. 3279.)

§ 59-77. When personal representative may take inventory; receiver.

If the surviving partner should neglect or refuse to have such inventory made, the personal representative of the deceased partner may have the same made in accordance with the provisions of G.S. 59-76. Should any surviving partner fail to take such an inventory or refuse to allow the personal representative of the deceased partner's estate to do so, such personal representative of the deceased partner's estate may forthwith apply to a court of competent jurisdiction for the appointment of a receiver for such partnership, who shall thereupon proceed to wind up the same and dispose of the assets thereof in accordance with law. (1901, c. 640, s. 2; Rev., s. 2541; C.S., s. 3280; 2000-140, s. 101(o); 2001-387, s. 116.)

§ 59-78. Notice to creditors.

Every surviving partner, within 30 days after the death of the deceased partner, shall notify all persons having claims against the partnership which were in existence at the time of the death of the deceased partner, to exhibit the same to the surviving partner within six months from the date of first publication of such notice. The notice shall be published once a week for four consecutive weeks in a newspaper qualified to publish legal advertisements, if any such newspaper is published in the county. If there is no newspaper published in the county, but there is a newspaper having general circulation in the county, then at the option of the surviving partner the notice shall be published in the newspaper having general circulation in the county and posted at the courthouse or the notice shall be posted at the courthouse and four other public places in the county. (1901, c. 640, s. 3; Rev., s. 2542; C.S., s. 3281; 1951, c. 381, s. 2; 1973, c. 1410, ss. 1, 2.)

§ 59-79. Debts paid pro rata; liens.

All debts and demands against a copartnership, where one partner has died, shall be paid pro rata, except debts which are a specific lien on property belonging to the partnership. (1901, c. 640, s. 4; Rev., s. 2543; C.S., s. 3282.)

§ 59-80. Effect of failure to present claim in six months.

In an action brought on a claim which was not presented within six months from the first publication of the general notice to creditors, the surviving partner shall not be chargeable for any assets that he may have paid in satisfaction of any debts before such action was commenced, nor shall any costs be recovered in such action against the surviving partner. (1901, c. 640, s. 5; Rev., s. 2544; C.S., s. 3283; 1973, c. 1410, s. 3.)

§ 59-81. Procedure for purchase by surviving partner.

(a) Appraisal of Property. - The surviving partner may, if he so desire, make application to the clerk of the superior court of the county in which the partnership existed, after first giving notice to the executor or administrator of the time of the hearing of such application, for the appointment of three judicious, disinterested appraisers, one of whom may be named by the surviving partner, one by the representative of the deceased partner's estate, and the third named by the two appraisers selected, whose duty it shall be to make out under oath a full and complete inventory and appraisement of the entire assets of the partnership, including real estate if there be any, together with a schedule of the debts and liabilities thereof, and to deliver the same to the surviving partner; they shall also deliver a copy to the executor or administrator, and file a copy with the clerk of the court.

(b) Surviving Partner May Purchase. - The surviving partner may, with the consent of the executor or administrator of the deceased partner and the approval of the clerk of the superior court by whom such executor or administrator was appointed, purchase the interest of such deceased partner in the partnership assets at the appraised value thereof, including the good will of the business, first deducting therefrom the debts and liabilities of the partnership, for cash or upon giving to the executor or administrator his promissory note or notes, with good approved security, and satisfactory to the executor or administrator, for the payment of the interest of such deceased partner in the partnership assets.

(c) Surviving Partner to Give Bond. - In case the surviving partner shall avail himself of the privilege of purchasing such interest as provided for in this section, he shall give bond to the executor or administrator with surety for the payment of the debts and liabilities of the partnership, and for the performance of all contracts for which the partnership is liable.

(d) Sale of Real Estate. - In case of such sale of the real estate belonging to the partnership, the title to the real estate so purchased shall not pass until the sale thereof has been reported to and confirmed by the clerk of the superior court of the county in which the partnership was located, in a special proceeding to which the widow and heirs at law or devisees of the deceased partner are duly made parties. (1901, c. 640, s. 6; Rev., s. 2545; 1911, c. 12; C.S., s. 3284.)

§ 59-82. Surviving partner to account and settle.

In case the surviving partner shall not avail himself of the privilege of purchasing the interest of the deceased partner, he shall, within six months from the date of the first publication of notice to creditors, file with the clerk of the superior court of the county where the partnership was located, an account, under oath, stating his action as surviving partner, and shall come to a settlement with the executor or administrator of the deceased partner: Provided, that the clerk of the superior court shall have power, upon good cause shown, to extend the time within which said final settlement shall be made. The surviving partner for his services in settling the partnership estate shall receive commissions to be allowed by the court. (1901, c. 640, s. 7; Rev., s. 2546; C.S., s. 3285; 1947, c. 781; 1957, c. 783, s. 6; 1973, c. 1410, s. 4.)

§ 59-83. Accounting compelled.

In case any surviving partner fails to come to a settlement with the executor or administrator of the deceased partner within the time prescribed by law, the clerk of the superior court may, at the instance of such executor, administrator or other person interested in such deceased partnership estate, cite the surviving partners to a final settlement as provided for by law in the case of executors and administrators. (1901, c. 640, s. 8; Rev., s. 2547; C.S., s. 3286.)

§ 59-84. Settlement otherwise provided for.

When the original articles of partnership in force at the death of any partner or the will of a deceased partner make provision for the settlement of the deceased partner's interest in the partnership, and for a disposition thereof different from that provided for in this Chapter, the interest of such deceased partner in the partnership shall be settled and disposed of in accordance with the provisions of such articles of partnership or of such will. (1901, c. 640, s. 6; Rev., s. 2545; C.S., s. 3287.)

Article 3A.

Miscellaneous Provisions.

§ 59-84.1. Partnership to comply with "assumed name" statute; income taxation.

(a) Every partnership other than a limited partnership shall comply with, and be subject to, the provisions of Articles 14 and 15 of Chapter 66 of the General Statutes in all cases in which the same are applicable.

(b) A partnership, including a registered limited liability partnership and a foreign limited liability partnership, and a partner of one of these partnerships are subject to taxation under Article 4 of Chapter 105 of the General Statutes in accordance with their classification for federal income tax purposes. Accordingly, if any such partnership is classified for federal income tax purposes as a C corporation as defined in G.S. 105-131(b)(2) or an S corporation as defined in G.S. 105-131(b)(8), the partnership and its partners are subject to tax under Article 4 of Chapter 105 of the General Statutes to the same extent as a C corporation or an S corporation, as the case may be, and its shareholders. If any such partnership is classified for federal income tax purposes as a partnership, the partnership and its partners are subject to tax under Article 4 of Chapter 105 of the General Statutes accordingly. If any such partnership is classified for federal income tax purposes as other than a corporation or a partnership, the partnership and its partners are subject to tax under Article 4 of Chapter 105 of the General Statutes in a manner consistent with that classification. This section does not require a partnership, including any registered limited liability partnership or foreign limited liability partnership authorized to transact business in this State, to obtain an administrative ruling from the Internal Revenue Service on its classification under the Internal Revenue Code. (1951, c. 381, s. 9; 1993, c. 354, s. 5; 2001-387, s. 117.)

Article 3B.

Registered Limited Liability Partnerships.

§ 59-84.2. Registered limited liability partnerships.

(a) A partnership whose internal affairs are governed by the laws of this State, other than a limited partnership, may become a registered limited liability partnership by filing with the Secretary of State an application stating all of the following:

(1) The name of the partnership.

(2) The street address, and the mailing address if different from the street address, of its principal office and the county in which the principal office is located.

(3) The name and street address, and the mailing address if different from the street address, of the partnership's registered agent and registered office for service of process.

(4) The county in this State in which the registered office is located.

(5) Repealed by Session Laws 2001-387, s. 156(b), effective January 1, 2002.

(6) Repealed by Session Laws 2001-387, s. 156(b), effective January 1, 2002.

(7) The fiscal year end of the partnership.

(a1)   The terms and conditions on which a partnership becomes a limited liability partnership must be approved in the manner provided in the partnership agreement; provided, however, if the partnership agreement does not contain any such provision, the terms and conditions shall be approved (i) in the case of a partnership having a partnership agreement that expressly considers obligations to contribute to the partnership, in the manner necessary to amend those provisions, or (ii) in any other case, in the manner necessary to amend the partnership agreement.

(b)   Repealed by Session Laws 2001-387, s. 156(b), effective January 1, 2002.

(c)   Repealed by Session Laws 2001-387, s. 156(b), effective January 1, 2002.

(d)   Repealed by Session Laws 2001-387, s. 156(b), effective January 1, 2002.

(e)   Repealed by Session Laws 2001-387, s. 156(b), effective January 1, 2002.

(f)   Repealed by Session Laws 2001-387, s. 156(b), effective January 1, 2002.

(f1)   A partnership becomes a registered limited liability partnership when its application for registration becomes effective.

(g)   The status of a registered limited liability partnership and the liability of its partners is not affected by errors or later changes in the information required to be contained in the application for registration.

(h)   A partnership shall promptly amend its registration to reflect any change in the information contained in its application for registration, other than changes that are properly included in other documents filed with the Secretary of State. A registration is amended by filing a certificate of amendment with the Secretary of State. The certificate of amendment shall set forth:

(1)   The name of the partnership as reflected on the application for registration.

(2)   The date of filing of the application for registration.

(3) The amendment to the application for registration.

(i) Each registered limited liability partnership must maintain a registered office and registered agent as required by Article 4 of Chapter 55D of the General Statutes and is subject to service on the Secretary of State under that Article.

(j) A partnership may cancel its registration by filing a certificate of cancellation with the Secretary of State. The certificate of cancellation shall set forth:

(1) The name of the partnership as reflected on the application for registration;

(2) The date of filing of the application for registration;

(3) A mailing address to which the Secretary of State may mail a copy of any process served on the Secretary of State under this subsection;

(4) A commitment to file with the Secretary of State a statement of any subsequent change in its mailing address; and

(5) The effective date and time of cancellation if it is not to be effective at the time of filing the certificate.

Cancellation of registration terminates the authority of the partnership's registered agent to accept service of process, notice, or demand, and appoints the Secretary of State as agent to accept service on behalf of the partnership with respect to any action or proceeding based upon any cause of action arising in this State, or arising out of business transacted in this State, during the time the partnership was registered as a registered limited liability partnership. Service on the Secretary of State of any such process, notice, or demand shall be made by delivering to and leaving with the Secretary of State, or with any clerk authorized by the Secretary of State to accept service of process, duplicate copies of such process, notice, or demand and the fee required by G.S. 59-35.2. Upon receipt of process, notice, or demand in the manner provided in this section, the Secretary of State shall immediately mail a copy of the process, notice, or demand by registered or certified mail, return receipt requested, to the partnership at the mailing address designated pursuant to this subsection.

(k) If a registered limited liability partnership is dissolved but its business is continued by some of its partners with or without others in a new partnership under the same name, then (i) the new partnership shall automatically succeed to the registration of the dissolved original partnership as a registered limited liability partnership and (ii) the dissolved original partnership shall be deemed to be registered as a registered limited liability partnership until the winding up of its affairs is completed. (1993, c. 354, s. 5; 1999-362, ss. 6, 7; 2000-140, ss. 53, 101(p); 2001-358, s. 51(a); 2001-387, ss. 118, 156, 173, 175(a); 2001-413, s. 6; 2002-58, s. 5.)

§ 59-84.3. Name of registered limited liability partnerships.

A registered limited liability partnership's name must meet the requirements of G.S. 55D-20 and G.S. 55D-21. (1993, c. 354, s. 5; 1999-362, ss. 6, 8; 2001-358, s. 39; 2001-387, ss. 173, 175(a); 2001-413, s. 6.)

§ 59-84.4. Annual report for Secretary of State.

(a) Each registered limited liability partnership and each foreign limited liability partnership authorized to transact business in this State shall deliver to the Secretary of State for filing an annual report, in a form prescribed by the Secretary of State, that sets forth all of the following:

(1) The name of the registered limited liability partnership or foreign limited liability partnership and the state or country under whose law it is formed.

(2) The street address, and the mailing address if different from the street address, of the registered office, the county in which the registered office is located, and the name of its registered agent at that office in this State, and a statement of any change of the registered office or registered agent, or both.

(3) The street address and telephone number of its principal office.

(4) A brief description of the nature of its business.

(5) The fiscal year end of the partnership.

If the information contained in the most recently filed annual report has not changed, a certification to that effect may be made instead of setting forth the information required by subdivisions (2) through (4) of this subsection. The Secretary of State shall make available the form required to file an annual report.

(b) Information in the annual report must be current as of the date the annual report is executed on behalf of the registered limited liability partnership or the foreign limited liability partnership.

(c) The annual report shall be delivered to the Secretary of State by the fifteenth day of the fourth month following the close of the registered or foreign limited liability partnership's fiscal year.

(d) If an annual report does not contain the information required by this section, the Secretary of State shall promptly notify the reporting registered or foreign limited liability partnership in writing and return the report to it for correction. If the report is corrected to contain the information required by this section and delivered to the Secretary of State within 30 days after the effective date of notice, it is deemed to be timely filed.

(e) Amendments to any previously filed annual report may be filed with the Secretary of State at any time for the purpose of correcting, updating, or augmenting the information contained in the annual report.

(f) The Secretary of State may revoke the registration of a registered limited liability partnership or foreign limited liability partnership if the Secretary of State determines that:

(1) The registered limited liability partnership or foreign limited liability partnership has not paid, within 60 days after they are due, any penalties, fees, or other payments due under this Chapter;

(2) The registered limited liability partnership or foreign limited liability partnership does not deliver its annual report to the Secretary of State on or before the date it is due;

(3) The registered limited liability partnership or foreign limited liability partnership has been without a registered agent or registered office in this State for 60 days or more; or

(4) The registered limited liability partnership or foreign limited liability partnership does not notify the Secretary of State within 60 days of the change, resignation, or discontinuance that its registered agent or registered office has been changed, that its registered agent has resigned, or that its registered office has been discontinued.

(g) If the Secretary of State determines that one or more grounds exist under subsection (f) of this section for revoking the registration of the registered limited liability partnership or foreign limited liability partnership, the Secretary of State shall mail the registered limited liability partnership or foreign limited liability partnership written notice of that determination. If, within 60 days after the notice is mailed, the registered limited liability partnership or foreign limited liability partnership does not correct each ground for revocation or demonstrate to the reasonable satisfaction of the Secretary of State that each ground does not exist, the Secretary of State shall revoke the registration of a registered limited liability partnership or foreign limited liability partnership by signing a certificate of revocation that recites the ground or grounds for revocation and its effective date. The Secretary of State shall file the original certificate of revocation and mail a copy to the registered limited liability partnership or foreign limited liability partnership.

(h) A registered limited liability partnership or foreign limited liability partnership whose registration is revoked under this section may apply to the Secretary of State for reinstatement. If, at the time the registered limited liability partnership applies for reinstatement, the name of the registered limited liability partnership is not distinguishable from the name of another entity authorized to be used under G.S. 55D-21, then the registered limited liability partnership must change its name to a name that is distinguishable upon the records of the Secretary of State from the name of the other entity before the Secretary of State may prepare a certificate of reinstatement. The procedures for reinstatement and for the appeal of any denial of the registered limited liability partnership or foreign limited liability partnership's application for reinstatement shall be the same procedures applicable to business corporations under G.S. 55-14-22, 55-14-23, and 55-14-24. The effect of reinstatement of a limited liability partnership shall be the same as for a corporation under G.S. 55-14-22. (1999-362, s. 9; 2001-387, s. 119; 2001-390, s. 13.)

Article 4.

Business under Assumed Name Regulated.

§§ 59-85 through 59-88: Transferred to §§ 66-68 to 66-71 by Session Laws 1951, c. 381, s. 7.

§ 59-89. Transferred to § 66-72 by Session Laws 1951, c. 381, s. 8.

Article 4A.

Foreign Limited Liability Partnerships.

§ 59-90. Law governing foreign limited liability partnership.

(a) The law of the state or jurisdiction under which a foreign limited liability partnership is formed governs relations among the partners and between the partners and the partnership and the liability of partners for obligations of the partnership.

(b) A foreign limited liability partnership may not be denied a statement of foreign registration by reason of any difference between the law under which the partnership was formed and the law of this State.

(c) A statement of foreign registration does not authorize a foreign limited liability partnership to engage in any business or exercise any power that a partnership may not engage in or exercise in this State as a registered limited liability partnership. (1999-362, s. 10.)

§ 59-91. Statement of foreign registration.

(a) Before transacting business in this State, a foreign limited liability partnership must file an application for registration as a foreign limited liability partnership. The application must contain:

(1) The name of the foreign limited liability partnership that satisfies the requirements of the state or other jurisdiction under whose law it is formed and meets the requirements of Article 3 of Chapter 55D of the General Statutes.

(2) The street address, and the mailing address if different from the street address, of the partnership's principal office, and the county in which the principal office is located.

(3) The name and street address, and the mailing address if different from the street address, for the partnership's registered agent and registered office for service of process, and the county in which the registered office is located.

(4), (5) Repealed by Session Laws 2001-387, s. 157(b).

(6) The fiscal year end of the partnership.

The foreign limited liability partnership shall deliver with the completed application a certificate of existence, or a document with similar import, duly authenticated by the Secretary of State or other official having custody of the records of registered limited liability partnerships in the state or country under whose law it is registered.

(b) Each foreign limited liability partnership maintaining a statement of foreign registration in this State must maintain a registered office and registered agent as required by Article 4 of Chapter 55D of the General Statutes and is subject to service on the Secretary of State under that Article.

(c) through (g) Repealed by Session Laws 2001-387, s. 157(b).

(h) A foreign limited liability partnership authorized to transact business in this State shall be subject to the provisions of G.S. 59-84.4 regarding annual reports and revocation of registration.

(i) A foreign limited liability partnership becomes registered as a foreign limited liability partnership when its application for registration becomes effective.

(j) A foreign limited liability partnership shall promptly amend its registration to reflect any change in the information contained in its application for registration, other than changes that are properly included in other documents filed with the Secretary of State. A registration is amended by filing a certificate of amendment with the Secretary of State. The certificate of amendment shall set forth:

(1)   The name of the foreign limited liability partnership under which it is registered in this State;

(2)   The date of filing of the application for registration; and

(3)   The amendment to the application for registration.

(k)   A foreign limited liability partnership may cancel its registration by filing a certificate of cancellation with the Secretary of State. The certificate of cancellation shall set forth:

(1)   The name of the foreign limited liability partnership under which it is registered in this State;

(2)   The date of filing of the application for registration;

(3)   A mailing address to which the Secretary of State may mail a copy of any process served on the Secretary of State under this subsection;

(4)   A commitment to file with the Secretary of State a statement of any subsequent change in its mailing address; and

(5)   The effective date and time of cancellation if it is not to be effective at the time of filing the certificate.

Cancellation of registration terminates the authority of the foreign limited liability partnership's registered agent to accept service of process, notice, or demand and appoints the Secretary of State as agent to accept such service on behalf of the foreign limited liability partnership with respect to any action or proceeding based upon any cause of action arising in this State, or arising out of business transacted in this State, during the time the foreign limited liability partnership was registered in this State. Service on the Secretary of State of any such process, notice, or demand shall be made by delivering to and leaving with the Secretary of State, or with any clerk authorized by the Secretary of State to accept service of process, duplicate copies of such process, notice, or demand and the fee required by G.S. 59-35.2. Upon receipt of process, notice, or demand in the manner herein provided, the Secretary of State shall immediately mail a copy of the process, notice, or demand by registered or certified mail, return receipt requested, to the foreign limited liability partnership at the mailing address designated pursuant to this subsection.

(l)   Whenever a foreign limited liability partnership authorized to transact business in this State ceases its separate existence as a result of a statutory merger or consolidation permitted by the laws of the state or country under which it was organized, or converts into another type of entity as permitted by those laws, the surviving or resulting entity shall apply for a certificate of withdrawal for the foreign limited liability partnership by delivering to the Secretary of State for filing a copy of the articles of merger, consolidation, or conversion or a certificate reciting the facts of the merger, consolidation, or conversion, duly authenticated by the Secretary of State or other official having custody of limited liability partnership records in the state or country under the laws of which the foreign limited liability partnership was organized. If the surviving or resulting entity is not authorized to transact business or conduct affairs in this State, the articles or certificate must be accompanied by an application which must set forth:

(1)   The name of the foreign liability limited partnership [sic] authorized to transact business in this State, the type of entity and name of the surviving or resulting entity, and a statement that the surviving or resulting entity is not authorized to transact business or conduct affairs in this State;

(2)   A statement that the surviving or resulting entity consents that service of process based on any cause of action arising in this State, or arising out of business transacted in this State, during the time the foreign limited liability partnership was authorized to transact business in this State, may thereafter be made by service thereof on the Secretary of State;

(3)   A mailing address to which the Secretary of State may mail a copy of any process served upon the Secretary under subdivision (2) of this subsection; and

(4)   A commitment to file with the Secretary of State a statement of any subsequent change in its mailing address.

(m)   If the Secretary of State finds that the articles or certificate and the application for withdrawal, if required, conform to law, the Secretary of State shall:

(1) Endorse on the articles or certificate and the application for withdrawal, if required, the word "filed" and the hour, day, month, and year of filing thereof;

(2) File the articles or certificate and the application, if required;

(3) Issue a certificate of withdrawal; and

(4) Send to the surviving or resulting entity or its representative the certificate of withdrawal, together with a copy of the application, if required, affixed thereto.

(n) After the withdrawal of the foreign limited liability partnership is effective, service of process on the Secretary of State in accordance with subsection (l) of this section shall be made by delivering to and leaving with the Secretary of State, or with any clerk authorized by the Secretary of State to accept service of process, duplicate copies of such process and the fee required by G.S. 59-35.2. Upon receipt of process in the manner herein provided, the Secretary of State shall immediately mail a copy of the process by registered or certified mail, return receipt requested, to the surviving or resulting entity at the mailing address designated pursuant to subsection (l) of this section. (1999-362, s. 10; 2000-140, s. 54; 2001-358, ss. 40, 51(b); 2001-387, ss. 120, 157, 173, 175(a); 2001-413, s. 6.)

§ 59-92. Effect of failure to register.

(a) A foreign limited liability partnership transacting business in this State may not maintain an action or proceeding in this State unless it has in effect a registration as a foreign limited liability partnership.

(b) The failure of a foreign limited liability partnership to have in effect a registration as a foreign limited liability partnership does not impair the validity of a contract or act of the foreign limited liability partnership or preclude it from defending an action or proceeding in this State.

(c) A limitation on personal liability of a partner is not waived solely by transacting business in this State without a registration as a foreign limited liability partnership.

(d) A foreign limited liability partnership failing to register as a foreign limited liability partnership as required by this Article shall be liable to the State for the years or parts thereof during which it transacted business in this State without having registered in an amount equal to all fees and taxes which would have been imposed by law upon the foreign limited liability partnership had it duly applied for and received such permission, plus interest and all penalties imposed by law for failure to pay such fees and taxes. In addition, the foreign limited liability partnership shall be liable for a civil penalty of ten dollars ($10.00) for each day, but not to exceed a total of one thousand dollars ($1,000) for each year or part thereof, it transacts business in this State without having registered. The Attorney General may bring actions to recover all amounts due the State under the provisions of this subsection. (1999-362, s. 10.)

§ 59-93. Activities not constituting transacting business.

(a) Without excluding other activities that may not constitute transacting business in this State, a foreign limited liability partnership shall not be considered to be transacting business in this State for the purposes of this Article by reason of carrying on in this State any one or more of the following activities:

(1) Maintaining or defending any action or suit or any administrative or arbitration proceeding or effecting the settlement thereof or the settlement of claims or disputes;

(2) Holding meetings of its partners or carrying on other activities concerning its internal affairs;

(3) Maintaining bank accounts or borrowing money in this State, with or without security, even if such borrowings are repeated and continuous transactions;

(4) Maintaining offices or agencies for the transfer, exchange, and registration of the partnership's own securities, or appointing and maintaining trustees or depositories with relation to those securities;

(5) Soliciting or procuring orders, whether by mail or through employees or agents or otherwise, where the orders require acceptance without this State before becoming binding contracts;

(6) Making or investing in loans with or without security including servicing of mortgages or deeds of trust through independent agencies within the State, the conducting of foreclosure proceedings and sales, the acquiring of property at foreclosure sale, and the management and rental of such property for a reasonable time while liquidating its investment, provided no office or agency therefor is maintained in this State;

(7) Taking security for or collecting debts due to it or enforcing any rights in property securing the same;

(8) Transacting business in interstate commerce;

(9) Conducting an isolated transaction completed within a period of six months and not in the course of a number of repeated transactions of like nature;

(10) Selling through independent contractors; and

(11) Owning, without more, real or personal property.

(b) This section does not apply in determining the contacts or activities that may subject a foreign limited liability partnership to service of process, taxation, or regulation under any other law of this State. (1999-362, s. 10.)

§ 59-94. Action by Attorney General.

The Attorney General may maintain an action to restrain a foreign limited liability partnership from transacting business in this State in violation of this Article. (1999-362, s. 10.)

§§ 59-95 through 59-100. Reserved for future codification purposes.

Article 5.

Revised Uniform Limited Partnership Act.

Part 1. General Provisions.

§ 59-101. Short title.

This Article may be cited as the Revised Uniform Limited Partnership Act. (1985 (Reg. Sess., 1986), c. 989, s. 2.)

§ 59-102. Definitions.

As used in this Article, unless the context otherwise requires:

(1) "Business" means any lawful trade, investment, or other purpose or activity, whether or not the trade, investment, purpose, or activity is carried on for profit.

(1a) "Business entity" means a domestic corporation (including a professional corporation as defined in G.S. 55B-2), a foreign corporation (including a foreign professional corporation as defined in G.S. 55B-16), a domestic or foreign nonprofit corporation, a domestic or foreign limited liability company, a domestic limited partnership, a foreign limited partnership, a registered limited liability partnership, a foreign limited liability partnership, or any other partnership as defined in G.S. 59-36 whether or not formed under the laws of this State.

(1b) "Certificate of limited partnership" means the certificate referred to in G.S. 59-201, and the certificate as amended.

(2) "Conformed copy" shall include a photostatic or other photographic copy of the original document.

(3) "Contribution" means any cash, property, services rendered, or a promissory note or other binding obligation to contribute cash or property or to perform services, which a partner contributes to a limited partnership in his capacity as a partner.

(3a) "Domestic corporation" has the same meaning as in G.S. 55-1-40.

(3b) "Domestic limited liability company" has the same meaning as the term "LLC" in G.S. 57D-1-03.

(3c) "Domestic nonprofit corporation" means a corporation as defined in G.S. 55A-1-40.

(4) "Event of withdrawal of a general partner" means an event that causes a person to cease to be a general partner as provided in G.S. 59-402.

(4a) "Foreign corporation" has the same meaning as in G.S. 55-1-40.

(4b) "Foreign limited liability company" has the same meaning as the term "foreign LLC" in G.S. 57D-1-03.

(4c) "Foreign limited liability limited partnership" means a foreign limited partnership whose general partners have limited liability for the obligations of the foreign limited partnership under a provision similar to the provisions of G.S. 59-403(b) pertaining to general partners in limited liability limited partnerships.

(5) "Foreign limited partnership" means a partnership formed under the laws of any state, province, country, or other jurisdiction other than this State and having as partners one or more general partners and one or more limited partners, and includes, for all purposes of the laws of the State of North Carolina, a limited liability limited partnership.

(5a) "Foreign nonprofit corporation" means a foreign corporation as defined in G.S. 55A-1-40.

(6) "General partner" means a person who has been admitted to a limited partnership as a general partner in accordance with the partnership agreement and named in the certificate of limited partnership as a general partner.

(6a) "Limited liability limited partnership" and "registered limited liability limited partnership" mean a limited partnership that is registered under and complies with G.S. 59-210.

(7) "Limited partner" means a person who has been admitted to a limited partnership as a limited partner in accordance with the partnership agreement.

(8) "Limited partnership" and "domestic limited partnership" mean a partnership formed by two or more persons under the laws of this State and

having one or more general partners and one or more limited partners, and includes, for all purposes of the laws of the State of North Carolina, a limited liability limited partnership.

(9) "Partner" means a limited or general partner.

(10) "Partnership agreement" means any valid agreement of the partners as to the affairs of a limited partnership, the conduct of its business, and the responsibilities and rights of its partners. The term "partnership agreement" includes any written or oral agreement, whether or not the agreement is set forth in a document referred to by the partners as a "partnership agreement", and includes any amendment agreed upon by the partners unanimously or in accordance with the terms of the agreement. The term also includes any agreement of the partners to waive or revise the terms of the partnership agreement in one or more specific instances and not necessarily on an ongoing or permanent basis.

(11) "Partnership interest" means a partner's share of the allocations of income, gain, loss, deduction or credit of a limited partnership and the right to receive distributions of cash or other partnership assets.

(12) "Person" means a natural person, domestic or foreign partnership, domestic or foreign limited partnership, domestic or foreign limited liability company, trust, estate, unincorporated association, domestic or foreign corporation, domestic or foreign nonprofit corporation, or another entity.

(12a) "Principal office" means the office (in or out of this State) where the principal executive offices of a limited liability limited partnership or foreign limited partnership are located, in the case of a limited liability limited partnership as designated in its most recent annual report filed with the Secretary of State or, if no annual report has yet been filed, in its application for registration as a limited liability limited partnership, or in the case of a foreign limited partnership as most recently designated in its application for registration as a foreign limited partnership or a certificate filed pursuant to G.S. 59-905.

(13) "State" means a state, territory, or possession of the United States, the District of Columbia, or the Commonwealth of Puerto Rico. (1985 (Reg. Sess., 1986), c. 989, s. 2; 1999-362, s. 11; 1999-369, s. 4.2; 2001-387, s. 121; 2001-487, ss. 62(w), (x); 2013-157, s. 16.)

§ 59-103. Name.

The name of the limited partnership must meet any requirements of Article 3 of Chapter 55D of the General Statutes. (1985 (Reg. Sess., 1986), c. 989, s. 2; 1987, c. 531, s. 1; 1995, c. 539, s. 34; 2001-358, s. 32; 2001-387, ss. 122, 155, 172, 173, 175(a); 2001-413, s. 6.)

§ 59-104: Repealed by Session Laws 2001-358, s. 33.

§ 59-105. Registered office and registered agent.

(a) Each limited partnership must maintain a registered office and registered agent as required by Article 4 of Chapter 55D of the General Statutes and is subject to service on the Secretary of State under that Article.

(b) Limited partnerships formed prior to October 1, 1986, shall file a certificate of limited partnership with the Office of the Secretary of State pursuant to G.S. 59-201(a) designating the address of the registered office of the limited partnership and the identity of the registered agent at such address.

(b1) through (e) Repealed by Session Laws 2001-358, s. 50(a). (1985 (Reg. Sess., 1986), c. 989, s. 2; 1987, c. 531, s. 2; 1989, c. 209; 2000-140, s. 101(q); 2001-358, s. 50(a); 2001-387, ss. 123, 155, 173, 175(a); 2001-413, s. 6.)

§ 59-106. Records to be kept.

(a) Each limited partnership shall keep in this State at an office in this State:

(1) A current list of the full name and last known mailing address of each partner set forth in alphabetical order;

(2) A copy of the certificate of limited partnership and all certificates of amendment thereto, together with executed copies of any powers of attorney pursuant to which any certificate has been executed;

(3) Copies of the limited partnership's federal, State and local income tax returns and reports, if any, for the three most recent years;

(4) Copies of any then effective written partnership agreements and copies of any financial statements of the limited partnership for the three most recent years; and

(5) A written record that contains:

a. The amount of cash and a description and statement of the agreed value of the other property or services contracted by each partner and which each partner has agreed to contribute;

b. The times at which or events on the happening of which any additional contributions agreed to be made by each partner are to be made;

c. Any right of a partner to receive distribution of property, including cash from the limited partnership; and

d. Events upon the happening of which the limited partnership is to be dissolved and its affairs wound up.

The written record required pursuant to this subdivision may be part of a written partnership agreement or may be contained in one or more other documents or records.

(b) The books and records are subject to inspection and copying at the reasonable request, and at the expense, of any partner during ordinary business hours. (1985 (Reg. Sess., 1986), c. 989, s. 2; 1987 (Reg. Sess., 1988), c. 1031, s. 2; 1997-456, s. 27; 1999-362, s. 12.)

§ 59-107. Nature of business.

A limited partnership may be formed for and carry on any lawful business. (1985 (Reg. Sess., 1986), c. 989, s. 2; 1999-362, s. 13.)

§ 59-108. Business transactions of partner with the partnership.

Except as provided in the partnership agreement, a partner may lend money to and transact other business with the limited partnership and, subject to G.S. 59-804 and other applicable law, has the same rights and obligations with respect thereto as a person who is not a partner. (1985 (Reg. Sess., 1986), c. 989, s. 2.)

§§ 59-109 through 59-200. Reserved for future codification purposes.

Part 2. Formation; Certificate of Limited Partnership.

§ 59-201. Certificate of limited partnership.

(a)   In order to form a limited partnership, a certificate of limited partnership must be executed and filed in the office of the Secretary of State and set forth:

(1)   The name of the limited partnership.

(2)   The address, including county and city or town, and street and number, if any, of the registered office and the name of the registered agent at such address for service of process required to be maintained by G.S. 55D-30.

(3)   If the limited partnership is to dissolve by a specific date, the latest date upon which the limited partnership is to dissolve. If no date for dissolution is specified, there shall be no limit on the duration of the limited partnership.

(4)   The name and the address, including county and city or town, and street and number, if any, of each general partner.

(5)   The address, including county and city or town, and street and number, if any, of the office at which the records referred to in G.S. 59-106 are kept, if such records are not kept at the registered office.

(b)   Unless a delayed effective date is specified in the certificate of limited partnership, a limited partnership is formed at the effective time and date of the filing of the certificate of limited partnership in the office of the Secretary of State if there has been substantial compliance with the requirements of this section.

(c) Domestic limited partnership filings filed prior to October 1, 1986, with the Office of Register of Deeds pursuant to G.S. 59-2(a)(2) shall evidence the existence of limited partnerships formed prior to October 1, 1986, and shall be public notice of only those matters contained in G.S. 59-201(a) and shall be used for no other purpose.

(d) A limited partnership may also be formed through the conversion of another business entity in accordance with Part 10A of this Article.

(e) If the limited partnership is to be a limited liability limited partnership at its formation, then instead of separately filing the application for registration as a limited liability limited partnership, the application for registration shall be included as part of the certificate of limited partnership. (1985 (Reg. Sess., 1986), c. 989, s. 2; 1987, c. 531, s. 3; 1987 (Reg. Sess., 1988), c. 1031, s. 3; 1997-485, s. 24; 1999-369, s. 4.3; 2000-140, s. 17; 2001-358, s. 50(b); 2001-387, ss. 124, 124A, 173, 175(a); 2001-413, s. 6.)

§ 59-202. Amendment to certificate.

(a) A certificate of limited partnership is amended by filing a certificate of amendment thereto in the office of the Secretary of State. The certificate shall set forth:

(1) The name of the limited partnership;

(2) The date of filing of the certificate; and

(3) The amendment to the certificate.

(b) Within 30 days after the happening of any of the following events an amendment to a certificate of limited partnership reflecting the occurrence of the event or events shall be filed:

(1) The admission of a new general partner;

(2) The withdrawal of a general partner; or

(3) The continuation of the business under G.S. 59-801 after an event of withdrawal of a general partner.

(c) A general partner who becomes aware that any statement in a certificate of limited partnership was false when made or that any arrangements or other facts described have changed, making the certificate inaccurate in any respect, shall promptly amend the certificate.

(d) Repealed by Session Laws 1987, c. 531, s. 4. (1985 (Reg. Sess., 1986), c. 989, s. 2; 1987, c. 531, s. 4.)

§ 59-203. Cancellation of certificate.

A certificate of limited partnership shall be cancelled upon the dissolution and the commencement of winding up of the partnership or at any other time that there are no limited partners. A certificate of cancellation shall be filed in the office of the Secretary of State and set forth:

(1) The name of the limited partnership;

(2) The date of filing of its certificate of limited partnership;

(3) The reason for filing the certificate of cancellation;

(4) The effective date of cancellation if it is not to be effective upon the filing of the certificate; and

(5) Any other information the partners filing the certificate determine. (1985 (Reg. Sess., 1986), c. 989, s. 2; 1997-485, s. 25.)

§ 59-204. Execution of documents.

(a) Each certificate required by this Article to be filed in the office of the Secretary of State shall be executed in the following manner:

(1) An original certificate of limited partnership must be signed by all general partners;

(2) A certificate of amendment must be signed by at least one general partner and by each other partner designated in the certificate as a new general partner; and

(3) A certificate of cancellation must be signed by all general partners.

Any other document submitted by a domestic or foreign limited partnership for filing pursuant to this or any other Chapter must be signed by at least one general partner.

(b) Any person may sign a certificate by an attorney-in-fact.

(b1) Repealed by Session Laws 2001-358, s. 10(c).

(c) The execution of a certificate or amendment by a general partner constitutes an affirmation under the penalties of perjury that the facts stated therein are true. (1985 (Reg. Sess., 1986), c. 989, s. 2; 1991, c. 153, s. 1; 1997-485, s. 22; 1999-369, s. 4.4; 2001-358, ss. 10(b), (c); 2001-387, ss. 125, 155, 173, 175(a); 2001-413, s. 6.)

§ 59-205. Execution by judicial act.

If a person fails or refuses to execute a certificate pursuant to G.S. 59-204, any other person who is adversely affected by the failure or refusal, may petition the court for the county in which the partnership's registered office is located to direct the execution of the certificate. If the court finds that it is proper for the certificate to be executed and that any person so designated has failed or refused to execute the certificate, it shall order an appropriate person to prepare, and the Secretary of State to record, an appropriate certificate. (1985 (Reg. Sess., 1986), c. 989, s. 2; 1999-362, s. 14.)

§ 59-206. Filing requirements.

A document required or permitted by this Article to be filed by the Secretary of State must be filed under Chapter 55D of the General Statutes. (1985 (Reg. Sess., 1986), c. 989, s. 2; 1987, c. 531, s. 5; 1991, c. 153, s. 2; 1995, c. 539, s.

35; 1997-485, ss. 17, 26; 1999-362, s. 15; 1999-369, ss. 4.5, 4.6; 2001-358, ss. 10(d), 34; 2001-387, ss. 126, 155, 173, 175(a); 2001-413, s. 6.)

§§ 59-206.1 through 59-206.2: Repealed by Session Laws 2001-358, s. 10(e), effective January 1, 2002.

§ 59-207. Liability for false statement in certificate.

If any certificate of limited partnership or certificate of amendment or cancellation contains a false statement, one who suffers loss by reliance on the statement may recover damages for the loss from:

(1) Any person who executes the certificate, or causes another to execute it on his behalf, and knew, and any general partner who knew or should have known, the statement to be false at the time the certificate was executed; and

(2) Any general partner who thereafter knows or should have known that any arrangement or other fact described in the certificate has changed, making the statement inaccurate in any respect within a sufficient time before the statement was relied upon reasonably to have enabled that general partner to cancel or amend the certificate, or to file a petition for its cancellation or amendment under G.S. 59-205. (1985 (Reg. Sess., 1986), c. 989, s. 2.)

§ 59-208. Notice.

The fact that a certificate of limited partnership is on file in the office of the Secretary of State is notice that the partnership is a limited partnership and the persons designated therein as general partners are general partners, but it is not notice of any other fact. (1985 (Reg. Sess., 1986), c. 989, s. 2.)

§ 59-209. Certificate of existence.

(a) Anyone may apply to the Secretary of State to furnish a certificate of existence for a domestic limited partnership or a certificate of authorization for a foreign limited partnership.

(b) A certificate of existence or authorization sets forth:

(1) The domestic limited partnership's name or the foreign limited partnership's name used in this State;

(2) That (i) the domestic limited partnership has filed a certificate of limited partnership under the law of this State, the effective date of the filing, and the period of the domestic limited partnership's duration, or (ii) the foreign limited partnership is authorized to transact business in this State;

(3) If the limited partnership has registered as a limited liability limited partnership, that the registration has not been cancelled or revoked;

(4) That a certificate of cancellation of the certificate of limited partnership has not been filed; and

(5) Other facts of record in the office of the Secretary of State that may be requested by the applicant.

(c) Subject to any qualification stated in the certificate, a certificate of existence or authorization issued by the Secretary of State may be relied upon as conclusive evidence that the domestic limited partnership has filed a certificate of limited partnership and has not filed a certificate of cancellation or that the foreign limited partnership is authorized to transact business in this State, and, if applicable, that the domestic limited partnership has registered as a limited liability limited partnership and that such registration has not been cancelled or revoked. (2001-387, s. 127.)

§ 59-210. Limited liability limited partnerships.

(a) To become a limited liability limited partnership, a limited partnership shall file with the Secretary of State an application stating:

(1) The name of the limited liability limited partnership, which must satisfy the requirements of Article 3 of Chapter 55D of the General Statutes.

(2) The street address, and mailing address if different from the street address, of its principal office, and the county in which the principal office is located.

(3) The fiscal year end of the limited liability limited partnership.

(b) The terms and conditions on which a limited partnership becomes a limited liability limited partnership shall be approved in the manner provided in the partnership agreement; provided, however, if the partnership agreement does not contain any such provision, the terms and conditions must be approved (i) in the case of a limited partnership having a partnership agreement that expressly considers obligations to contribute to the partnership, in the manner necessary to amend those provisions, or (ii) in any other case, in the manner necessary to amend the partnership agreement.

(c) A limited partnership becomes a limited liability limited partnership when its application for registration becomes effective.

(d) The status of a limited liability limited partnership and the liability of its partners is not affected by errors or later changes in the information required to be contained in the application for registration.

(e) A limited liability limited partnership shall promptly amend its registration to reflect any change in the information contained in its application for registration, other than changes that are properly included in other documents filed with the Secretary of State. A registration is amended by filing a certificate of amendment with the Secretary of State. The certificate of amendment shall set forth:

(1) The name of the limited liability limited partnership as reflected on the application for registration;

(2) The date of filing of the application for registration; and

(3) The amendment to the application for registration.

(f) A limited liability limited partnership may cancel its registration by filing a certificate of cancellation with the Secretary of State. The certificate of cancellation shall set forth:

(1) The name of the limited liability limited partnership as reflected on the application for registration;

(2) The date of filing of the application for registration; and

(3) The effective date and time of cancellation if it is not to be effective at the time of filing the certificate.

(g) A limited liability limited partnership shall be subject to the provisions of G.S. 59-84.4 as if it were a registered limited liability partnership. (2001-387, ss. 127, 158; 2001-413, s. 8.)

§§ 59-211 through 59-300. Reserved for future codification purposes.

Part 3. Limited Partners.

§ 59-301. Admission of limited partners.

(a) In connection with the formation of a limited partnership, a person is admitted as a limited partner upon the later to occur of:

(1) The formation of the limited partnership; or

(2) The time provided for becoming a limited partner pursuant to and upon compliance with the partnership agreement.

(b) After the formation of a limited partnership, a person may be admitted as an additional limited partner:

(1) In the case of a person acquiring a partnership interest directly from the limited partnership, at the time provided pursuant to, and upon the compliance with, the partnership agreement; and

(2) In the case of an assignee of a partnership interest of a partner who has the power, as provided in G.S. 59-704, to grant the assignee the right to become a limited partner, upon the exercise of that power and compliance with

any conditions limiting the grant or exercise of the power. (1985 (Reg. Sess., 1986), c. 989, s. 2; 1999-362, s. 16.)

§ 59-302. Voting.

The partnership agreement may grant to all or a specified group of the limited partners the right to vote (on a per capita or other basis) upon any matter. (1985 (Reg. Sess., 1986), c. 989, s. 2; 1999-362, s. 17.)

§ 59-303. Liability to third parties.

A limited partner is not liable for the obligations of a limited partnership by reason of being a limited partner and does not become liable for the obligations of a limited partnership by participating in the management or control of the business of the limited partnership. (1985 (Reg. Sess., 1986), c. 989, s. 2; 1997-456, s. 27; 1999-362, s. 18.)

§ 59-304. Person erroneously believing himself limited partner.

(a) Except as provided in subsection (b), a person who makes a contribution to a business enterprise and erroneously but in good faith believes that the person has become a limited partner in the enterprise is not a general partner in the enterprise and is not bound by its obligations by reason of making the contribution, receiving distributions from the enterprise, or exercising any rights of a limited partner, if, on ascertaining the mistake, he:

(1) Causes an appropriate certificate of limited partnership [or] certificate of amendment to be executed and filed; or

(2) Withdraws from future equity participation in the enterprise.

(b) A person who makes a contribution of the kind described in subsection (a) of this section is liable as a general partner to any third party who transacts business with the enterprise in the case in which:

(1) The third party actually believed in good faith that the person was a general partner at the time of the transaction; and

(2) The third party transacted business with the enterprise before either:

a. An appropriate certificate has been filed pursuant to subsection (a) of this section to reflect that the person is not a general partner; or

b. The person has given notice to the partnership of withdrawal from future equity participation and before the withdrawal was effective. (1985 (Reg. Sess., 1986), c. 989, s. 2; 1999-362, s. 19.)

§ 59-305. Information.

Each limited partner has the right to:

(1) Inspect and copy any of the partnership records required to be maintained by G.S. 59-106; and

(2) Obtain from the general partners from time to time upon reasonable demand (i) true and full information regarding the state of the business and financial condition of the limited partnership, (ii) promptly after becoming available, a copy of the limited partnership's federal, State, and local income tax returns for each year, and (iii) other information regarding the affairs of the limited partnership as is just and reasonable. (1985 (Reg. Sess., 1986), c. 989, s. 2; 1999-362, s. 20.)

§§ 59-306 through 59-400. Reserved for future codification purposes.

Part 4. General Partners.

§ 59-401. Admission of additional general partners.

Unless otherwise provided in the partnership agreement, after the filing of a limited partnership's original certificate of limited partnership, additional general partners may be admitted only with the specific written consent of each partner. (1985 (Reg. Sess., 1986), c. 989, s. 2.)

§ 59-402. Events of withdrawal.

Except as approved by the specific written consent of all partners at the time, a person ceases to be a general partner of a limited partnership upon the happening of any of the following events:

(1) The general partner withdraws from the limited partnership as provided in G.S. 59-602;

(2) The general partner ceases to be a member of the limited partnership as provided in G.S. 59-702;

(3) The general partner is removed as a general partner in accordance with the partnership agreement;

(4) Unless otherwise provided in writing in the partnership agreement, the general partner: (i) makes an assignment for the benefit of creditors; (ii) files a voluntary petition in bankruptcy; (iii) is adjudicated a bankrupt or insolvent; (iv) files a petition or answer seeking for himself any reorganization, arrangement, composition, readjustment, liquidation, dissolution, or similar relief under any statute, law, or regulation; (v) files an answer or other pleading admitting or failing to contest the material allegations of a petition filed against the general partner in any proceeding of this nature; or (vi) seeks, consents to, or acquiesces in the appointment of a trustee, receiver, or liquidator of the general partner or of all or any substantial part of the general partner's properties;

(5) Unless otherwise provided in writing in the partnership agreement, 120 days after the commencement of any proceeding against the general partner seeking reorganization, arrangement, composition, readjustment, liquidation, dissolution, or similar relief under any statute, law, or regulation, the proceeding has not been dismissed, or if within 90 days after the appointment without the general partner's consent or acquiescence of a trustee, receiver, or liquidator of the general partner or of all or any substantial part of his properties, the appointment is not vacated or stayed, or within 90 days after the expiration of any such stay, the appointment is not vacated;

(6) In the case of a general partner who is a natural person,

a. The general partner's death; or

b. The entry of an order by a court of competent jurisdiction adjudicating the general partner incompetent to manage his or her person or property;

(7) In the case of a general partner who is acting as a general partner by virtue of being a trustee of a trust, the termination of the trust (but not merely the substitution of a new trustee);

(8) In the case of a general partner that is a separate partnership, the dissolution and commencement of winding up of the separate partnership;

(9) In the case of a general partner that is a corporation, the filing of a certificate of dissolution, or its equivalent, for the corporation or the revocation of its charter;

(10) Unless otherwise provided in the partnership agreement, or with the consent of all partners, in the case of a general partner that is an estate, the distribution by the fiduciary of the estate's entire interest in the partnership;

(11) In the case of a general partner that is a limited liability company, the dissolution and commencement of winding up of the limited liability company; or

(12) In the case of a general partner that is not a natural person, trust, separate partnership, corporation, estate, or limited liability company, the termination of the general partner. (1985 (Reg. Sess., 1986), c. 989, s. 2; 1997-456, s. 27; 1999-362, ss. 21, 22; 2001-387, ss. 128, 129, 130, 131.)

§ 59-403. General powers and liabilities.

(a) Except as provided in this Article or in the partnership agreement, a general partner of a limited partnership has the rights and powers and is subject to the restrictions and liabilities of a partner in a partnership without limited partners.

(b) Except as provided in this Article, a general partner of a limited partnership that is not a limited liability limited partnership has the liabilities of a partner in a partnership without limited partners to persons other than the partnership and the other partners, and a general partner of a limited liability limited partnership has the liabilities of, and has the limitation on liability afforded to, a partner in a registered limited liability partnership under the North Carolina Uniform Partnership Act to persons other than the partnership and the other partners with respect to debts and obligations of the limited partnership incurred while it is a limited liability limited partnership. Except as provided in this Article or in the partnership agreement, a general partner of a limited partnership that is not a limited liability limited partnership has the liabilities of a partner in a partnership without limited partners to the partnership and to the other partners, and a general partner of a limited liability limited partnership has the liabilities of, and has the limitation on liability afforded to, a partner in a registered limited liability partnership under the North Carolina Uniform Partnership Act to the partnership and to the other partners.

(c) Unless otherwise provided in the partnership agreement, a general partner of a limited partnership has the power and authority to delegate to one or more other persons the general partner's rights and powers to manage and control the business and affairs of the limited partnership, including to delegate to agents, officers, and employees of the general partner or the limited partnership, and to delegate by a management agreement or another agreement with, or otherwise to, other persons. Unless otherwise provided in the partnership agreement, a delegation by a general partner of a limited partnership shall not cause the general partner to cease to be a general partner of the limited partnership and shall not reduce or absolve the general partner of the general partner's duties or obligations to the limited partnership or its other partners. (1985 (Reg. Sess., 1986), c. 989, s. 2; 1987, c. 531, s. 6; 2001-387, ss. 132, 133.)

§ 59-404. Contributions by a general partner.

A general partner of a limited partnership may make contributions to the partnership and share in the profits and losses of, and in distributions from, the limited partnership as a general partner. A general partner also may make contributions to and share in profits, losses, and distributions as a limited partner. A person who is both a general partner and a limited partner has the rights and powers, and is subject to the restrictions and liabilities, of a general partner and, except as provided in the partnership agreement, also has the powers, and is subject to the restrictions, of a limited partner to the extent of his participation in the partnership as a limited partner. (1985 (Reg. Sess., 1986), c. 989, s. 2.)

§ 59-405. Voting.

The partnership agreement may grant to all or certain identified general partners the right to vote (on a per capita or any other basis), separately or with all or any class of the limited partners, on any matter. (1985 (Reg. Sess., 1986), c. 989, s. 2.)

§§ 59-406 through 59-500. Reserved for future codification purposes.

Part 5. Finance.

§ 59-501. Form of contribution.

The contribution of a partner may be in cash, property, or services rendered, or a promissory note or other obligation to contribute cash or property or to perform services. (1985 (Reg. Sess., 1986), c. 989, s. 2.)

§ 59-502. Liability for contributions.

(a) Except as provided in the partnership agreement, a partner is obligated to the limited partnership to perform any enforceable promise to contribute cash or property or to perform services, even if the partner is unable to perform because of death, disability or any other reason. If a partner does not make the required contribution of property or services, the partner is obligated at the option of the limited partnership to contribute cash equal to that portion of the agreed value of the stated contribution that has not been made. As used in this section, the term "agreed value" means an amount or other measure of value as (i) is provided in the partnership agreement, or (ii) if not provided in the partnership agreement, is required to be set forth in the written records required pursuant to G.S. 59-106.

(b) Unless otherwise provided in the partnership agreement, the obligation of a partner to make a contribution or return money or other property paid or distributed in violation of this Article may be compromised only by consent of all the partners. Any such compromise, however, shall not affect the rights of a creditor whose claim arose prior to the date of the compromise.

(c) No promise by a limited partner to contribute to the limited partnership is enforceable unless in a writing signed by the limited partner. (1985 (Reg. Sess., 1986), c. 989, s. 2; 1999-362, s. 23.)

§ 59-503. Sharing income, gain, loss, deduction or credit.

Income, gain, loss, deduction or credit of a limited partnership shall be allocated among the partners, and among classes of partners, in the manner provided in the partnership agreement. To the extent the partnership agreement does not provide for the allocation of items of income, gain, loss, deduction, or credit, then those items shall be allocated on the basis of the agreed value of the contributions made by each partner to the extent they have been received by the partnership and have not been returned. As used in this section, the term "agreed value" means an amount or other measure of value as (i) is provided in the partnership agreement, or (ii) if not provided in the partnership agreement, is required to be set forth in the written records required pursuant to G.S. 59-106. (1985 (Reg. Sess., 1986), c. 989, s. 2; 1999-362, s. 24.)

§ 59-504. Sharing of distributions.

Distributions of cash or other assets of a limited partnership shall be made among the partners, and among classes of partners, in the manner provided in the partnership agreement. To the extent the partnership agreement does not provide for the sharing of distributions among the partners, distributions shall be made among the partners on the basis of the agreed value of the contributions made by each partner to the extent they have been received by the partnership and have not been returned. As used in this section, the term "agreed value" means an amount or other measure of value as (i) is provided in the partnership agreement, or (ii) if not provided in the partnership agreement, is required to be set forth in the written records required pursuant to G.S. 59-106. (1985 (Reg. Sess., 1986), c. 989, s. 2; 1999-362, s. 25.)

§§ 59-505 through 59-600. Reserved for future codification purposes.

Part 6. Distribution and Withdrawal.

§ 59-601. Interim distributions.

Except as provided in this Article, a partner is entitled to receive distributions from a limited partnership before his withdrawal from the limited partnership and before the dissolution and winding up thereof to the extent and at the times or upon the happening of the events specified in the partnership agreement. (1985 (Reg. Sess., 1986), c. 989, s. 2.)

§ 59-602. Withdrawal of general partner.

After filing of the original certificate of limited partnership, a general partner may withdraw from a limited partnership at any time by giving written notice to the other partners, but if the withdrawal violates the partnership agreement, the limited partnership may recover from the withdrawing general partner, in addition to its other remedies, any damages for breach of the partnership agreement and may offset the damages against the amount otherwise distributable or payable to the partner. (1985 (Reg. Sess., 1986), c. 989, s. 2; 1999-362, s. 26.)

§ 59-603. Withdrawal of limited partner.

A limited partner may withdraw from a limited partnership only at the time or upon the happening of events specified in writing in and in accordance with the partnership agreement, including any amendment or addendum to the partnership agreement agreed upon by the partners unanimously or in accordance with the terms of the agreement and made in connection with any permitted withdrawal. If the partnership agreement does not specify in writing the time or the events upon the happening of which a limited partner may withdraw, a limited partner may not withdraw prior to the time for the dissolution and winding up of the limited partnership. (1985 (Reg. Sess., 1986), c. 989, s. 2; 1999-362, s. 27.)

§ 59-604. Distribution upon withdrawal.

Except as provided in this Article, upon withdrawal any withdrawing partner is entitled to receive any distribution to which the partner is entitled under the partnership agreement and, if not otherwise provided in the agreement, the partner is entitled to receive, within a reasonable time after withdrawal, the fair value of the partner's partnership interest in the limited partnership as of the date of withdrawal, based upon the partner's right to share in distributions from the limited partnership. (1985 (Reg. Sess., 1986), c. 989, s. 2; 1999-362, s. 28.)

§ 59-605. Distribution in kind.

Except as provided in writing in the limited partnership agreement, (1) a partner, regardless of the nature of his contribution, has no right to demand and receive any distribution from a limited partnership in any form other than cash; and (2) a partner may not be compelled to accept a distribution of any asset in kind from a limited partnership to the extent that the percentage of the asset distributed to him exceeds a percentage of that asset which is equal to the percentage in which he shares in distributions from the limited partnership. (1985 (Reg. Sess., 1986), c. 989, s. 2.)

§ 59-606. Right to distribution.

Subject to the other provisions of Part 6 of this Article, at the time a partner becomes entitled to receive a distribution, the partner has the status of, and is entitled to all remedies available to, a creditor of the limited partnership with respect to the distribution. (1985 (Reg. Sess., 1986), c. 989, s. 2; 1999-362, s. 29.)

§ 59-607. Limitations on distribution.

A partner shall not receive a distribution from a limited partnership to the extent that, after giving effect to the distribution, all liabilities of the limited partnership, other than liabilities to partners on account of their partnership interests, exceed the fair value of the partnership assets. (1985 (Reg. Sess., 1986), c. 989, s. 2.)

§ 59-608. Liability upon return of contribution.

(a) If a partner has received the return of any part of his contribution without violation of the partnership agreement or this Article, he is liable to the limited partnership for a period of one year thereafter for the amount of the returned contribution, but only to the extent necessary to discharge the limited partnership's liabilities to creditors who extended credit to the limited partnership during the period the contribution was held by the partnership.

(b) If a partner has received the return of any part of his contribution in violation of the partnership agreement or this Article, he is liable to the limited partnership for a period of six years thereafter for the amount of the contribution wrongfully returned.

(c) A partner receives a return of the partner's contribution to the extent that a distribution to the partner reduces the partner's share of the fair value of the net assets of the limited partnership below the agreed value of the partner's contribution which has not been distributed to the partner. As used in this section, the term "agreed value" means an amount or other measure of value as (i) is provided in the partnership agreement, or (ii) if not provided in the partnership agreement, is required to be set forth in the written records required pursuant to G.S. 59-106. (1985 (Reg. Sess., 1986), c. 989, s. 2; 1999-362, s. 30.)

§§ 59-609 through 59-700. Reserved for future codification purposes.

Part 7. Assignment of Partnership Interest.

§ 59-701. Nature of partnership interest.

A partnership interest is personal property. (1985 (Reg. Sess., 1986), c. 989, s. 2.)

§ 59-702. Assignment of partnership interest.

Except as provided in the partnership agreement, a partnership interest is assignable in whole or in part. Subject to G.S. 59-801(3) an assignment of a partnership interest does not dissolve a limited partnership or entitle the assignee to become or to exercise any rights of a partner. An assignment entitles the assignee to receive, to the extent assigned, only the allocation and distribution to which the assignor would be entitled. Except as provided in the partnership agreement, a partner ceases to be a partner and to have the power to exercise any rights and powers of a partner upon assignment of all of the partner's partnership interest. Except as provided in the partnership agreement, neither the pledge or granting of a security interest in any or all of the partnership interest of a partner nor the pledge or granting of a lien or other encumbrance against any or all of the partnership interest of a partner shall cause the partner to cease to be a partner or cease to have the power to exercise any rights or powers of a partner. (1985 (Reg. Sess., 1986), c. 989, s. 2; 1987, c. 531, s. 7; 1999-362, s. 31.)

§ 59-703. Rights of creditor.

On application to a court of competent jurisdiction by any judgment creditor of a partner, the court may charge the partnership interest of the partner with payment of the unsatisfied amount of the judgment with interest. The general partners shall have no liability to a partner for payments to a judgment creditor pursuant to this provision. To the extent so charged, the judgment creditor has only the rights of an assignee of the partnership interest. This Article does not deprive any partner of the benefit of any exemption laws applicable to his partnership interest. (1985 (Reg. Sess., 1986), c. 989, s. 2.)

§ 59-704. Right of assignee to become limited partner.

(a) An assignee of a partnership interest, including an assignee of a general partner, may become a limited partner if and to the extent that (1) the assignor gives the assignee that right in accordance with authority described in the partnership agreement, or (2) all other partners consent.

(b) An assignee who has become a limited partner has, to the extent assigned, the rights and powers, and is subject to the restrictions and liabilities, of a limited partner under the partnership agreement and this Article. An assignee who becomes a limited partner also is liable for the obligations of the assignee's assignor to make and return contributions as provided in Parts 5 and 6 of this Article. However, the assignee is not obligated for liabilities that (i) are unknown to the assignee at the time the assignee became a limited partner and (ii) could not be ascertained from the written provisions of the partnership agreement.

(c) If an assignee of a partnership interest becomes a limited partner, the assignor is not released from his liability to the limited partnership under G.S. 59-207, 59-502, and 59-608. (1985 (Reg. Sess., 1986), c. 989, s. 2; 1999-362, s. 32.)

§ 59-705. Power of estate of deceased or incompetent partner.

If a partner who is an individual dies or a court of competent jurisdiction adjudges him to be incompetent to manage his person or his property, the partner's executor, administrator, guardian, conservator, or other legal representative may exercise all of the partner's rights for the purpose of settling his estate or administering his property, including any power the partner had to give an assignee the right to become a limited partner. If a partner is a corporation, trust, or other entity and is dissolved or terminated, the powers of that partner may be exercised by its legal representative or successor. (1985 (Reg. Sess., 1986), c. 989, s. 2.)

§§ 59-706 through 59-800. Reserved for future codification purposes.

Part 8. Dissolution.

§ 59-801. Nonjudicial dissolution.

(a) A limited partnership is dissolved and its affairs shall be wound up upon the happening of the first to occur of the following:

(1) At the time specified in the certificate of limited partnership or upon the happening of events specified in writing in the partnership agreement;

(2) Written consent of all partners;

(3) An event of withdrawal of a general partner unless:

a. At the time there is at least one other general partner, in which case, unless otherwise provided in a written partnership agreement or agreed upon by all remaining partners, (i) the limited partnership is not dissolved, (ii) the limited partnership shall not be wound up, and (iii) the business of the limited partnership shall be continued by the remaining general partners; or

b. Within 90 days after the withdrawal, all remaining partners, or a lesser number or portion of the partners provided in the partnership agreement, agree in writing to continue the business of the limited partnership and to the appointment of one or more additional general partners if necessary or desired, in which case the limited partnership is not dissolved and is not required to be wound up by reason of the event of withdrawal;

(3a) Ninety days after the withdrawal of the limited partnership's last limited partner, unless the limited partnership admits at least one limited partner before the end of the 90 days; or

(4) Entry of a decree of judicial dissolution under G.S. 59-802.

(b) The causes of dissolution of a limited partnership shall be governed solely by this Article. Article 2 of this Chapter, which governs the causes of dissolution of a partnership without limited partners, does not apply and shall not govern the causes of dissolution of a limited partnership. (1985 (Reg. Sess., 1986), c. 989, s. 2; 1999-362, s. 33.)

§ 59-802. Judicial dissolution.

On application by or for a partner the court may decree dissolution of a limited partnership whenever it is not reasonably practicable to carry on the business in conformity with the partnership agreement. The limited partnership's name becomes available for use by another entity as provided in 55D-21. (1985 (Reg. Sess., 1986), c. 989, s. 2; 2001-358, s. 36; 2001-387, ss. 173, 175(a); 2001-413, s. 6.)

§ 59-803. Winding up.

Except as provided in the partnership agreement, the general partners who have not wrongfully dissolved a limited partnership or, if none, the limited partners, may wind up the limited partnership's affairs; but the court may wind up the limited partnership's affairs upon application of any partner, his legal representative, or assignee. (1985 (Reg. Sess., 1986), c. 989, s. 2.)

§ 59-804. Distribution of assets.

Upon the winding up of a limited partnership, the assets shall be distributed as follows:

(1)   To creditors, including limited partners who are creditors, to the extent otherwise permitted by law, in satisfaction of liabilities of the limited partnership other than liabilities for distributions to partners under G.S. 59-601 or G.S. 59-604;

(2)   To general partners who are creditors to the extent otherwise permitted by law, in satisfaction of liabilities of the limited partnership other than liabilities for distributions to partners under G.S. 59-601 or G.S. 59-604;

(3)   Except as provided in the partnership agreement, to partners and former partners in satisfaction of liabilities for distributions under G.S. 59-601 or G.S. 59-604; and

(4) Except as provided in the partnership agreement, to partners first for the return of their contributions and secondly respecting their partnership interests, in the proportions in which the partners share in distributions. (1985 (Reg. Sess., 1986), c. 989, s. 2.)

§§ 59-805 through 59-900. Reserved for future codification purposes.

Part 9. Foreign Limited Partnerships.

§ 59-901. Law governing.

Subject to the Constitution of this State, (i) the laws of the jurisdiction under which a foreign limited partnership is organized govern its organization and internal affairs and the liability of its partners, and (ii) a foreign limited partnership may not be denied registration by reason of any difference between those laws and the laws of this State. (1985 (Reg. Sess., 1986), c. 989, s. 2; 1999-362, s. 34.)

§ 59-902. Registration.

(a) Before transacting business in this State, a foreign limited partnership shall procure a certificate of authority to transact business in this State from the Secretary of State. No foreign limited partnership shall be entitled to transact in this State any business which a limited partnership organized under this Article is not permitted to transact. In order to register, a foreign limited partnership shall deliver to the Secretary of State an application for registration as a foreign limited partnership, signed by a general partner and setting forth:

(1) The name of the foreign limited partnership and, if different, the name under which it proposes to register and transact business in this State;

(2) The jurisdiction and date of its formation;

(3) The date of formation and the period of duration;

(4) The street address, and the mailing address if different from the street address, of the principal office of the foreign limited partnership, and the county in which the principal office is located;

(5) The street address, and the mailing address if different from the street address, of the registered office of the foreign limited partnership in this State, the county in which the registered office is located, adn the name of its proposed registered agent in this State;

(6) If the certificate of limited partnership filed in the foreign limited partnership's state of organization is not required to include the names and addresses of the partners, a list of the names and addresses or, at the election of the foreign limited partnership, a list of the names and addresses of the general partners and the address, including county and city or town, and street and number, of the office at which is kept a list of the names and addresses of the limited partners and their capital contributions, together with an undertaking by the foreign limited partnership to keep such records until such foreign limited partnership's registration in this State is cancelled;

(7) A statement that in consideration of the issuance of a certificate of authority to transact business in this State, the foreign limited partnership appoints the Secretary of State of North Carolina as the agent to receive service of process, notice, or demand, whenever the foreign limited partnership fails to appoint or maintain a registered agent in this State or whenever any such registered agent cannot with reasonable diligence be found at the registered office;

(8) The names and addresses including county and city or town, and street and number, if any, of all of the general partners;

(8a) Whether the foreign limited partnership is a foreign limited liability partnership; and

(9) The effective date and time of the registration if it is not to be effective at the time of filing of the application.

(b) Without excluding other activities which shall not constitute transacting business in this State, a foreign limited partnership shall not be considered to be transacting business in this State, for the purpose of this Article, by reason of carrying on in this State any one or more of the following activities:

(1)	Maintaining or defending any action or suit or any administrative or arbitration proceeding, or effecting the settlement thereof or the settlement of claims or disputes;

(2)	Holding meetings of its partners or carrying on other activities concerning its internal affairs;

(3)	Maintaining bank accounts or borrowing money in this State, with or without security, even if such borrowings are repeated and continuous transactions;

(4)	Maintaining offices or agencies for the transfer, exchange, and registration of its securities, or appointing and maintaining trustees or depositaries with relation to its securities;

(5)	Soliciting or procuring orders, whether by mail or through employees or agents or otherwise, where such orders require acceptance without this State before becoming binding contracts;

(6)	Making or investing in loans with or without security including servicing of mortgages or deeds of trust through independent agencies within the State, the conducting of foreclosure proceedings and sale, the acquiring of property at foreclosure sale and the management and rental of such property for a reasonable time while liquidating its investment, provided no office or agency therefor is maintained in this State;

(7)	Taking security for or collecting debts due to it or enforcing any rights in property securing the same;

(8)	Transacting business in interstate commerce; and

(9)	Conducting an isolated transaction completed within a period of six months and not in the course of a number of repeated transactions of like nature.

(c)	Each foreign limited partnership authorized to transact business in this State must maintain a registered agent as required by Article 4 of Chapter 55D of the General Statutes and is subject to service on the Secretary of State under that Article.

(d) through (e) Repealed by Session Laws 2001-358, s. 50(b). (1985 (Reg. Sess., 1986), c. 989, s. 2; 1987, c. 531, s. 8.1; 2000-140, s. 55; 2001-358, s. 50(c); 2001-387, ss. 134, 159, 173, 175(a); 2001-413, s. 6; 2001-487, s. 62(y).)

§ 59-903. Issuance of registration.

If the Secretary of State finds that an application satisfies the requirements of this Article, the Secretary shall, when all requisite fees have been tendered as in this Article prescribed:

(1) Endorse on the application the word "filed", and the hour, day, month and year of the filing thereof;

(2) File in the office of the Secretary of State the application;

(3) Issue a certificate of authority to transact business in this State to which the Secretary shall affix the conformed copy of the application; and

(4) Send to the foreign limited partnership or its representative the certificate of authority, together with the conformed copy of the application affixed thereto. (1985 (Reg. Sess., 1986), c. 989, s. 2; 1987, c. 531, s. 8; 1997-485, s. 27; 1999-362, s. 35.)

§ 59-904. Name.

A foreign limited partnership may register with the Secretary of State under any name that meets the requirements of Article 3 of Chapter 55D of the General Statutes. (1985 (Reg. Sess., 1986), c. 989, s. 2; 2001-358, s. 35; 2001-387, ss. 135, 155, 173, 175(a); 2001-413, s. 6.)

§ 59-905. Changes and amendments.

If any statement in the application for registration of a foreign limited partnership was false when made or any arrangements or other facts described have changed, making the application inaccurate in any respect, the foreign limited partnership shall promptly file in the office of the Secretary of State an original and one conformed copy of a certificate, signed by a general partner, correcting such statement. (1985 (Reg. Sess., 1986), c. 989, s. 2.)

§ 59-906. Cancellation of registration.

A foreign limited partnership may cancel its registration by filing with the Secretary of State a certificate of cancellation signed by a general partner. A cancellation does not terminate the authority of the Secretary of State to accept service of process on the foreign limited partnership with respect to causes of action arising out of the transactions of business in this State. (1985 (Reg. Sess., 1986), c. 989, s. 2.)

§ 59-907. Transaction of business without registration.

(a) No foreign limited partnership transacting business in this State without permission obtained through a certificate of authority under this Article shall be permitted to maintain any action or proceeding in any court of this State unless such foreign limited partnership shall have obtained a certificate of authority prior to trial.

(b) The failure of a foreign limited partnership to obtain a certificate of authority to transact business in this State shall not impair the validity of any contract or act of the foreign limited partnership and shall not prevent the foreign limited partnership from defending any action or proceeding in any court of this State.

(c) A foreign limited partnership failing to obtain permission to transact business in this State as required by this Article or by prior statutes then applicable shall be liable to the State for the years or parts thereof during which it transacted business in this State without such permission in an amount equal to all fees and taxes which would have been imposed by law upon such foreign limited partnership had it duly applied for and received such permission plus interest and all penalties imposed by law for failure to pay such fees and taxes, plus five hundred dollars ($500.00) and costs. The Attorney General shall bring actions to recover all amounts due the State under the provisions of this section.

(d)   The Secretary of State is hereby directed to require that every foreign limited partnership transacting business in this State comply with the provisions of this Article. The Secretary of State is authorized to employ such assistants as shall be deemed necessary in his office for the purpose of enforcing the provisions of this Article and for making such investigations as shall be necessary to ascertain foreign limited partnerships now transacting business in this State which may have failed to comply with the provisions of this Article.

(e)   A limited partner of a foreign limited partnership is not liable as a general partner of the foreign limited partnership solely by reason of the foreign limited partnership's having transacted business in this State without registration.

(f)   A foreign limited partnership, by transacting business in this State without registration, appoints the Secretary of State as its agent for service of process with respect to causes of action arising out of the transaction of business in this State. (1985 (Reg. Sess., 1986), c. 989, s. 2; 1999-362, s. 36; 2000-140, s. 101(r).)

§ 59-908. Action by Attorney General.

The Attorney General may bring an action to restrain a foreign limited partnership from transacting business in this State in violation of this Article. (1985 (Reg. Sess., 1986), c. 989, s. 2.)

§ 59-909. Withdrawal of foreign limited partnership by reason of a merger, consolidation, or conversion.

(a)   Whenever a foreign limited partnership authorized to transact business in this State ceases its separate existence as a result of a statutory merger or consolidation permitted by the laws of the state or country under which it was organized, or converts into another type of entity as permitted by those laws, the surviving or resulting entity shall apply for a certificate of withdrawal for the foreign limited partnership by delivering to the Secretary of State for filing a copy of the articles of merger, consolidation, or conversion or a certificate reciting the facts of the merger, consolidation, or conversion, duly authenticated by the Secretary of State or other official having custody of limited partnership records in the state or country under the laws of which the foreign limited partnership was organized. If the surviving or resulting entity is not authorized to transact business or conduct affairs in this State, the articles or certificate must be accompanied by an application which must set forth:

(1)   The name of the foreign limited partnership authorized to transact business in this State, the type of entity and name of the surviving or resulting entity, and a statement that the surviving or resulting entity is not authorized to transact business or conduct affairs in this State;

(2)   A statement that the surviving or resulting entity consents that service of process based on any cause of action arising in this State, or arising out of business transacted in this State, during the time the foreign limited partnership was authorized to transact business in this State, may thereafter be made by service thereof on the Secretary of State;

(3)   A mailing address to which the Secretary of State may mail a copy of any process served upon the Secretary under subdivision (a)(2) of this section; and

(4)   A commitment to file with the Secretary of State a statement of any subsequent change in its mailing address.

(b)   If the Secretary of State finds that the articles or certificate and the application for withdrawal, if required, conform to law, the Secretary of State shall:

(1)   Endorse on the articles or certificate and the application for withdrawal, if required, the word "filed" and the hour, day, month, and year of filing thereof;

(2)   File the articles or certificate and the application, if required;

(3)   Issue a certificate of withdrawal; and

(4)   Send to the surviving or resulting entity or its representative the certificate of withdrawal, together with the exact or conformed copy of the application, if required, affixed thereto.

(c) After the withdrawal of the foreign limited partnership is effective, service of process on the Secretary of State in accordance with subsection (a) of this section shall be made by delivering to and leaving with the Secretary of State, or with any clerk authorized by the Secretary of State to accept service of process, duplicate copies of the process and the fee required by G.S. 59-1106(b). Upon receipt of process in the manner provided in this subsection, the Secretary of State shall immediately mail a copy of the process by registered or certified mail, return receipt requested, to the surviving or resulting entity at the mailing address designated pursuant to subsection (a) of this section. (1999-369, s. 4.7; 2001-387, ss. 136, 137; 2001-487, s. 62(z).)

§§ 59-910 through 59-1000. Reserved for future codification purposes.

Part 10. Derivative Actions.

§ 59-1001. Right of action.

A limited partner may bring an action in the right of a limited partnership to recover a judgment in its favor if general partners with authority to do so have refused to bring the action or if an effort to cause those general partners to bring the action is not likely to succeed. (1985 (Reg. Sess., 1986), c. 989, s. 2.)

§ 59-1002. Proper plaintiff.

In a derivative action, the plaintiff must be a partner at the time of bringing the action and (i) must have been a partner at the time of the transaction that is the subject of the complaint or (ii) the plaintiff's status as a partner must have devolved upon the partner by operation of law or pursuant to the terms of the partnership agreement from a person who was a partner at the time of the transaction. (1985 (Reg. Sess., 1986), c. 989, s. 2; 1999-362, s. 37.)

§ 59-1003. Pleading.

In a derivative action, the complaint shall set forth with particularity the effort of the plaintiff to secure initiation of the action by a general partner or the reasons for not making the effort. (1985 (Reg. Sess., 1986), c. 989, s. 2.)

§ 59-1004. Expenses.

(a) If a derivative action is successful, in whole or in part, or if anything is received by the plaintiff as a result of a judgment, compromise, or settlement of any action or claim, the court may award the plaintiff reasonable expenses, including reasonable attorney's fees, and shall direct him to remit to the limited partnership the remainder of those proceeds received by him.

(b) In any such action, the court, upon final judgment and a finding that the action was brought without reasonable cause, may require the plaintiff or plaintiffs to pay to the defendant or defendants the reasonable expenses, including attorneys' fees, incurred by them in defense of the action. (1985 (Reg. Sess., 1986), c. 989, s. 2.)

§ 59-1005. Dismissal of action.

Such action shall not be discontinued, dismissed, compromised or settled without the approval of the court. If the court shall determine that the interest of the partners or of the creditors of the partnership will be substantially affected by such discontinuance, dismissal, compromise, or settlement, the court, in its discretion, may direct that notice, by publication or otherwise, shall be given to such partners or creditors whose interest it determines will be so affected. If notice is so directed to be given, the court may determine which one or more of the parties to the action shall bear the expense of giving the same, in such amount as the court shall be awarded as costs of the action. (1985 (Reg. Sess., 1986), c. 989, s. 2.)

§ 59-1006. Construction.

The provisions of this Article shall not be construed to deprive a partner of whatever rights of action he may possess in his individual capacity. (1985 (Reg. Sess., 1986), c. 989, s. 2.)

§§ 59-1007 through 59-1049. Reserved for future codification purposes.

Part 10A. Conversion to Limited Partnership.

§ 59-1050. Conversion.

A business entity other than a domestic limited partnership may convert to a domestic limited partnership if:

(1) The conversion is permitted by the laws of the state or country governing the organization and internal affairs of the converting business entity; and

(2) The converting business entity complies with the requirements of this part and, to the extent applicable, the laws referred to in subdivision (1) of this section. (1999-369, s. 4.8; 2001-387, s. 139.)

§ 59-1051. Plan of conversion.

(a) The converting business entity shall approve a written plan of conversion containing:

(1) The name of the converting business entity, its type of business entity, and the state or country whose laws govern its organization and internal affairs;

(2) The name of the resulting domestic limited partnership into which the converting business entity shall convert;

(3) The terms and conditions of the conversion; and

(4) The manner and basis for converting the interests in the converting business entity into interests, obligations, or securities of the resulting domestic limited partnership or into cash or other property in whole or in part.

(a1) The plan of conversion may contain other provisions relating to the conversion.

(a2) The provisions of the plan of conversion, other than the provisions required by subdivisions (1) and (2) of subsection (a) of this section, may be made dependent on facts objectively ascertainable outside the plan of conversion if the plan of conversion sets forth the manner in which the facts will operate upon the affected provisions. The facts may include any of the following:

(1) Statistical or market indices, market prices of any security or group of securities, interest rates, currency exchange rates, or similar economic or financial data.

(2) A determination or action by the converting business entity or by any other person, group, or body.

(3) The terms of, or actions taken under, an agreement to which the converting business entity is a party, or any other agreement or document.

(b) The plan of conversion shall be approved in accordance with the laws of the state or country governing the organization and internal affairs of the converting business entity.

(c) After a plan of conversion has been approved as provided in subsection (b) of this section, but before a certificate of limited partnership for the resulting domestic limited partnership becomes effective, the plan of conversion may be amended or abandoned to the extent permitted by the laws that govern the organization and internal affairs of the converting business entity. (1999-369, s. 4.8; 2001-387, s. 140; 2005-268, s. 56.)

§ 59-1052. Filing of certificate of limited partnership.

(a) After a plan of conversion has been approved by the converting business entity as provided in G.S. 59-1051, a certificate of limited partnership shall be delivered to the Secretary of State for filing. In addition to the matters required or permitted by G.S. 59-201, the certificate of limited partnership shall contain articles of conversion stating:

(1)   That the domestic limited partnership is being formed pursuant to a conversion of another business entity;

(2)   The name of the converting business entity, its type of business entity, and the state or country whose laws govern its organization and internal affairs; and

(3)   That a plan of conversion has been approved by the converting business entity in the manner required by law.

If the plan of conversion is abandoned after the certificate of limited partnership has been filed with the Secretary of State but before the certificate of limited partnership becomes effective, an amendment withdrawing the certificate of limited partnership shall be delivered to the Secretary of State for filing prior to the time the articles of organization become effective.

(b)   The conversion takes effect when the certificate of limited partnership becomes effective.

(c)   Repealed by Session Laws 2001-387, s. 141.

(d)   Certificates of conversion shall also be registered as provided in G.S. 47-18.1. (1999-369, s. 4.8; 2001-387, s. 141; 2002-159, s. 34(b).)

§ 59-1053. Effects of conversion.

When the conversion takes effect:

(1)   The converting business entity ceases its prior form of organization and continues in existence as the resulting domestic limited partnership;

(2)   The title to all real estate and other property owned by the converting business entity continues vested in the resulting domestic limited partnership without reversion or impairment;

(3) All liabilities of the converting business entity continue as liabilities of the resulting domestic limited partnership;

(4) A proceeding pending by or against the converting business entity may be continued as if the conversion did not occur; and

(5) The interests in the converting business entity that are to be converted into interests, obligations, or securities of the resulting domestic limited partnership or into the right to receive cash or other property are thereupon so converted, and the former holders of interests in the converting business entity are entitled only to the rights provided in the plan of conversion.

The conversion shall not affect the liability or absence of liability of any holder of an interest in the converting business entity for any acts, omissions, or obligations of the converting business entity made or incurred prior to the effectiveness of the conversion. The cessation of the existence of the converting business entity in its prior form of organization in the conversion shall not constitute a dissolution or termination of the converting business entity. (1999-369, s. 4.8; 2000-140, s. 101(s).)

§ 59-1054: Recodified as § 59-1070 by Session Laws 2001-387, s. 143.

§ 59-1055: Recodified as § 59-1071 by Session Laws 2001-387, s. 143.

§ 59-1056: Recodified as § 59-1072 by Session Laws 2001-387, s. 143.

§ 59-1057: Recodified as § 59-1073 by Session Laws 2001-387, s. 143.

§ 59-1058. Reserved for future codification purposes.

§ 59-1059. Reserved for future codification purposes.

Part 10B. Conversion of Limited Partnership.

§ 59-1060. Conversion.

A domestic limited partnership may convert to a different business entity if:

(1) The conversion is permitted by the laws of the state or country governing the organization and internal affairs of such other business entity; and

(2) The converting domestic limited partnership complies with the requirements of this Part and, to the extent applicable, the laws referred to in subdivision (1) of this section. (2001-387, s. 142.)

§ 59-1061. Plan of conversion.

(a) The converting domestic limited partnership shall approve a written plan of conversion containing:

(1) The name of the converting domestic limited partnership;

(2) The name of the resulting business entity into which the domestic limited partnership shall convert, its type of business entity, and the state or country whose laws govern its organization and internal affairs;

(3) The terms and conditions of the conversion; and

(4) The manner and basis for converting the interests in the domestic limited partnership into interests, obligations, or securities of the resulting business entity or into cash or other property in whole or in part.

(a1) The plan of conversion may contain other provisions relating to the conversion.

(a2) The provisions of the plan of conversion, other than the provisions required by subdivisions (1) and (2) of subsection (a) of this section, may be made dependent on facts objectively ascertainable outside the plan of conversion if the plan of conversion sets forth the manner in which the facts will operate upon the affected provisions. The facts may include any of the following:

(1) Statistical or market indices, market prices of any security or group of securities, interest rates, currency exchange rates, or similar economic or financial data.

(2) A determination or action by the converting domestic limited partnership or by any other person, group, or body.

(3) The terms of, or actions taken under, an agreement to which the converting domestic limited partnership is a party, or any other agreement or document.

(b) The plan of conversion shall be approved by the domestic limited partnership in the manner provided for the approval of the conversion in a written partnership agreement or, if there is no provision, by the unanimous consent of its partners. If any partner of the converting domestic limited partnership has or will have personal liability for any existing or future obligation of the resulting business entity solely as a result of holding an interest in the resulting business entity, then in addition to the requirements of the preceding sentence, approval of the plan of conversion by the domestic limited partnership shall require the consent of each such partner. The converting domestic limited partnership shall provide a copy of the plan of conversion to each partner of the converting domestic limited partnership at the time provided in a written partnership agreement or, if there is no such provision, prior to its approval of the plan of conversion.

(c) After a plan of conversion has been approved by a domestic limited partnership but before the articles of conversion become effective, the plan of conversion (i) may be amended as provided in the plan of conversion, or (ii) may be abandoned (subject to any contractual rights) as provided in the plan of conversion or written partnership agreement or, if not so provided, as determined by the general partners of the domestic limited partnership in accordance with G.S. 59-403. (2001-387, s. 142; 2001-487, s. 62(aa); 2005-268, s. 57.)

§ 59-1062. Articles of conversion.

(a) After a plan of conversion has been approved by the converting domestic limited partnership as provided in G.S. 59-1061, the converting domestic limited partnership shall deliver articles of conversion to the Secretary of State for filing. The articles of conversion shall state:

(1) The name of the converting domestic limited partnership;

(2) The name of the resulting business entity, its type of business entity, the state or country whose laws govern its organization and internal affairs, and, if the resulting business entity is not authorized to transact business or conduct affairs in this State, a designation of its mailing address and a commitment to file with the Secretary of State a statement of any subsequent change in its mailing address; and

(3) That a plan of conversion has been approved by the domestic limited partnership as required by law.

(b) If the domestic limited partnership is converting to a business entity whose formation, or whose status as a registered limited liability partnership as defined in G.S. 59-32, requires the filing of a document with the Secretary of State, then, notwithstanding subsection (a) of this section, the articles of conversion shall be included as part of that document and shall contain the information required by the laws governing the organization and internal affairs of the resulting business entity.

(c) If the plan of conversion is abandoned after the articles of conversion have been filed with the Secretary of State but before the articles of conversion become effective, the converting domestic limited partnership shall deliver to the Secretary of State for filing prior to the time the articles of conversion become effective an amendment of the articles of conversion withdrawing the articles of conversion.

(d) The conversion takes effect when the articles of conversion become effective.

(e) Certificates of conversion shall also be registered as provided in G.S. 47-18.1. (2001-387, s. 142; 2001-487, s. 62(bb).)

§ 59-1063. Effects of conversion.

(a) When the conversion takes effect:

(1) The converting domestic limited partnership ceases its prior form of organization and continues in existence as the resulting business entity;

(2) The title to all real estate and other property owned by the converting domestic limited partnership continues vested in the resulting business entity without reversion or impairment;

(3) All liabilities of the converting domestic limited partnership continue as liabilities of the resulting business entity;

(4) A proceeding pending by or against the converting domestic limited partnership may be continued as if the conversion did not occur; and

(5) The interests in the converting domestic limited partnership that are to be converted into interests, obligations, or securities of the resulting business entity or into the right to receive cash or other property are thereupon so converted, and the former holders of interests in the converting domestic limited partnership are entitled only to the rights provided in the plan of conversion.

The conversion shall not affect the liability or absence of liability of any holder of an interest in the converting domestic limited partnership for any acts, omissions, or obligations of the converting domestic limited partnership made or incurred prior to the effectiveness of the conversion. The cessation of the existence of the converting domestic limited partnership in its form of organization as a domestic limited partnership in the conversion shall not constitute a dissolution or termination of the converting domestic limited partnership.

(b) If the resulting business entity is not a domestic corporation or a domestic limited liability company when the conversion takes effect, the resulting business entity is deemed:

(1) To agree that it may be served with process in this State for enforcement of (i) any obligation of the converting domestic limited partnership, and (ii) any obligation of the resulting business entity arising from the conversion; and

(2) To have appointed the Secretary of State as its agent for service of process in any such proceeding. Service on the Secretary of State of any such process shall be made by delivering to and leaving with the Secretary of State, or with any clerk authorized by the Secretary of State to accept service of process, duplicate copies of the process and the fee required by G.S. 59-1106(b). Upon receipt of service of process on behalf of a resulting business entity in the manner provided for in this section, the Secretary of State shall

immediately mail a copy of the process by registered or certified mail, return receipt requested, to the resulting business entity. If the resulting business entity is authorized to transact business or conduct affairs in this State, the address for mailing shall be its principal office designated in the latest document filed with the Secretary of State that is authorized by law to designate the principal office or, if there is no principal office on file, its registered office. If the resulting business entity is not authorized to transact business or conduct affairs in this State, the address for mailing shall be the mailing address designated pursuant to G.S. 59-1062(a)(2). (2001-387, s. 142.)

§§ 59-1064 through 59-1069. Reserved for future codification purposes.

Part 10C. Merger.

§ 59-1070. Merger.

A domestic limited partnership may merge with one or more other domestic limited partnerships or other business entities if:

(1)   The merger is permitted by the laws of the state or country governing the organization and internal affairs of each other merging business entity; and

(2)   Each merging domestic limited partnership and each other merging business entity comply with the requirements of this Part, and, to the extent applicable, the laws referred to in subdivision (1) of this section. (1999-369, s. 4.8; 2001-387, ss. 143, 144.)

§ 59-1071. Plan of merger.

(a)   Each merging domestic limited partnership and each other merging business entity shall approve a written plan of merger containing:

(1)   For each merging business entity, its name, type of business entity, and the state or country whose laws govern its organization and internal affairs;

(2) The name of the merging business entity that shall survive the merger;

(3) The terms and conditions of the merger;

(4) The manner and basis for converting the interests in each merging business entity into interests, obligations, or securities of the surviving business entity or into cash or other property in whole or in part; and

(5) If the surviving business entity is a domestic limited partnership, any amendments to its certificate of limited partnership that are to be made in connection with the merger.

(a1) The plan of merger may contain other provisions relating to the merger.

(a2) The provisions of the plan of merger, other than the provisions referred to in subdivisions (1), (2), and (5) of subsection (a) of this section, may be made dependent on facts objectively ascertainable outside the plan of merger if the plan of merger sets forth the manner in which the facts will operate upon the affected provisions. The facts may include any of the following:

(1) Statistical or market indices, market prices of any security or group of securities, interest rates, currency exchange rates, or similar economic or financial data.

(2) A determination or action by the domestic limited partnership or by any other person, group, or body.

(3) The terms of, or actions taken under, an agreement to which the domestic limited partnership is a party, or any other agreement or document.

(b) In the case of a merging domestic limited partnership, the plan of merger must be approved in the manner provided in a written partnership agreement that is binding on all the partners for approval of a merger with the type of business entity contemplated in the plan of merger, or, if there is no provision, by the unanimous consent of its partners. If any partner of a merging domestic limited partnership has or will have personal liability for any existing or future obligation of the surviving business entity solely as a result of holding an interest in the surviving business entity, then in addition to the requirements of the preceding sentence, approval of the plan of merger by the domestic limited partnership shall require the consent of that partner. In the case of each other merging business entity, the plan of merger must be approved in accordance with the laws of the state or country governing the organization and internal affairs of the merging business entity.

(c) After a plan of merger has been approved by a domestic limited partnership, but before the articles of merger become effective, the plan of merger (i) may be amended as provided in the plan of merger, or (ii) may be abandoned (subject to any contractual rights) as provided in the plan of merger or a written partnership agreement that is binding on all the partners or, if there is no such provision, as determined by the unanimous consent of the partners. (1999-369, s. 4.8; 2001-387, ss. 143, 145; 2005-268, s. 58.)

§ 59-1072. Articles of merger.

(a) After a plan of merger has been approved by each merging domestic limited partnership and each other merging business entity as provided in G.S. 59-1071, the surviving business entity shall deliver articles of merger to the Secretary of State for filing. The articles of merger shall set forth:

(1) Repealed by Session Laws 2005-268, s. 59, effective October 1, 2005.

(2) For each merging business entity, its name, type of business entity, and the state or country whose laws govern its organization and internal affairs.

(3) The name of the merging business entity that will survive the merger and, if the surviving business entity is not authorized to transact business or conduct affairs in this State, a designation of its mailing address and a commitment to file with the Secretary of State a statement of any subsequent change in its mailing address.

(3a) If the surviving business entity is a domestic limited partnership, any amendment to its certificate of limited partnership as provided in the plan of merger.

(4) A statement that the plan of merger has been approved by each merging business entity in the manner required by law.

(5) Repealed by Session Laws 2005-268, s. 59, effective October 1, 2005.

If the plan of merger is amended after the articles of merger have been filed but before the articles of merger become effective, and any statement in the articles of merger becomes incorrect as a result of the amendment, the surviving business entity promptly shall deliver to the Secretary of State for filing prior to the time the articles of merger become effective an amendment to the articles of merger correcting the incorrect statement. If the articles of merger are abandoned after the articles of merger are filed but before the articles of merger become effective, the surviving business entity shall deliver to the Secretary of State for filing prior to the time the articles of merger become effective an amendment reflecting abandonment of the plan of merger.

(b) A merger takes effect when the articles of merger become effective.

(c) Certificates of merger shall also be registered as provided in G.S. 47-18.1. (1999-369, s. 4.8; 2001-387, ss. 143, 146; 2001-487, s. 62(cc); 2005-268, s. 59.)

§ 59-1073. Effects of merger.

(a) When the merger takes effect:

(1) Each other merging business entity merges into the surviving business entity, and the separate existence of each merging business entity except the surviving business entity ceases;

(2) The title to all real estate and other property owned by each merging business entity is vested in the surviving business entity without reversion or impairment;

(3) The surviving business entity has all liabilities of each merging business entity;

(4) A proceeding pending by or against any merging business entity may be continued as if the merger did not occur, or the surviving business entity may be substituted in the proceeding for a merging business entity whose separate existence ceases in the merger;

(5) If a domestic limited partnership is the surviving business entity, its certificate of limited partnership shall be amended to the extent provided in the articles of merger;

(6) The interests in each merging business entity that are to be converted into interests, obligations, or securities of the surviving business entity or into the right to receive cash or other property are thereupon so converted, and the former holders of the interests are entitled only to the rights provided to them in the plan of merger or, in the case of former holders of shares in a domestic corporation as defined in G.S. 55-1-40, any rights they have under Article 13 of Chapter 55 of the General Statutes; and

(7) If the surviving business entity is not a domestic corporation, the surviving business entity is deemed to agree that it will promptly pay to the shareholders of any merging domestic corporation exercising appraisal rights the amount, if any, to which they are entitled under Article 13 of Chapter 55 of the General Statutes and otherwise to comply with the requirements of Article 13 as if it were a surviving domestic corporation in the merger.

The merger shall not affect the liability or absence of liability of any holder of an interest in a merging business entity for any acts, omissions, or obligations of any merging business equity made or incurred prior to the effectiveness of the merger. The cessation of separate existence of a merging business entity in the merger shall not constitute a dissolution or termination of such merging business entity.

(b) If the surviving business entity is not a domestic limited liability company, a domestic corporation, a domestic nonprofit corporation, or a domestic limited partnership, when the merger takes effect the surviving business entity is deemed:

(1) To agree that it may be served with process in this State in any proceeding for enforcement of (i) any obligation of any merging domestic limited liability company, domestic corporation, domestic nonprofit corporation, domestic limited partnership or other partnership as defined in G.S. 59-36 that is formed under the laws of this State, (ii) the appraisal rights of shareholders of any merging domestic corporation under Article 13 of Chapter 55 of the General Statutes, and (iii) any obligation of the surviving business entity arising from the merger; and

(2) To have appointed the Secretary of State as its agent for service of process in any such proceeding. Service on the Secretary of State of any such process shall be made by delivering to and leaving with the Secretary of State, or with any clerk authorized by the Secretary of State to accept service of process, duplicate copies of the process and the fee required by G.S. 59-1106(b). Upon receipt of service of process on behalf of a surviving business entity in the manner provided for in this section, the Secretary of State shall immediately mail a copy of the process by registered or certified mail, return receipt requested, to the surviving business entity. If the surviving business entity is authorized to transact business or conduct affairs in this State, the address for mailing shall be its principal office designated in the latest document filed with the Secretary of State that is authorized by law to designate the principal office or, if there is no principal office on file, its registered office. If the surviving business entity is not authorized to transact business or conduct affairs in this State, the address for mailing shall be the mailing address designated pursuant to G.S. 59-1072(a)(3). (1999-369, s. 4.8; 2001-387, ss. 143, 147; 2005-268, s. 60; 2007-385, s. 6.; 2011-347, ss. 19, 20.)

§§ 59-1074 through 59-1100. Reserved for future codification purposes.

Part 11. Miscellaneous.

§ 59-1101. Construction and application.

This Article shall be so applied and construed to effectuate its general purpose to make uniform the law with respect to the subject of this Article among states enacting it. (1985 (Reg. Sess., 1986), c. 989, s. 2.)

§ 59-1102. Rules for cases not provided for in this Article.

In any case not provided for in this Article the provisions of Article 2 of this Chapter govern. (1985 (Reg. Sess., 1986), c. 989, s. 2.)

§ 59-1103. Severability.

If any provision of this Article or its application to any person or circumstance is held invalid, the invalidity does not affect other provisions or applications of the Article which can be given effect without the invalid provision or application, and to this end the provisions of this Article are severable. (1985 (Reg. Sess., 1986), c. 989, s. 2.)

§ 59-1104. Effective date and repeal.

(a)   Except as set forth below, the effective date of this Article is October 1, 1986, and Article 1 of Chapter 59 of the North Carolina General Statutes is hereby repealed subject to the following:

(1)   G.S. 59-501, 59-502, and 59-608 shall apply only to contributions and distributions made after the effective date;

(2)   G.S. 59-704 applies only to assignments made after the effective date;

(3)   G.S. 59-804 shall not be construed so as to change the priority of creditors for transactions entered into prior to the effective date;

(4)   Unless agreed otherwise by the partners, the applicable provisions of existing law governing allocation of profits and losses (rather than the provisions of G.S. 59-503), distribution to a withdrawing partner (rather than the provisions of G.S. 59-604), and the distribution of assets upon the winding up of a limited partnership (rather than the provisions of G.S. 59-804) shall govern limited partnerships formed before the effective date of this Article herein.[;]

(5)   The repeal of any prior statutory provision by this Article shall not impair, or otherwise affect, the organization or continued existence of a limited partnership existing at the effective date of this Article, nor shall the repeal by this Article of any such prior provision be construed so as to impair any contract or to affect any right accrued prior to the effective date of this Article; but such limited partnerships shall be subject to the procedural and other requirements of this Article except as otherwise specified in G.S. 59-1104(a). Provided, that failure to comply with the requirements of this Article by such limited partnerships shall not cause loss of limited liability.

(b) Any foreign limited partnership formed under the laws of another jurisdiction doing business in this State prior to the effective date shall within two years thereafter comply with Part 9 of Article 5 of Chapter 59. (1985 (Reg. Sess., 1986), c. 989, s. 2; 1987, c. 531, ss. 9, 10.)

§ 59-1105: Repealed by Session Laws 2001-387, s. 148, effective January 1, 2002.

§ 59-1106. Filing, service, and copying fees.

(a) The Secretary of State shall collect the following fees when the documents described in this subsection are delivered to the Secretary of State for filing:

Document
Fee

(1) Certificate of limited partnership which does not include an application for registration as a limited liability limited partnership $50.00

(2) Certificate of limited partnership which includes an application for registration as a limited liability limited partnership 125.00

(3) Certificate of amendment 25.00

(4) Certificate of cancellation 25.00

(5) Application for reservation of name 10.00

(6) Notice of transfer of reserved name 10.00

(7) Application for registration of name ....
10.00

(8) Application for renewal of registration name ....
10.00

(9) Limited partnership's or foreign limited partnership's statement of change of registered agent or registered office or both ....
5.00

(10) Agent's statement of change of registered office for each affected partnership ....
5.00

(11) Agent's statement of resignation ....
No Fee

(12) Designation of registered agent or registered office or both ....
5.00

(13) Application for registration as foreign limited partnership ....
50.00

(14) Certificate of amendment of registration as foreign limited partnership
25.00

(15) Cancellation of registration as foreign limited partnership ....
25.00

(16) Application for certificate of withdrawal by reason of merger, consolidation, or conversion
.... 10.00

(17) Articles of merger ....
50.00

(18) Articles of conversion (other than articles of conversion included as part of another document) ....
50.00

(19) Application for registration as a limited liability limited partnership (other than an application included in the certificate of limited partnership) 125.00

(20) Certificate of amendment of registration as a limited liability limited partnership 25.00

(21) Certificate of cancellation of registration as a limited liability limited partnership 25.00

(22) Annual report for a limited liability limited partnership 200.00

(23) Any other document required or permitted to be filed under this Article 10.00

(b) The Secretary of State shall collect a fee of ten dollars ($10.00) each time process is served on the Secretary under this Article. The party to a proceeding causing service of process is entitled to recover this fee as costs if the party prevails in the proceeding.

(c) The Secretary of State shall collect the following fees for copying, comparing, and certifying a copy of any filed document relating to a domestic or foreign limited partnership:

(1) One dollar ($1.00) a page for copying or comparing a copy to the original; and

(2) Fifteen dollars ($15.00) for a paper certificate.

(3) Ten dollars ($10.00) for an electronic certificate.

(d) Repealed by Session Laws 2001-387, s. 171(b), effective January 1, 2002. (1985 (Reg. Sess., 1986), c. 989, s. 2; 1991, c. 574, s. 3; 1995, c. 539, s. 37; 1997-485, s. 13; 2001-358, ss. 10(f), 37; 2001-387, ss. 149, 171(a), 171(b), 173, 175(a); 2001-413, s. 6; 2002-126, s. 29A.31.)

§ 59-1107. Income taxation.

A limited partnership, a foreign limited partnership authorized to transact business in this State, and a partner of one of these partnerships are subject to taxation under Article 4 of Chapter 105 of the General Statutes in accordance with their classification for federal income tax purposes. Accordingly, if a limited partnership or a foreign limited partnership authorized to transact business in this State is classified for federal income tax purposes as a C corporation as defined in G.S. 105-131(b)(2) or an S corporation as defined in G.S. 105-131(b)(8), the partnership and its partners are subject to tax under Article 4 of Chapter 105 of the General Statutes to the same extent as a C corporation or an S corporation, as the case may be, and its shareholders. If a limited partnership or a foreign limited partnership authorized to transact business in this State is classified for federal income tax purposes as a partnership, the partnership and its partners are subject to tax under Article 4 of Chapter 105 of the General Statutes accordingly. If a limited partnership or a foreign limited partnership authorized to transact business in this State is classified for federal income tax purposes as other than a corporation or a partnership, the partnership and its partners are subject to tax under Article 4 of Chapter 105 of the General Statutes in a manner consistent with that classification. This section does not require a limited partnership or a foreign limited partnership to obtain an administrative ruling from the Internal Revenue Service on its classification under the Internal Revenue Code. (2001-387, s. 150.)

Chapter 59B.

Uniform Unincorporated Nonprofit Association Act.

§ 59B-1. Short title.

This Chapter may be cited as the Uniform Unincorporated Nonprofit Association Act. (2006-226, s. 1.)

§ 59B-2. Definitions.

In this Chapter:

(1) "Member" means a person who, under the rules or practices of a nonprofit association, may participate in the selection of persons authorized to manage the affairs of the nonprofit association or in the development of policy of the nonprofit association.

(2) "Nonprofit association" means an unincorporated organization, other than one created by a trust and other than a limited liability company, consisting of two or more members joined by mutual consent for a common, nonprofit purpose. However, joint tenancy, tenancy in common, or tenancy by the entireties does not by itself establish a nonprofit association, even if the co-owners share use of the property for a nonprofit purpose.

(3) "Person" means an individual, corporation, limited liability company, business trust, estate, trust, partnership, association, joint venture, government, governmental subdivision, agency, or instrumentality, or any other legal or commercial entity.

(4) "State" means a state of the United States, the District of Columbia, the Commonwealth of Puerto Rico, or any territory or insular possession subject to the jurisdiction of the United States. (2006-226, s. 1.)

§ 59B-3. Supplementary general principles of law and equity.

Principles of law and equity supplement this Chapter unless displaced by a particular provision of it. (2006-226, s. 1.)

§ 59B-4. Title to property; choice of law.

Real and personal property in this State may be acquired, held, encumbered, and transferred by a nonprofit association, whether or not the nonprofit association or a member has any other relationship to this State. (2006-226, s. 1.)

§ 59B-5. Real and personal property; nonprofit association as devisee or beneficiary.

(a) A nonprofit association is a legal entity separate from its members for the purposes of acquiring, holding, encumbering, and transferring real and personal property.

(b) A nonprofit association, in its name, may acquire, hold, encumber, or transfer an estate or interest in real or personal property.

(c) A nonprofit association may be a beneficiary of a trust or contract or a devisee.

(d) Any judgments and executions against a nonprofit association bind its real and personal property in like manner as if it were incorporated. (2006-226, s. 1; 2011-284, s. 59.)

§ 59B-6. Statement of authority as to real property.

(a) A nonprofit association may execute and record a statement of authority to transfer an estate or interest in real property in the name of the nonprofit association.

(b) An estate or interest in real property in the name of a nonprofit association may be transferred by a person so authorized in a statement of authority recorded in the office of the register of deeds in the county in which a transfer of the property would be recorded.

(c) A statement of authority must be set forth in a document styled "affidavit" that contains all of the following:

(1) The name of the nonprofit association.

(2) Reserved for future codification purposes.

(3) The street address, and the mailing address if different from the street address, of the nonprofit association, and the county in which it is located, or, if the nonprofit association does not have an address in this State, its address out-of-state.

(4) That the association is an unincorporated nonprofit association.

(5) The name or office of a person authorized to transfer an estate or interest in real property held in the name of the nonprofit association.

(6) That the association has duly authorized the member or agent executing the statement to do so.

(d) A statement of authority must be sworn to and subscribed in the same manner as an affidavit by a member or agent who is not the person authorized to transfer the estate or interest.

(e) The register of deeds shall collect a fee for recording a statement of authority in the amount authorized by G.S. 161-10(a)(1). The register of deeds shall index the name of the nonprofit association and the member or agent signing the statement of authority or any subsequent document relating thereto as Grantor and the name of the appointee as Grantee.

(f) An amendment, including a termination, of a statement of authority must meet the requirements for execution and recording of an original statement. Unless terminated earlier, a recorded statement of authority or its most recent amendment expires by operation of law five years after the date of the most recent recording.

(g) If the record title to real property is in the name of a nonprofit association and the statement of authority is recorded in the office of the register of deeds in the county in which a transfer of real property would be recorded, the authority of the person or officer named in a statement of authority is conclusive in favor of a person who gives value without notice that the person or officer lacks authority. (2006-226, s. 1.)

§ 59B-7. Liability of members or other persons.

(a) A nonprofit association is a legal entity separate from its members for the purposes of determining and enforcing rights, duties, and liabilities.

(b) A person is not liable for the contract, tort, or other obligations of a nonprofit association merely because the person is a member, is authorized to participate in the management of the affairs of the nonprofit association, or is referred to as a "member" by the nonprofit association.

(c) Reserved for future codification purposes.

(d) A tortious act or omission of a member or other person for which a nonprofit association is liable is not imputed to a person merely because the person is a member of the nonprofit association, is authorized to participate in the management of the affairs of the nonprofit association, or is referred to as a "member" by the nonprofit association.

(e) A member of, or a person referred to as a "member" by, a nonprofit association may assert a claim against or on behalf of the nonprofit association. A nonprofit association may assert a claim against a member or a person referred to as a "member" by the nonprofit association. (2006-226, s. 1.)

§ 59B-8. Capacity to assert and defend; standing.

(a) A nonprofit association, in its name, may institute, defend, intervene, or participate in a judicial, administrative, or other governmental proceeding or in an arbitration, mediation, or any other form of alternative dispute resolution.

(b) A nonprofit association may assert a claim in its name on behalf of its members or persons referred to as "members" by the nonprofit association if one or more of them have standing to assert a claim in their own right, the interests the nonprofit association seeks to protect are germane to its purposes, and neither the claim asserted nor the relief requested requires the participation of a member or a person referred to as a "member" by the nonprofit association. (2006-226, s. 1.)

§ 59B-9. Effect of judgment or order.

A judgment or order against a nonprofit association is not by itself a judgment or order against a member, a person referred to as a "member" by the nonprofit association, or a person authorized to participate in the management of the affairs of the nonprofit association. (2006-226, s. 1.)

§ 59B-10. Disposition of personal property of inactive nonprofit association.

If a nonprofit association has been inactive for three years or longer, or a different period specified in a document of the nonprofit association, a person in possession or control of personal property of the nonprofit association may transfer custody of the property:

(1)   If a document of the nonprofit association or document of gift specifies a person to whom transfer is to be made under these circumstances, to that person; or

(2)   If no person is so specified, to a nonprofit association, nonprofit corporation, or other nonprofit entity pursuing broadly similar purposes, or to a government or governmental subdivision, agency, or instrumentality. (2006-226, s. 1.)

§ 59B-11. Appointment of agent to receive service of process.

(a)   A nonprofit association may file in the office of the Secretary of State a statement appointing an agent authorized to receive service of process, notice, or demand required or permitted by law to be served on a nonprofit association.

(b)   A statement appointing an agent must set forth all of the following:

(1)   The name of the nonprofit association.

(2)   Reserved for future codification purposes.

(3)   The street address, and the mailing address if different from the street address, of the nonprofit association, and the county in which it is located, or, if the nonprofit association does not have an address in this State, its address out-of-state.

(4)   The name of the person in this State authorized to receive service of process and the person's address, including the street address, in this State.

(c)   A statement appointing an agent must be signed and acknowledged by a person authorized to manage the affairs of a nonprofit association. The statement must also be signed and acknowledged by the person appointed agent, who thereby accepts the appointment. The appointed agent may resign by filing a resignation in the office of the Secretary of State and giving written notice to the nonprofit association at its last known address.

(d) The sole duty of the appointed agent to the nonprofit association is to forward to the nonprofit association at its last known address any notice, process, or demand that is served on the appointed agent.

(e) The Secretary of State is not an agent for service of any process, notice, or demand on any nonprofit association.

(f) The Secretary of State shall collect the following fees when the documents described in this subsection are delivered to the Secretary of State for filing:

             Document Fee

(1) Statement appointing an agent to receive service of process $5.00

(2) Amendment of statement appointing an agent 5.00

(3) Cancellation of statement appointing an agent 5.00

(4) Agent's statement of resignation No fee

(g) An amendment to or cancellation of a statement appointing an agent to receive service of process must meet the requirements for execution of an original statement. (2006-226, s. 1.)

§ 59B-12. Claim not abated by change.

A claim for relief against a nonprofit association does not abate merely because of a change in its members or persons authorized to manage the affairs of the nonprofit association. (2006-226, s. 1.)

§ 59B-13. Venue.

For purposes of venue, a nonprofit association is a resident of a county in which it has an office or maintains a place of operation or, if on due inquiry no office or place of operation can be found, in which any officer resides. (2006-226, s. 1.)

§ 59B-14. Uniformity of application and construction.

This Chapter shall be applied and construed to effectuate its general purpose to make uniform the law with respect to the subject of this Chapter among states enacting it. (2006-226, s. 1.)

§ 59B-15. Effect as to conveyances by trustees; prior deeds validated.

(a) Nothing in this Chapter changes the law with reference to the holding and conveyance of land by the trustees of churches under Chapter 61 of the General Statutes where the land is conveyed to and held by the trustees.

(b) All deeds executed before January 1, 2007, in conformity with former G.S. 39-24 and former G.S. 39-25 are declared to be sufficient to pass title to real estate. (1939, c. 133, ss. 3, 4; 2006-226, s. 2(b).)

Chapter 60.

Railroads and Other Carriers.

§§ 60-1 through 60-81. Repealed by Session Laws 1963, c. 1165, s. 1.

§§ 60-82 through 60-87. Transferred to §§ 74A-1 to 74A-6 by Session Laws 1963, c. 1165, s. 2.

§§ 60-88 through 60-146. Repealed by Session Laws 1963, c. 1165, s. 1.

Chapter 61.

Religious Societies.

§ 61-1. Trustees may be appointed and removed.

(a) The conference, synod, convention or other ecclesiastical body representing any church or religious denomination within the State, as also the religious societies and congregations within the State, may from time to time and at any time appoint in such manner as such body, society or congregation may deem proper, a suitable number of persons as trustees for such church, denomination, religious society, or congregation. The body appointing may remove such trustees or any of them, and fill all vacancies caused by death or otherwise.

(b) A person serving as a trustee appointed pursuant to subsection (a) of this section or a director or officer of a religious society shall be immune individually from civil liability for monetary damages, except to the extent covered by insurance, for any act or failure to act arising out of this service, except where the person:

(1) Is compensated for his services beyond reimbursement for expenses,

(2) Was not acting within the scope of his official duties,

(3) Was not acting in good faith,

(4) Committed gross negligence or willful or wanton misconduct that resulted in the damage or injury,

(5) Derived an improper personal financial benefit from the transaction,

(6) Incurred the liability from the operation of a motor vehicle, or

(7) Is sued in an action that would qualify as a derivative action if the organization were a for-profit corporation or as a member's or director's

derivative action under G.S. 55A-28.1 or G.S. 55A-28.2 if the organization were a nonprofit corporation.

The immunity in this subsection is personal to the officers, directors, and trustees and does not immunize the organization for the acts or omissions of the officers, directors, or trustees. (1796, c. 457, ss. 1, 2; 1844, c. 47; 1848, c. 76; R.C., c. 97; Code, ss. 3667, 3668; Rev., ss. 2670, 2671; C.S., s. 3568; 1987, c. 799, s. 1.)

§ 61-2. Trustees may hold property.

The trustees and their successors have power to receive donations, and to purchase, take and hold property, real and personal, in trust for such church or denomination, religious society or congregation; and they may sue or be sued in all proper actions, for or on account of the donations and property so held or claimed by them, and for and on account of any matters relating thereto. They shall be accountable to the churches, denominations, societies and congregations for the use and management of such property, and shall surrender it to any person authorized to demand it. (1796, c. 457, ss. 1, 3; 1844, c. 47; 1848, c. 76; R.C., c. 97; Code, ss. 3667, 3668; Rev., ss. 2670, 2671; C.S., s. 3569.)

§ 61-3. Title to lands vested in trustees, or in societies.

All glebes, lands and tenements, heretofore purchased, given, or devised for the support of any particular ministry, or mode of worship, and all churches and other houses built for the purpose of public worship, and all lands and donations of any kind of property or estate that have been or may be given, granted or devised to any church or religious denomination, religious society or congregation within the State for their respective use, shall be and remain forever to the use and occupancy of that church or denomination, society or congregation for which the glebes, lands, tenements, property and estate were so purchased, given, granted or devised, or for which such churches, chapels or other houses of public worship were built; and the estate therein shall be deemed and held to be absolutely vested, as between the parties thereto, in the trustees respectively of such churches, denominations, societies and congregations, for their several use, according to the intent expressed in the conveyance, gift, grant or will; and in case there shall be no trustees, then in such churches, denominations, societies and congregations, respectively, according to such intent. (1776, c. 107; 1796, c. 457, s. 4; R.C., c. 97, s. 1; Code, s. 3665; Rev., s. 2672; C.S., s. 3570.)

§ 61-4. Trustees may convey property.

The trustees of any religious body may mortgage or sell and convey in fee simple any land owned by such body, when directed so to do by such church, congregation, society or denomination, or its committee, board or body having charge of its finances, and all such conveyances so made or heretofore made, or hereafter to be made, shall be effective to pass the land in fee simple to the purchaser or to the mortgagee for the purposes in such conveyances or mortgage expressed; and they may sell or mortgage its personal property. (1855, c. 384; 1889, c. 484; Rev., s. 2673; C.S., s. 3571.)

§ 61-5. Authority of bishops, ministers, etc., to acquire, hold and transfer property; prior transfers validated.

Whenever the laws, rules, or ecclesiastic polity of any church or religious sect, society or denomination, commits to its duly elected or appointed bishop, minister or other ecclesiastical officer, authority to administer its affairs, such duly elected or appointed bishop, minister or other ecclesiastical officer shall have power to acquire by gift, purchase or otherwise, and to hold, improve, mortgage, sell and convey the property, real or personal, of any such church or religious sect, society or denomination, for the purposes, in the manner and otherwise as authorized and permitted by its laws, rules or ecclesiastic polity; and in the event of the transfer, removal, resignation or death of any such bishop, minister or other ecclesiastical officer, the title and all rights with respect to any such property shall pass to and become vested in his duly elected or appointed successor immediately upon appointment or election, and pending appointment or election of such successor, such title and rights shall be vested in such person or persons as shall be designated by the laws, rules or ecclesiastic polity of such church or religious sect, society or denomination.

All deeds, deeds of trust, mortgages, wills or other instruments made prior to March 24, 1939, to or by a duly elected or appointed bishop, minister or other ecclesiastical officer, who, at the time of the making of any such deed, deed of trust, mortgage, will or other instrument, or thereafter, had authority to administer the affairs of any church, religious sect, society or denomination under its laws, rules or ecclesiastic polity, transferring property, real or personal, of any such church or religious sect, society or denomination, are hereby ratified and declared valid; and all transfers of title and rights with respect to property, prior to March 24, 1939, from a predecessor bishop, minister or other ecclesiastical officer who has resigned or died, or has been transferred or removed, to his duly elected or appointed successor, by the laws, rules or ecclesiastic polity of any such church, or religious sect, society or denomination, either by written instruments or solely by virtue of the election or appointment of such successor, are also hereby ratified and declared valid.

This section shall not affect vested rights, or repeal any of the provisions of G.S. 61-1 to 61-4, or of G.S. 36-21 to 36-23. (1939, c. 177.)

§ 61-6. House on vacant land vests title.

All houses and edifices erected for public religious worship on vacant lands, or on lands of the State not for other purposes intended or appropriated, together with two acres adjoining the same, shall hereafter be held and kept sacred for divine worship, to and for the use of the society by which the same was originally established. (1778, c. 132, s. 6; R.C., c. 97, s. 2; Code, s. 3666; Rev., s. 2674; C.S., s. 3572.)

§ 61-7. Governing body of assembly authorized to adopt traffic regulations.

(a)   The governing body of any religious organization or assembly may by appropriate resolution establish rules and regulations with respect to the use of the streets, roads, alleys, driveways, and parking lots on the grounds or premises owned or under the exclusive control of such organization, and it shall be unlawful for any person to park a motor vehicle or other vehicle on the streets, roads or on the premises of a religious assembly where parking has been prohibited by the religious assembly by the erection of "No Parking" signs at each space on the street, road or on the premises where parking is prohibited. Each space in which parking is prohibited shall be clearly designated as such by a sign no smaller than 24 inches by 24 inches. All rules and regulations adopted pursuant to the authority of this section shall be recorded in the proceedings of said governing body and copies thereof shall be filed in the office of the Secretary of State of North Carolina.

(b) It shall be unlawful for any person to park a motor vehicle or other vehicle in a parking space on the streets, roads, or premises of a religious assembly where the parking space has been designated by the religious assembly as being limited to a named individual or to a person holding a named position with the assembly; provided, that such private parking space or private parking lot be clearly designated as such by a sign no smaller than 24 inches by 24 inches prominently displayed at the entrance to the parking lot, if within a parking lot, and provided further that the private parking spaces within the lot or the private parking spaces on the streets, roads or on the premises of the religious assembly be clearly marked by signs setting forth the name of each individual for whom the space is reserved or the name of the position held with the assembly for which space is reserved.

(c) It shall be unlawful for any person to park a motor vehicle or other vehicle on the streets or roads of a religious assembly, except where parking is expressly designated, so as to interfere with, or obstruct the free flow of vehicular traffic on the streets or roads within the assembly grounds.

(d) It shall be unlawful for any person to park a motor vehicle or other vehicle at the entrance to any driveway on the grounds of a religious assembly so as to block the driveway.

(e) Any vehicle parked in violation of subsections (a), (b), (c), or (d) may be removed by the assembly, or its agents, or its employees to a place of storage and the registered owner of such motor vehicle shall become liable for removal and storage charges. Any person who removes a vehicle pursuant to subsections (a), (b), (c), or (d) shall not be held liable for damages for the removal of the vehicle to the owner, lienholder or other person legally entitled to the possession of the vehicle removed; however, any person who intentionally or negligently damages a vehicle in the removal of such vehicle, or intentionally or negligently inflicts injury upon any person in the removal of such vehicle, may be held liable for damages.

(f) A "religious assembly" is defined as being a corporation or association formed for the purpose of providing a resort community for religious and recreational purposes and where the streets and roads are solely maintained by the religious assembly without governmental funds. (1977, c. 398, s. 1; 1989, c. 644, s. 3; 1989, c. 644, s. 3.)

Chapter 62.

Public Utilities.

Article 1.

General Provisions.

§ 62-1. Short title.

This Chapter shall be known and may be cited as the Public Utilities Act. (1963, c. 1165, s. 1.)

§ 62-2. Declaration of policy.

(a) Upon investigation, it has been determined that the rates, services and operations of public utilities as defined herein, are affected with the public interest and that the availability of an adequate and reliable supply of electric power and natural gas to the people, economy and government of North Carolina is a matter of public policy. It is hereby declared to be the policy of the State of North Carolina:

(1) To provide fair regulation of public utilities in the interest of the public;

(2) To promote the inherent advantage of regulated public utilities;

(3) To promote adequate, reliable and economical utility service to all of the citizens and residents of the State;

(3a) To assure that resources necessary to meet future growth through the provision of adequate, reliable utility service include use of the entire spectrum of demand-side options, including but not limited to conservation, load management and efficiency programs, as additional sources of energy supply and/or energy demand reductions. To that end, to require energy planning and fixing of rates in a manner to result in the least cost mix of generation and demand-reduction measures which is achievable, including consideration of appropriate rewards to utilities for efficiency and conservation which decrease utility bills;

(4)   To provide just and reasonable rates and charges for public utility services without unjust discrimination, undue preferences or advantages, or unfair or destructive competitive practices and consistent with long-term management and conservation of energy resources by avoiding wasteful, uneconomic and inefficient uses of energy;

(4a)   To assure that facilities necessary to meet future growth can be financed by the utilities operating in this State on terms which are reasonable and fair to both the customers and existing investors of such utilities; and to that end to authorize fixing of rates in such a manner as to result in lower costs of new facilities and lower rates over the operating lives of such new facilities by making provisions in the rate-making process for the investment of public utilities in plants under construction;

(5)   To encourage and promote harmony between public utilities, their users and the environment;

(6)   To foster the continued service of public utilities on a well-planned and coordinated basis that is consistent with the level of energy needed for the protection of public health and safety and for the promotion of the general welfare as expressed in the State energy policy;

(7)   To seek to adjust the rate of growth of regulated energy supply facilities serving the State to the policy requirements of statewide development;

(8)   To cooperate with other states and with the federal government in promoting and coordinating interstate and intrastate public utility service and reliability of public utility energy supply;

(9)   To facilitate the construction of facilities in and the extension of natural gas service to unserved areas in order to promote the public welfare throughout the State and to that end to authorize the creation of expansion funds for natural gas local distribution companies or gas districts to be administered under the supervision of the North Carolina Utilities Commission; and

(10) To promote the development of renewable energy and energy efficiency through the implementation of a Renewable Energy and Energy Efficiency Portfolio Standard (REPS) that will do all of the following:

a. Diversify the resources used to reliably meet the energy needs of consumers in the State.

b. Provide greater energy security through the use of indigenous energy resources available within the State.

c. Encourage private investment in renewable energy and energy efficiency.

d. Provide improved air quality and other benefits to energy consumers and citizens of the State.

(b) To these ends, therefore, authority shall be vested in the North Carolina Utilities Commission to regulate public utilities generally, their rates, services and operations, and their expansion in relation to long-term energy conservation and management policies and statewide development requirements, and in the manner and in accordance with the policies set forth in this Chapter. Nothing in this Chapter shall be construed to imply any extension of Utilities Commission regulatory jurisdiction over any industry or enterprise that is not subject to the regulatory jurisdiction of said Commission.

Because of technological changes in the equipment and facilities now available and needed to provide telephone and telecommunications services, changes in regulatory policies by the federal government, and changes resulting from the court-ordered divestiture of the American Telephone and Telegraph Company, competitive offerings of certain types of telephone and telecommunications services may be in the public interest. Consequently, authority shall be vested in the North Carolina Utilities Commission to allow competitive offerings of local exchange, exchange access, and long distance services by public utilities defined in G.S. 62-3(23)a.6. and certified in accordance with the provisions of G.S. 62-110, and the Commission is further authorized after notice to affected parties and hearing to deregulate or to exempt from regulation under any or all provisions of this Chapter: (i) a service provided by any public utility as defined in G.S. 62-3(23)a.6. upon a finding that such service is competitive and that such deregulation or exemption from regulation is in the public interest; or (ii) a public utility as defined in G.S. 62-3(23)a.6., or a portion of the business of such public utility, upon a finding that the service or business of such public utility is competitive and that such deregulation or exemption from regulation is in the public interest.

Notwithstanding the provisions of G.S. 62-110(b) and G.S. 62-134(h), the following services provided by public utilities defined in G.S. 62-3(23)a.6. are sufficiently competitive and shall no longer be regulated by the Commission: (i) intraLATA long distance service; (ii) interLATA long distance service; and (iii) long distance operator services. A public utility providing such services shall be permitted, at its own election, to file and maintain tariffs for such services with the Commission up to and including September 1, 2003. Nothing in this subsection shall limit the Commission's authority regarding certification of providers of such services or its authority to hear and resolve complaints against providers of such services alleged to have made changes to the services of customers or imposed charges without appropriate authorization. For purposes of this subsection, and notwithstanding G.S. 62-110(b), "long distance services" shall not include existing or future extended area service, local measured service, or other local calling arrangements, and any future extended area service shall be implemented consistent with Commission rules governing extended area service existing as of May 1, 2003.

The North Carolina Utilities Commission may develop regulatory policies to govern the provision of telecommunications services to the public which promote efficiency, technological innovation, economic growth, and permit telecommunications utilities a reasonable opportunity to compete in an emerging competitive environment, giving due regard to consumers, stockholders, and maintenance of reasonably affordable local exchange service and long distance service.

(b1)   Broadband service provided by public utilities as defined in G.S. 62-3(23)a.6. is sufficiently competitive and shall not be regulated by the Commission.

(c)   The policy and authority stated in this section shall be applicable to common carriers of passengers by motor vehicle and their regulation by the North Carolina Utilities Commission only to the extent that they are consistent with the provisions of the Bus Regulatory Reform Act of 1985. (1963, c. 1165, s. 1; 1975, c. 877, s. 2; 1977, c. 691, s. 1; 1983 (Reg. Sess., 1984), c. 1043, s. 1; 1985, c. 676, s. 3; 1987, c. 354; 1989, c. 112, s. 1; 1991, c. 598, s. 1; 1995, c. 27, s. 1; 1995 (Reg. Sess., 1996), c. 742, ss. 29-32; 1998-132, s. 18; 2003-91, s. 1; 2005-95, s. 1; 2007-397, s. 1.)

§ 62-3. Definitions.

As used in this Chapter, unless the context otherwise requires, the term:

(1) "Broadband service" means any service that consists of or includes a high-speed access capability to transmit at a rate of not less than 200 kilobits per second in either the upstream or downstream direction and either (i) is used to provide access to the Internet, or (ii) provides computer processing, information storage, information content, or protocol conversion, including any service applications or information service provided over such high-speed access service. "Broadband service" does not include intrastate service that was tariffed by the Commission and in effect as of the effective date of this subdivision.

(1a) "Broker," with regard to motor carriers of passengers, means any person not included in the term "motor carrier" and not a bona fide employee or agent of any such carrier, who or which as principal or agent engages in the business of selling or offering for sale any transportation of passengers by motor carrier, or negotiates for or holds himself, or itself, out by solicitation, advertisements, or otherwise, as one who sells, provides, furnishes, contracts, or arranges for such transportation for compensation, either directly or indirectly.

(1b) "Bus company" means any common carrier by motor vehicle which holds itself out to the general public to engage in the transportation by motor vehicle in intrastate commerce of passengers over fixed routes or in charter operations, or both, except as exempted in G.S. 62-260.

(2) "Certificate" means a certificate of public convenience and necessity issued by the Commission to a public utility or a certificate of authority issued by the Commission to a bus company.

(3) "Certified mail" means such mail only when a return receipt is requested.

(4) "Charter operations" with regard to bus companies means the transportation of a group of persons for sightseeing purposes, pleasure tours, and other types of special operations, or the transportation of a group of persons who, pursuant to a common purpose and under a single contract, and for a fixed charge for the vehicle, have acquired the exclusive use of a passenger-carrying motor vehicle to travel together as a group to a specified

destination or for a particular itinerary, either agreed upon in advance or modified by the chartered group after having left the place of origin.

(5) "Commission" means the North Carolina Utilities Commission.

(6) "Common carrier" means any person, other than a carrier by rail, which holds itself out to the general public to engage in transportation of persons or household goods for compensation, including transportation by bus, truck, boat or other conveyance, except as exempted in G.S. 62-260.

(7) "Common carrier by motor vehicle" means any person which holds itself out to the general public to engage in the transportation by motor vehicle in intrastate commerce of persons or household goods or any class or classes thereof for compensation, whether over regular or irregular routes, or in charter operations, except as exempted in G.S. 62-260.

(7a) "Competing local provider" means any person applying for a certificate to provide local exchange or exchange access services in competition with a local exchange company.

(8), (9) Repealed by Session Laws 1995, c. 523, s. 1.

(9a) "Fixed route" means the specific highway or highways over which a bus company is authorized to operate between fixed termini.

(10) "Foreign commerce" means commerce between any place in the United States and any place in a foreign country, or between places in the United States through any foreign country.

(11) "Franchise" means the grant of authority by the Commission to any person to engage in business as a public utility, whether or not exclusive or shared with others or restricted as to terms and conditions and whether described by area or territory or not, and includes certificates, and all other forms of licenses or orders and decisions granting such authority.

(12) "Highway" means any road or street in this State used by the public or dedicated or appropriated to public use.

(13) "Industrial plant" means any plant, mill, or factory engaged in the business of manufacturing.

(14) "Interstate commerce" means commerce between any place in a state and any place in another state or between places in the same state through another state.

(15) "Intrastate commerce" means commerce between points and over a route or within a territory wholly within this State, which commerce is not a part of a prior or subsequent movement to or from points outside of this State in interstate or foreign commerce, and includes all transportation within this State for compensation in interstate or foreign commerce which has been exempted by Congress from federal regulation.

(16) "Intrastate operations" means the transportation of persons or household goods for compensation in intrastate commerce.

(16a) "Local exchange company" means a person holding, on January 1, 1995, a certificate to provide local exchange services or exchange access services.

(17) "Motor carrier" means a common carrier by motor vehicle.

(18) "Motor vehicle" means any vehicle, machine, tractor, semi-trailer, or any combination thereof, which is propelled or drawn by mechanical power and used upon the highways within the State.

(19) "Municipality" means any incorporated community, whether designated in its charter as a city, town, or village.

(20) Repealed by Session Laws 1995, c. 523, s. 1.

(21) "Person" means a corporation, individual, copartnership, company, association, or any combination of individuals or organizations doing business as a unit, and includes any trustee, receiver, assignee, lessee, or personal representative thereof.

(22) "Private carrier" means any person, other than a carrier by rail, not included in the definitions of common carrier, which transports in intrastate commerce in its own vehicle or vehicles property of which such person is the owner, lessee, or bailee, when such transportation is for the purpose of sale, lease, rent, or bailment, or when such transportation is purely an incidental adjunct to some other established private business owned and operated by such person other than the transportation of household goods for compensation.

(23) a. "Public utility" means a person, whether organized under the laws of this State or under the laws of any other state or country, now or hereafter owning or operating in this State equipment or facilities for:

1. Producing, generating, transmitting, delivering or furnishing electricity, piped gas, steam or any other like agency for the production of light, heat or power to or for the public for compensation; provided, however, that the term "public utility" shall not include persons who construct or operate an electric generating facility, the primary purpose of which facility is for such person's own use and not for the primary purpose of producing electricity, heat, or steam for sale to or for the public for compensation;

2. Diverting, developing, pumping, impounding, distributing or furnishing water to or for the public for compensation, or operating a public sewerage system for compensation; provided, however, that the term "public utility" shall not include any person or company whose sole operation consists of selling water to less than 15 residential customers, except that any person or company which constructs a water system in a subdivision with plans for 15 or more lots and which holds itself out by contracts or other means at the time of said construction to serve an area containing more than 15 residential building lots shall be a public utility at the time of such planning or holding out to serve such 15 or more building lots, without regard to the number of actual customers connected;

3. Transporting persons or household goods by street, suburban or interurban bus for the public for compensation;

4. Transporting persons or household goods by motor vehicles or any other form of transportation for the public for compensation, except motor carriers exempted in G.S. 62-260, carriers by rail, and carriers by air;

5. Transporting or conveying gas, crude oil or other fluid substance by pipeline for the public for compensation;

6. Conveying or transmitting messages or communications by telephone or telegraph, or any other means of transmission, where such service is offered to the public for compensation.

b. The term "public utility" shall for rate-making purposes include any person producing, generating or furnishing any of the foregoing services to another person for distribution to or for the public for compensation.

c. The term "public utility" shall include all persons affiliated through stock ownership with a public utility doing business in this State as parent corporation or subsidiary corporation as defined in G.S. 55-2 to such an extent that the Commission shall find that such affiliation has an effect on the rates or service of such public utility.

d. The term "public utility," except as otherwise expressly provided in this Chapter, shall not include a municipality, an authority organized under the North Carolina Water and Sewer Authorities Act, electric or telephone membership corporation; or any person not otherwise a public utility who furnishes such service or commodity only to himself, his employees or tenants when such service or commodity is not resold to or used by others; provided, however, that any person other than a nonprofit organization serving only its members, who distributes or provides utility service to his employees or tenants by individual meters or by other coin-operated devices with a charge for metered or coin-operated utility service shall be a public utility within the definition and meaning of this Chapter with respect to the regulation of rates and provisions of service rendered through such meter or coin-operated device imposing such separate metered utility charge. If any person conducting a public utility shall also conduct any enterprise not a public utility, such enterprise is not subject to the provisions of this Chapter. A water or sewer system owned by a homeowners' association that provides water or sewer service only to members or leaseholds of members is not subject to the provisions of this Chapter.

e. The term "public utility" shall include the University of North Carolina insofar as said University supplies telephone service, electricity or water to the public for compensation from the University Enterprises defined in G.S. 116-41.1(9).

f. The term "public utility" shall include the Town of Pineville insofar as said town supplies telephone services to the public for compensation. The territory to be served by the Town of Pineville in furnishing telephone services, subject to the Public Utilities Act, shall include the town limits as they exist on May 8, 1973, and shall also include the area proposed to be annexed under the town's ordinance adopted May 3, 1971, until January 1, 1975.

g. The term "public utility" shall not include a hotel, motel, time share or condominium complex operated primarily to serve transient occupants, which imposes charges to occupants for local, long-distance, or wide area telecommunication services when such calls are completed through the use of facilities provided by a public utility, and provided further that the local services received are rated in accordance with the provisions of G.S. 62-110(d) and the applicable charges for telephone calls are prominently displayed in each area where occupant rooms are located.

h. The term "public utility" shall not include the resale of electricity by (i) a campground operated primarily to serve transient occupants, or (ii) a marina; provided that (i) the campground or marina charges no more than the actual cost of the electricity supplied to it, (ii) the amount of electricity used by each campsite or marina slip occupant is measured by an individual metering device, (iii) the applicable rates are prominently displayed at or near each campsite or marina slip, and (iv) the campground or marina only resells electricity to campsite or marina slip occupants.

i. The term "public utility" shall not include the State, the Office of Information Technology Services, or the Microelectronics Center of North Carolina in the provision or sharing of switched broadband telecommunications services with non-State entities or organizations of the kind or type set forth in G.S. 143B-426.39.

j. The term "public utility" shall not include any person, not otherwise a public utility, conveying or transmitting messages or communications by mobile radio communications service. Mobile radio communications service includes one-way or two-way radio service provided to mobile or fixed stations or receivers using mobile radio service frequencies.

k. The term "public utility" shall not include a regional natural gas district organized and operated pursuant to Article 28 of Chapter 160A of the General Statutes.

l. The term "public utility" shall include a city or a joint agency under Part 1 of Article 20 of Chapter 160A of the General Statutes that provides service as defined in G.S. 62-3(23)a.6. and is subject to the provisions of G.S. 160A-340.1.

(24) "Rate" means every compensation, charge, fare, tariff, schedule, toll, rental and classification, or any of them, demanded, observed, charged or collected by any public utility, for any service product or commodity offered by it

to the public, and any rules, regulations, practices or contracts affecting any such compensation, charge, fare, tariff, schedule, toll, rental or classification.

(25) "Route" means the course or way which is traveled; the road or highway over which motor vehicles operate.

(26) "Securities" means stock, stock certificates, bonds, notes, debentures, or other evidences of ownership or of indebtedness, and any assumption or guaranty thereof.

(27) "Service" means any service furnished by a public utility, including any commodity furnished as a part of such service and any ancillary service or facility used in connection with such service.

(27a) "Small power producer" means a person or corporation owning or operating an electrical power production facility with a power production capacity which, together with any other facilities located at the same site, does not exceed 80 megawatts of electricity and which depends upon renewable resources for its primary source of energy. For the purposes of this section, renewable resources shall mean: hydroelectric power. A small power producer shall not include persons primarily engaged in the generation or sale of electricity from other than small power production facilities.

(28) The word "State" means the State of North Carolina; "state" means any state.

(29) "Town" means any unincorporated community or collection of people having a geographical name by which it may be generally known and is so generally designated.

(30) "Panel" means a panel of three commissioners, a division of the Utilities Commission authorized for the purpose of carrying out certain functions of the Commission. (1913, c. 127, s. 7; C.S., s. 1112(b); 1933, c. 134, ss. 3, 8; c. 307, s. 1; 1937, c. 108, s. 2; 1941, cc. 59, 97; 1947, c. 1008, s. 3; 1949, c. 1132, s. 4; 1953, c. 1140, s. 1; 1957, c. 1152, s. 13; 1959, c. 639, ss. 12, 13; 1963, c. 1165, s. 1; 1967, c. 1094, ss. 1, 2; 1971, c. 553; c. 634, s. 1; cc. 894, 895; 1973, c. 372, s. 1; 1975, c. 243, s. 2; cc. 254, 415; 1979, c. 652, s. 1; 1979, 2nd Sess., c. 1219, s. 1; 1981 (Reg. Sess., 1982), c. 1186, s. 2; 1985, c. 676, s. 4; 1987, c. 445, s. 2; 1989, c. 110; 1993, c. 349, s. 1; 1993 (Reg. Sess., 1994), c. 777, s. 1(b); 1995, c. 27, ss. 2, 3; c. 509, s. 34; c. 523, s. 1; 1997-426, s. 8; 1997-437,

s. 1; 1998-128, ss. 1-3; 2004-199, s. 1; 2004-203, s. 37(a); 2005-95, s. 2; 2011-84, s. 2(a).)

§ 62-4. Applicability of Chapter.

This Chapter shall not terminate the preexisting Commission or appointments thereto, or any certificates, permits, orders, rules or regulations issued by it or any other action taken by it, unless and until revoked by it, nor affect in any manner the existing franchises, territories, tariffs, rates, contracts, service regulations and other obligations and rights of public utilities, unless and until altered or modified by or in accordance with the provisions of this Chapter. (1963, c. 1165, s. 1.)

§§ 62-5 through 62-9. Reserved for future codification purposes.

Article 2.

Organization of Utilities Commission.

§ 62-10. Number; appointment; terms; qualifications; chairman; vacancies; compensation; other employment prohibited.

(a)   The North Carolina Utilities Commission shall consist of seven commissioners who shall be appointed by the Governor subject to confirmation by the General Assembly by joint resolution. The names of commissioners to be appointed by the Governor shall be submitted by the Governor to the General Assembly for confirmation by the General Assembly on or before May 1, of the year in which the terms for which the appointments are to be made are to expire. Upon failure of the Governor to submit names as herein provided, the Lieutenant Governor and Speaker of the House jointly shall submit the names of a like number of commissioners to the General Assembly on or before May 15 of the same year for confirmation by the General Assembly. Regardless of the way in which names of commissioners are submitted, confirmation of commissioners must be accomplished prior to adjournment of the then current session of the General Assembly. This subsection shall be subject to the provisions of subsection (c) of this section.

(b)   The terms of the commissioners now serving shall expire at the conclusion of the term for which they were appointed which shall remain as before with two regular eight-year terms expiring on July 1 of each fourth year after July 1, 1965, and the fifth term expiring on July 1 of each eighth year after July 1, 1963. The terms of office of utilities commissioners thereafter shall be six years commencing on July 1 of the year in which the predecessor terms expired, and ending on July 1 of the sixth year thereafter.

(c)   In order to increase the number of commissioners to seven, the names of two additional commissioners shall be submitted to the General Assembly on or before May 27, 1975, for confirmation by the General Assembly as provided in G.S. 62-10(a). The commissioners so appointed and confirmed shall serve new terms commencing on July 1, 1975, one of which shall be for a period of two years (with the immediate successor serving for a period of six years), and one of which shall be for a period of two years.

Thereafter, the terms of office of the additional commissioners shall be for six years as provided in G.S. 62-10(b).

(d)   A commissioner in office shall continue to serve until his successor is duly confirmed and qualified but such holdover shall not affect the expiration date of such succeeding term.

(e)   On July 1, 1965, and every four years thereafter, one of the commissioners shall be designated by the Governor to serve as chairman of the Commission for the succeeding four years and until his successor is duly confirmed and qualifies. Upon death or resignation of the commissioner appointed as chairman, the Governor shall designate the chairman from the remaining commissioners and appoint a successor as hereinafter provided to fill the vacancy on the Commission.

(f)   In case of death, incapacity, resignation or vacancy for any other reason in the office of any commissioner prior to the expiration of his term of office, the name of his successor shall be submitted by the Governor within four weeks after the vacancy arises to the General Assembly for confirmation by the General Assembly. Upon failure of the Governor to submit the name of the successor, the Lieutenant Governor and Speaker of the House jointly shall submit the name of a successor to the General Assembly within six weeks after the vacancy arises. Regardless of the way in which names of commissioners are submitted, confirmation of commissioners must be accomplished prior to the adjournment of the then current session of the General Assembly.

(g)   If a vacancy arises or exists pursuant to either subsection (a) or (c) or (f) of this section when the General Assembly is not in session, and the appointment is deemed urgent by the Governor, the commissioner may be appointed and serve on an interim basis pending confirmation by the General Assembly.

(h)   The salary of each commissioner and that of the commissioner designated as chairman shall be set by the General Assembly in the Current Operations Appropriations Act. In lieu of merit and other increment raises paid to regular State employees, each commissioner, including the commissioner designated as chairman, shall receive as longevity pay an amount equal to four and eight-tenths percent (4.8%) of the annual salary set forth in the Current Operations Appropriations Act payable monthly after five years of service, and nine and six-tenths percent (9.6%) after 10 years of service. "Service" means service as a member of the Utilities Commission.

(h1)   In addition to compensation for their services, each member of the Commission who lives at least 50 miles from the City of Raleigh shall be paid a weekly travel allowance for each week the member travels to the City of Raleigh from the member's home for business of the Commission. The allowance shall be calculated for each member by multiplying the actual round-trip mileage from that member's home to the City of Raleigh by the rate-per-mile which is the business standard mileage rate set by the Internal Revenue Service in Rev. Proc. 93-51, December 27, 1993.

(i)   The standards of judicial conduct provided for judges in Article 30 of Chapter 7A of the General Statutes shall apply to members of the Commission. Members of the Commission shall be liable to impeachment for the causes and in the manner provided for judges of the General Court of Justice in Chapter 123 of the General Statutes. Members of the Commission shall not engage in any other employment, business, profession, or vocation while in office.

(j)   Except as provided in subsection (h1) of this section, members of the Commission shall be reimbursed for travel and subsistence expenses at the rates allowed to State officers and employees by G.S. 138-6(a). (1941, c. 97, s. 2; 1949, c. 1009, s. 1; 1959, c. 1319; 1963, c. 1165, s. 1; 1967, c. 1238; 1975, c. 243, s. 3; c. 867, ss. 1, 2; 1977, c. 468, s. 1; c. 913, s. 2; 1983 (Reg. Sess.,

1984), c. 1116, s. 91; 1989, c. 781, s. 41.2; 1993 (Reg. Sess., 1994), c. 769, s. 7.4(b); 1996, 2nd Ex. Sess., c. 18, s. 28.2(b); 1997-443, s. 33.5; 1999-237, s. 28.21(a), (b); 2011-145, s. 14.8A(a).)

§ 62-11. Oath of office.

Each utilities commissioner before entering upon the duties of his office shall file with the Secretary of State his oath of office to support the Constitution and laws of the United States and the Constitution and laws of the State of North Carolina, and to well and truly perform the duties of his said office as utilities commissioner, and that he is not the agent or attorney of any public utility, or an employee thereof, and that he has no interest in any public utility. (1933, c. 134, s. 5; 1935, c. 280; 1939, c. 404; 1941, c. 97; 1963, c. 1165, s. 1.)

§ 62-12. Organization of Commission; adoption of rules and regulations therefor.

To facilitate the work of the Commission and for administrative purposes, the chairman of the Commission, with the consent and approval of the Commission, may organize the work of the Commission in several hearing divisions and operating departments and may designate a member of the Commission as the head of any division or divisions and assign to members of the Commission various duties in connection therewith. Subject to the provisions of the North Carolina Human Resources Act (Article 2 of Chapter 143 of the General Statutes), the Commission shall prepare and adopt rules and regulations governing the personnel, departments or divisions and all internal affairs and business of the Commission. (1941, c. 97, s. 3; 1949, c. 1009, s. 2; 1957, c. 1062, s. 1; 1963, c. 1165, s. 1; 2013-382, s. 9.1(c).)

§ 62-13. Chairman to direct Commission.

(a) The chairman shall be the chief executive and administrative officer of the Commission.

(b) The chairman shall determine whether matters pending before the Commission shall be considered or heard initially by the full Commission, a panel of three commissioners, a hearing commissioner, or a hearing examiner. Subject to the rules of the Commission, the chairman shall assign members of the Commission to proceedings and shall assign members to preside at proceedings before the full Commission or a panel of three commissioners.

(c) The chairman, the presiding commissioner, hearing commissioner, or hearing examiner shall hear and determine procedural motions or petitions not determinative of the merits of the proceedings and made prior to hearing; and at hearing shall make all rulings on motions and objections.

(d) The chairman acting alone, or any three commissioners, may initiate investigations, complaints, or any other proceedings within the jurisdiction of the Commission. (1941, c. 97, s. 4; 1957, c. 1062, s. 2; 1963, c. 1165, s. 1; 1975, c. 243, ss. 9, 10; 1977, c. 468, s. 2; c. 913, s. 2.)

§ 62-14. Commission staff; structure and function.

(a) The Commission is authorized and empowered to employ hearing examiners; court reporters; a chief clerk and deputy clerk; a commission attorney and assistant commission attorney; transportation and pipeline safety inspectors; and such other professional, administrative, technical, and clerical personnel as the Commission may determine to be necessary in the proper discharge of the Commission's duty and responsibility as provided by law. The chairman shall organize and direct the work of the Commission staff.

(b) The salaries and compensation of all such personnel shall be fixed in the manner provided by law for fixing and regulating salaries and compensation by other State agencies.

(c) The chairman, within allowed budgetary limits and as allowed by law, shall authorize and approve travel, subsistence and related expenses of such personnel, incurred while traveling on official business. (1963, c. 1165, s. 1; 1977, c. 468, s. 3.)

§ 62-15. Office of executive director; public staff, structure and function.

(a) There is established in the Commission the office of executive director, whose salary and longevity pay shall be the same as that fixed for members of the Commission. "Service" for purposes of longevity pay means service as executive director of the public staff. The executive director shall be appointed by the Governor subject to confirmation by the General Assembly by joint resolution. The name of the executive director appointed by the Governor shall be submitted to the General Assembly on or before May 1 of the year in which the term of his office begins. The term of office for the executive director shall be six years, and the initial term shall begin July 1, 1977. The executive director may be removed from office by the Governor in the event of his incapacity to serve; and the executive director shall be removed from office by the Governor upon the affirmative recommendation of a majority of the Commission, after consultation with the Joint Legislative Commission on Governmental Operations of the General Assembly. In case of a vacancy in the office of executive director for any reason prior to the expiration of his term of office, the name of his successor shall be submitted by the Governor to the General Assembly, not later than four weeks after the vacancy arises. If a vacancy arises in the office when the General Assembly is not in session, the executive director shall be appointed by the Governor to serve on an interim basis pending confirmation by the General Assembly.

(b) There is established in the Commission a public staff. The public staff shall consist of the executive director and such other professional, administrative, technical, and clerical personnel as may be necessary in order for the public staff to represent the using and consuming public, as hereinafter provided. All such personnel shall be appointed, supervised, and directed by the executive director. The public staff shall not be subject to the supervision, direction, or control of the Commission, the chairman, or members of the Commission.

(c) Except for the executive director, the salaries and compensation of all such personnel shall be fixed in the manner provided by law for fixing and regulating salaries and compensation by other State agencies.

(d) It shall be the duty and responsibility of the public staff to:

(1) Review, investigate, and make appropriate recommendations to the Commission with respect to the reasonableness of rates charged or proposed to be charged by any public utility and with respect to the consistency of such rates

with the public policy of assuring an energy supply adequate to protect the public health and safety and to promote the general welfare,

(2)   Review, investigate, and make appropriate recommendations to the Commission with respect to the service furnished, or proposed to be furnished by any public utility;

(3)   Intervene on behalf of the using and consuming public, in all Commission proceedings affecting the rates or service of any public utility;

(4)   When deemed necessary by the executive director in the interest of the using and consuming public, petition the Commission to initiate proceedings to review, investigate, and take appropriate action with respect to the rates or service of public utilities;

(5)   Intervene on behalf of the using and consuming public in all certificate applications filed pursuant to the provisions of G.S. 62-110.1, and provide assistance to the Commission in making the analysis and plans required pursuant to the provisions of G.S. 62-110.1 and 62-155;

(6)   Intervene on behalf of the using and consuming public in all proceedings wherein any public utility proposes to reduce or abandon service to the public;

(7)   Investigate complaints affecting the using and consuming public generally which are directed to the Commission, members of the Commission, or the public staff and where appropriate make recommendations to the Commission with respect to such complaints;

(8)   Make studies and recommendations to the Commission with respect to standards, regulations, practices, or service of any public utility pursuant to the provisions of G.S. 62-43; provided, however, that the public staff shall have no duty, responsibility, or authority with respect to the enforcement of natural gas pipeline safety laws, rules, or regulations;

(9)   When deemed necessary by the executive director, in the interest of the using and consuming public, intervene in Commission proceedings with respect to transfers of franchises, mergers, consolidations, and combinations of public utilities pursuant to the provisions of G.S. 62-111;

(10) Investigate and make appropriate recommendations to the Commission with respect to applications for certificates by radio common carriers, pursuant to the provisions of Article 6A of this Chapter;

(11) Review, investigate, and make appropriate recommendations to the Commission with respect to contracts of public utilities with affiliates or subsidiaries, pursuant to the provisions of G.S. 62-153;

(12) When deemed necessary by the executive director, in the interest of the using and consuming public, advise the Commission with respect to securities, regulations, and transactions, pursuant to the provisions of Article 8 of this Chapter.

(e) The public staff shall have no duty, responsibility, or authority with respect to the laws, rules or regulations pertaining to the physical facilities or equipment of common, contract and exempt carriers, the registration of vehicles or of insurance coverage of vehicles of common, contract and exempt carriers; the licensing, training, or qualifications of drivers or other persons employed by common, contract and exempt carriers, or the operation of motor vehicle equipment by common, contract and exempt carriers in the State.

(f) The executive director representing the public staff shall have the same rights of appeal from Commission orders or decisions as other parties to Commission proceedings.

(g) Upon request, the executive director shall employ the resources of the public staff to furnish to the Commission, its members, or the Attorney General, such information and reports or conduct such investigations and provide such other assistance as may reasonably be required in order to supervise and control the public utilities of the State as may be necessary to carry out the laws providing for their regulation.

(h) The executive director is authorized to employ, subject to approval by the State Budget Officer, expert witnesses and such other professional expertise as the executive director may deem necessary from time to time to assist the public staff in its participation in Commission proceedings, and the compensation and expenses therefor shall be paid by the utility or utilities participating in said proceedings. Such compensation and expenses shall be treated by the Commission, for rate-making purposes, in a manner generally consistent with its treatment of similar expenditures incurred by utilities in the presentation of their cases before the Commission. An accounting of such compensation and expenses shall be reported annually to the Joint Legislative Commission on Governmental Operations and to the Speaker of the House of Representatives and the President Pro Tempore of the Senate.

(i)   The executive director, within established budgetary limits, and as allowed by law, shall authorize and approve travel, subsistence, and related necessary expenses of the executive director or members of the public staff, incurred while traveling on official business. (1949, c. 1009, s. 3; 1963, c. 1165, s. 1; 1977, c. 468, s. 4; 1981, c. 475; 1983, c. 717, s. 12.1; 1985, c. 499, s. 4; 1989, c. 781, s. 41.3; 1989 (Reg. Sess., 1990), c. 1024, s. 13; 1999-237, s. 28.21A; 2011-291, ss. 2.8, 2.9.)

§ 62-16. Repealed by Session Laws 1977, c. 468, s. 5.

§ 62-17. Annual reports; monthly or quarterly release of certain information; publication of procedural orders and decisions.

(a)   It shall be the duty of the Commission to make and publish annual reports to the Governor of Commission activities, including copies of its general orders and regulations, comparative statistical data on the operation of the various public utilities in the State, comparisons of rates in North Carolina with rates elsewhere, a detailed report of its investigative division, a review of significant developments in the fields of utility law, economics and planning, a report of pending matters before the Commission, and a digest of the principal decisions of the Commission and the North Carolina courts affecting public utilities. A monthly or quarterly release of such information shall be made if the Commission deems it advisable or if the Governor shall so request.

(a1)   The public staff of the Commission shall make and publish annual reports to the General Assembly on its activities in the interest of the using and consuming public.

(b)   The Commission shall publish in a separate volume at least once each year its final decisions made on the merits in formal proceedings before the Commission, and may include significant procedural orders and decisions. (1899, c. 164, s. 27; Rev., s. 1117; 1911, c. 211, s. 9; 1913, c. 10, s. 1; C.S., s.

1065; 1933, c. 134, s. 8; 1941, c. 97; 1955, c. 981; 1957, c. 1152, s. 1; 1963, c. 1165, s. 1; 1977, c. 468, s. 6.)

§ 62-18. Records of receipts and disbursements; payment into treasury.

(a)   The Commission shall keep a record showing in detail all receipts and disbursements.

(b)   Except as provided in G.S. 62-110.3, all license fees and seal taxes, all money received from fines and penalties, and all other fees paid into the office of the Utilities Commission shall be turned in to the State treasury. (1899, c. 164, ss. 26, 33, 34; Rev., ss. 1114, 1115; C.S., ss. 1063, 1064; 1933, c. 134, s. 8; 1941, c. 97; 1963, c. 1165, s. 1; 1987, c. 490, s. 1.)

§ 62-19. Public record of proceedings; chief clerk; seal.

(a)   The Commission shall keep in the office of the chief clerk at all times a record of its official acts, rulings, orders, decisions, and transactions, and a current calendar of its scheduled activities and hearings, which shall be public records of the State of North Carolina.

(b)   Upon receipt by the Commission, the chief clerk shall furnish to the executive director copies of all rates, tariffs, contracts, applications, petitions, pleadings, complaints, and all other documents filed with the Commission and shall furnish to the executive director copies of all orders and decisions entered by the Commission.

(c)   The Commission shall have and adopt a seal with the words "North Carolina Utilities Commission" and such other design as it may prescribe engraved thereon by which it shall authenticate its proceedings and of which the courts shall take judicial notice. Where an exemplified copy of Commission records and proceedings is required for full faith and credit outside of the State, such records and proceedings shall be attested by the chief clerk, or deputy clerk, and the seal of the Commission annexed, and there shall be affixed a certificate of a member of the Commission that the said attestation is in proper form. Such exemplification shall constitute an authenticated or exemplified copy of an official record of a court of record of the State of North Carolina. (1933, c. 134, ss. 13, 15; 1941, c. 97; 1963, c. 1165, s. 1; 1977, c. 468, s. 7.)

§ 02-20. Participation by Attorney General in Commission proceedings.

The Attorney General may intervene, when he deems it to be advisable in the public interest, in proceedings before the Commission on behalf of the using and consuming public, including utility users generally and agencies of the State. The Attorney General may institute and originate proceedings before the Commission in the name of the State, its agencies or citizens, in matters within the jurisdiction of the Commission. The Attorney General may appear before such State and federal courts and agencies as he deems it advisable in matters affecting public utility services. In the performance of his responsibilities under this section, the Attorney General shall have the right to employ expert witnesses, and the compensation and expenses therefor shall be paid from the Contingency and Emergency Fund. The Commission shall furnish the Attorney General with copies of all applications, petitions, pleadings, order and decisions filed with or entered by the Commission. The Attorney General shall have access to all books, papers, studies, reports and other documents filed with the Commission. (1949, c. 989, s. 1; c. 1029, s. 3; 1959, c. 400; 1963, c. 1165, s. 1; 1977, c. 468, s. 8.)

§ 62-21. Repealed by Session Laws 1977, c. 468, s. 9.

§ 62-22. Utilities Commission and Department of Revenue to coordinate facilities for rate making and taxation purposes.

The Commission, at the request of the Department of Revenue, shall make available to the Department of Revenue the services of such of the personnel of the Commission as may be desired and required for the purpose of furnishing to the Department of Revenue advice and information as to the value of properties of public utilities, the valuations of which for ad valorem taxation are required by law to be determined by the Department of Revenue. It shall be the duty of the Commission and the Department of Revenue, with regard to the assessment and valuation of properties of public utilities doing business in North Carolina, to coordinate the activities of said agencies so that each of them shall receive the benefit of the exchange of information gathered by them with respect to the valuations of public utilities property for rate making and taxation purposes, and the facilities of each of said agencies shall be made fully available to both of them. (1949, c. 1029, s. 3; 1963, c. 1165, s. 1; 1973, c. 476, s. 193.)

§ 62-23. Commission as an administrative board or agency.

The Commission is hereby declared to be an administrative board or agency of the General Assembly created for the principal purpose of carrying out the administration and enforcement of this Chapter, and for the promulgation of rules and regulations and fixing utility rates pursuant to such administration; and in carrying out such purpose, the Commission shall assume the initiative in performing its duties and responsibilities in securing to the people of the State an efficient and economic system of public utilities in the same manner as commissions and administrative boards generally. In proceedings in which the Commission is exercising functions judicial in nature, it shall act in a judicial capacity as provided in G.S. 62-60. The Commission shall separate its administrative or executive functions, its rule making functions, and its functions judicial in nature to such extent as it deems practical and advisable in the public interest. (1963, c. 1165, s. 1.)

§§ 62-24 through 62-29. Reserved for future codification purposes.

Article 3.

Powers and Duties of Utilities Commission.

§ 62-30. General powers of Commission.

The Commission shall have and exercise such general power and authority to supervise and control the public utilities of the State as may be necessary to carry out the laws providing for their regulation, and all such other powers and duties as may be necessary or incident to the proper discharge of its duties. (1933, c. 134, s. 2; 1941, c. 97; 1963, c. 1165, s. 1.)

§ 62-31. Power to make and enforce rules and regulations for public utilities.

The Commission shall have and exercise full power and authority to administer and enforce the provisions of this Chapter, and to make and enforce reasonable and necessary rules and regulations to that end. (1907, c. 469, s. 1a; 1913, c. 127, s. 2; C.S., s. 1037; 1933, c. 134, s. 8; 1941, c. 97; 1947, c. 1008, s. 2; 1949, c. 1132, s. 3; 1963, c. 1165, s. 1.)

§ 62-32. Supervisory powers; rates and service.

(a) Under the rules herein prescribed and subject to the limitations hereinafter set forth, the Commission shall have general supervision over the rates charged and service rendered by all public utilities in this State.

(b) Except as provided in this Chapter for bus companies, the Commission is hereby vested with all power necessary to require and compel any public utility to provide and furnish to the citizens of this State reasonable service of the kind it undertakes to furnish and fix and regulate the reasonable rates and charges to be made for such service. (1913, c. 127, s. 7; C.S., s. 1112(b); 1933, c. 134, s. 3; 1937, c. 108, s. 2; 1941, cc. 59, 97; 1959, c. 639, s. 12; 1963, c. 1165, s. 1; 1985, c. 676, s. 5.)

§ 62-33. Commission to keep informed as to utilities.

The Commission shall at all times keep informed as to the public utilities, their rates and charges for service, and the service supplied and the purposes for which it is supplied. (1933, c. 134, s. 16; 1937, c. 165; 1939, c. 365, ss. 1, 2; 1941, c. 97; 1963, c. 1165, s. 1.)

§ 62-34. To investigate companies under its control; visitation and inspection.

(a) The Commission shall from time to time visit the places of business and investigate the books and papers of all public utilities to ascertain if all the orders, rules and regulations of the Commission have been complied with, and shall have full power and authority to examine all officers, agents and employees of such public utilities, and all other persons, under oath or otherwise, and to compel the production of papers and the attendance of witnesses to obtain the information necessary for carrying into effect and otherwise enforcing the provisions of this Chapter.

(b) Members of the Commission, Commission staff, and public staff may during all reasonable hours enter upon any premises occupied by any public utility, for the purpose of making the examinations and tests and exercising any power provided for in this Article, and may set up and use on such premises any apparatus and appliances necessary therefor. Such public utility shall have the right to be represented at the making of such examinations, tests and inspections. (1899, c. 164, s. 1; Rev., s. 1064; 1913, c. 127, ss. 1, 2, 7; 1917, c. 194; C.S., s. 1060; 1933, c. 134, s. 8; c. 307, s. 14; 1941, c. 97; 1963, c. 1165, s. 1; 1977, c. 468, s. 10.)

§ 62-35. System of accounts.

(a) The Commission may establish a system of accounts to be kept by the public utilities under its jurisdiction, or may classify said public utilities and establish a system of accounts for each class, and prescribe the manner of keeping such accounts.

(b) The Commission may require any public utility under its jurisdiction to keep separate or allocate the revenue from and the cost of doing interstate and intrastate business in North Carolina.

(c) The Commission may ascertain, determine, and prescribe what are proper and adequate charges for depreciation of the several classes of property for each public utility. The Commission may prescribe such changes in such charges for depreciation as it finds necessary. (Ex. Sess. 1913, c. 20, s. 14; C.S., s. 1088; 1931, c. 455; 1933, c. 134, s. 8; c. 307, s. 13; 1941, c. 97; 1963, c. 1165, s. 1.)

§ 62-36. Reports by utilities; canceling certificates for failure to file.

The Commission may require any public utility to file annual reports in such form and of such content as the Commission may require and special reports concerning any matter about which the Commission is authorized to inquire or to keep informed, or which it is required to enforce. All reports shall be under oath when required by the Commission. The Commission may issue an order, without notice or hearing, canceling or suspending any certificate of convenience and necessity or any certificate of authority 30 days after the date of service of the order for failing to file the required annual report at the time it was due. In the event the report is filed during the 30-day period, the order of cancellation or suspension shall be null and void. (1931, c. 455; 1933, c. 134, s. 8; c. 307, s. 15; 1941, c. 97; 1959, c. 639, ss. 7, 8; 1963, c. 1165, s. 1; 1985, c. 676, s. 6.)

§ 62-36.1. Natural gas planning.

(a) The Commission shall require each franchised natural gas local distribution company to file reports with the Commission detailing its plans for providing natural gas service in areas of its franchise territory in which natural gas service is not available. Commission rules shall require that each local distribution company shall update its report at least every two years.

(b) The Commission shall develop rules to carry out the intent of subsection (a) of this section, and to produce an orderly system for reviewing current levels of natural gas service and planning the orderly expansion of natural gas service to areas not served. These rules shall provide for expansion of service by each franchised natural gas local distribution company to all areas of its franchise territory by July 1, 1998 or within three years of the time the franchise territory is awarded, whichever is later, and shall provide that any local distribution company that the Commission determines is not providing adequate service to at least some portion of each county within its franchise territory by July 1, 1998 or within three years of the time the franchise territory is awarded, whichever is later, shall forfeit its exclusive franchise rights to that portion of its territory not being served.

(b1) The Commission shall issue a certificate of public convenience and necessity in accordance with the provisions of Article 6 of this Chapter for natural gas service for all areas of the State for which certificates have not been issued. Issuance of certificates shall be completed by January 1, 1997, and shall be made after a hearing process in which any person capable of providing natural gas service to an area of the State for which no certificate has been issued or for which no application has been made by July 1, 1995, may apply to the Commission to be considered for the issuance of a certificate under the provisions of this subsection. In issuing a certificate for any unfranchised area of the State, the Commission shall consider the timeliness with which each applicant could begin providing adequate, reliable, and economical service to that area, as well as any other criteria the Commission finds to be relevant, and the Commission may issue a certificate covering less than the total area applied for by an applicant. If the Commission issues a certificate covering less than the total area applied for by the applicant, the applicant may refuse the certificate. In the event that the Commission receives no application for issuance of a certificate for service to a particular area of the State, or in the event a certificate for service to a particular area is not awarded for any reason, the Commission shall issue a certificate for that area to a person or persons to whom a certificate has already been issued.

(c)   Within 180 days after all local distribution companies have filed their initial or biennial update reports, the Commission and the Public Staff shall independently provide analyses and summaries of those reports, together with status reports of natural gas service in the State, to the Joint Legislative Commission on Governmental Operations. (1989, c. 338, s. 1; 1993 (Reg. Sess., 1994), c. 560, s. 1; 1995, c. 216, s. 1; c. 271, s. 1; 2011-291, s. 2.10; 2012-194, s. 16.)

§ 62-36A. Natural gas planning.

(a)   The Commission shall require each franchised natural gas local distribution company to file reports with the Commission detailing its plans for providing natural gas service in areas of its franchise territory in which natural gas service is not available. Commission rules shall require that each local distribution company shall update its report at least every two years.

(b)   The Commission shall develop rules to carry out the intent of subsection (a) of this section, and to produce an orderly system for reviewing current levels of natural gas service and planning the orderly expansion of natural gas service to areas not served. These rules shall provide for expansion of service by each franchised natural gas local distribution company to all areas of its franchise territory by July 1, 1998 or within three years of the time the franchise territory is awarded, whichever is later, and shall provide that any local distribution company that the Commission determines is not providing adequate service to at least some portion of each county within its franchise territory by July 1, 1998 or within three years of the time the franchise territory is awarded, whichever is later, shall forfeit its exclusive franchise rights to that portion of its territory not being served.

(b1)   The Commission shall issue a certificate of public convenience and necessity in accordance with the provisions of Article 6 of this Chapter for natural gas service for all areas of the State for which certificates have not been issued. Issuance of certificates shall be completed by January 1, 1997, and shall be made after a hearing process in which any person capable of providing natural gas service to an area of the State for which no certificate has been issued or for which no application has been made by July 1, 1995, may apply to the Commission to be considered for the issuance of a certificate under the provisions of this subsection. In issuing a certificate for any unfranchised area of the State, the Commission shall consider the timeliness with which each applicant could begin providing adequate, reliable, and economical service to that area, as well as any other criteria the Commission finds to be relevant, and the Commission may issue a certificate covering less than the total area applied for by an applicant. If the Commission issues a certificate covering less than the total area applied for by the applicant, the applicant may refuse the certificate. In the event that the Commission receives no application for issuance of a certificate for service to a particular area of the State, or in the event a certificate for service to a particular area is not awarded for any reason, the Commission shall issue a certificate for that area to a person or persons to whom a certificate has already been issued.

(c)   Within 180 days after all local distribution companies have filed their initial or biennial update reports, the Commission and the Public Staff shall independently provide analyses and summaries of those reports, together with status reports of natural gas service in the State, to the Joint Legislative Commission on Governmental Operations. (1989, c. 338, s. 1; 1993 (Reg. Sess., 1994), c. 560, s. 1; 1995, c. 216, s. 1; c. 271, s. 1; 2011-291, s. 2.10.)

§ 62-36B. Regulation of natural gas service agreements.

Whenever the Commission, after notice and hearing, finds that additional natural gas service agreements (including "backhaul" agreements) with interstate or intrastate pipelines will provide increased competition in North Carolina's natural gas industry and (i) will likely result in lower costs to consumers without substantially increasing the risks of service interruptions to customers, or (ii) will substantially reduce the risks of service interruptions without unduly increasing costs to consumers, the Commission may enter and serve an order directing the franchised natural gas local distribution company to negotiate in good faith to enter into such service agreements within a reasonable time. In considering costs to consumers under this section, the Commission may consider both short-term and long-term costs. (1989 (Reg. Sess., 1990), c. 962, s. 5.)

§ 62-37. Investigations.

(a) The Commission may, on its own motion and whenever it may be necessary in the performance of its duties, investigate and examine the condition and management of public utilities or of any particular public utility. In conducting such investigation the Commission may proceed either with or without a hearing as it may deem best, but shall make no order without affording the parties affected thereby notice and hearing.

(b) If after such an investigation, or investigation and hearing, the Commission, in its discretion, is of the opinion that the public interest shall be served by an appraisal of any properties in question, the investigation of any particular construction, the audit of any accounts or books, the investigation of any contracts, or the practices, contracts or other relations between the public utility in question and any holding or finance agency with which such public utility may be affiliated, it shall be the duty of the Commission to report its findings and recommendation to the Governor and Council of State with request for an allotment from the Contingency and Emergency Fund to defray the expense thereof, which may be granted as provided by law for expenditures from such fund or may be denied. Provided, however, that the Commission is authorized to order any such appraisal, investigations, or audit to be undertaken by a competent, qualified, and independent firm selected by the Commission, the cost of such appraisal, investigation or audit to be borne by the public utility in question. Notwithstanding any other provisions of this Chapter, the Commission is authorized to initiate a full and complete management audit of any public utility company once every five years, by a competent, qualified, and independent firm, such audit to thoroughly examine the efficiency and effectiveness of management decisions among other factors as directed by the Commission. The cost of such audit is to be borne by the particular public utility subject to the audit; provided, however, that carriers subject to regulation by and auditing of the Interstate Commerce Commission shall not be required to bear the expense of additional audit of accounts or management audit required hereunder. (1931, c. 455; 1933, c. 134, s. 8; c. 307, s. 16; 1941, c. 97; 1963, c. 1165, s. 1; 1975, c. 867, s. 4.)

§ 62-38. Power to regulate public utilities in municipalities.

The Commission shall have the same power and authority to regulate the operation of privately owned public utilities within municipalities as it has to regulate such public utilities operating outside of municipalities, with the exception of the rights of such municipalities to grant franchises for such operation under G.S. 160A-319, and such public utilities shall be subject to the provisions of this Chapter in the same manner as public utilities operating outside municipalities. (1917, c. 136, subch. 3, s. 3; C.S., ss. 2783, 2784, 2785; 1933, c. 134, s. 8; 1941, c. 97; 1963, c. 1165, s. 1; 1989, c. 770, s. 11.)

§ 62-39. To regulate crossings of telephone, telegraph, electric power lines and pipelines and rights-of-way of railroads and other utilities by another utility.

(a) The Commission, upon its own motion or upon petition of any public utility or upon petition of the North Carolina Rural Electrification Authority on behalf of any electric membership corporation, shall have the power and authority, after notice and hearing, to order that the lines and right-of-way of any public utility or electric membership corporation may be crossed by any other public utility or electric membership corporation. The Commission, in all such cases, may require any such crossings to be constructed and maintained in a safe manner and in accord with accepted and approved standards of safety and may prescribe the manner in which such construction shall be done.

(b) The Commission shall also have the power and authority to discontinue and prohibit such crossings where they are unnecessary and can reasonably be avoided and to order changes in existing crossings when deemed necessary.

(c) In all cases in which the Commission orders such crossings to be made or changed and when the parties affected cannot agree upon the cost of the construction of such crossings or the damages to be paid to one of the parties for the privilege of crossing the lines of such party, it shall be the duty of the Commission to apportion the cost of such construction and to fix the damage, if any, to be paid and to apportion the damages, if any, among the parties in such manner as may be just and equitable.

(d) This section shall not be construed to limit the right of eminent domain conferred upon public utilities and electric membership corporations by the laws of this State or to limit the right and duty conferred by law with respect to crossing of railroads and highways or railroads crossing railroads, but the duty imposed and the remedy given by this section shall be in addition to other duties and remedies now prescribed by law. Any party shall have the right of appeal from any final order or decision or determination of the Commission as provided by law for appeals from orders or decisions or final determinations of the Commission. (1913, c. 130, s. 1; C.S., s. 1052; 1933, c. 134, s. 8; 1941, c. 97; 1949, c. 1029, s. 1; 1963, c. 1165, s. 1.)

§ 62-40. To hear and determine controversies submitted.

When a public utility embraced in this Chapter has a controversy with another person and all the parties to such controversy agree in writing to submit such controversy to the Commission as arbitrator, the Commission shall act as such, and after due notice to all parties interested shall proceed to hear the same, and its award shall be final. Such award in cases where land or an interest in land is concerned shall immediately be certified to the clerk of the superior court of the county or counties in which said land, or any part thereof, is situated, and shall by such clerk be docketed in the judgment docket for such county, and from such docketing shall have the same effect as a judgment of the superior court for such county. Parties may appear in person or by attorney before such arbitrator. (1899, c. 164, s. 25; Rev., s. 1073; C.S., s. 1059; 1933, c. 134, s. 8; 1941, c. 97; 1963, c. 1165, s. 1.)

§ 62-41. To investigate accidents involving public utilities; to promote general safety program.

The Commission may conduct a program of accident prevention and public safety covering all public utilities with special emphasis on highway safety and transport safety and may investigate the causes of any accident on a highway involving a public utility. Any information obtained upon such investigation shall be reduced to writing and a report thereof filed in the office of the Commission, which shall be subject to public inspection but such report shall not be admissible in evidence in any civil or criminal proceeding arising from such accident. The Commission may adopt reasonable rules and regulations for the safety of the public as affected by public utilities and the safety of public utility employees. The Commission shall cooperate with and coordinate its activities for public utilities with similar programs of the Division of Motor Vehicles, the Insurance Department, the Industrial Commission and other organizations engaged in the promotion of highway safety and employee safety. (1899, c. 164, s. 24; Rev., s. 1065; C.S., s. 1061; 1933, c. 134, s. 8; 1941, c. 97; 1963, c. 1165, s. 1; 1975, c. 716, s. 5; 1995 (Reg. Sess., 1996), c. 673, s. 2.)

§ 62-42. Compelling efficient service, extensions of services and facilities, additions and improvements.

(a)   Except as otherwise limited in this Chapter, whenever the Commission, after notice and hearing had upon its own motion or upon complaint, finds:

(1)   That the service of any public utility is inadequate, insufficient or unreasonably discriminatory, or

(2)   That persons are not served who may reasonably be served, or

(3)   That additions, extensions, repairs or improvements to, or changes in, the existing plant, equipment, apparatus, facilities or other physical property of any public utility, of any two or more public utilities ought reasonably to be made, or

(4)   That it is reasonable and proper that new structures should be erected to promote the security or convenience or safety of its patrons, employees and the public, or

(5)   That any other act is necessary to secure reasonably adequate service or facilities and reasonably and adequately to serve the public convenience and necessity, the Commission shall enter and serve an order directing that such

additions, extensions, repairs, improvements, or additional services or changes shall be made or affected within a reasonable time prescribed in the order. This section shall not apply to terminal or terminal facilities of motor carriers of property.

(b)   If such order is directed to two or more public utilities, the utilities so designated shall be given such reasonable time as the Commission may grant within which to agree upon the portion or division of the cost of such additions, extensions, repairs, improvements or changes which each shall bear. If at the expiration of the time limited in the order of the Commission, the utility or utilities named in the order shall fail to file with the Commission a statement that an agreement has been made for division or apportionment of the cost or expense, the Commission shall have the authority, after further hearing in the same proceeding, to make an order fixing the portion of such cost or expense to be borne by each public utility affected and the manner in which the same shall be paid or secured.

(c)   Repealed by Session Laws 2013-187, s. 1, effective July 1, 2013. (1933, c. 307, s. 10; 1949, c. 1029, s. 2; 1963, c. 1165, s. 1; 1965, c. 287, s. 6; 1985, c. 676, s. 7; 2013-187, s. 1.)

§ 62-43. Fixing standards, classifications, etc.; testing service.

(a)   The Commission may, after notice and hearing, had upon its own motion or upon complaint, ascertain and fix just and reasonable standards, classifications, regulations, practices, or service to be furnished, imposed, observed or followed by any or all public utilities; ascertain and fix adequate and reasonable standards for the measurement of quantity, quality, pressure, initial voltage or other condition pertaining to the supply of the product, commodity or service furnished or rendered by any and all public utilities; prescribe reasonable regulations for the examination and testing of such product, commodity or service and for the measurement thereof; establish or approve reasonable rules, regulations, specifications and standards to secure the accuracy of all meters and appliances for measurement; and provide for the examination and testing of any and all appliances used for the measurement of any product, commodity or service of any public utility.

(b)   The Commission shall fix, establish and promulgate standards of quality and safety for gas furnished by a public utility and prescribe rules and regulations for the enforcement of and obedience to the same. (1919, c. 32; C.S., s. 1055; 1933, c. 134, s. 8; c. 307, s. 11; 1941, c. 97; 1963, c. 1165, s. 1.)

§ 62-44. Commission may require continuous telephone lines.

The Commission may, upon its own motion or upon written complaint by any person, after notice and hearing, require any two or more telephone or telegraph utilities to establish and maintain through lines within the State between two or more localities, which cannot be communicated with or reached by the lines of either utility alone, where the lines or wires of such utilities form a continuous line of communication, or could be made to do so by the construction and maintenance of suitable connections or the joint use of equipment, or the transfer of messages at common points. The rate for such service shall be just and reasonable and the Commission shall have power to establish the same, and declare the portion thereof to which each utility affected thereby is entitled and the manner in which the same must be secured and paid. All necessary construction, maintenance and equipment in order to establish such service shall be constructed and maintained in such manner and under such rules, with such divisions of expense and labor, as may be required by the Commission. (1933, c. 307, s. 9; 1963, c. 1165, s. 1.)

§ 62-45. Determination of cost and value of utility property.

The Commission, after notice and hearing, may ascertain and fix the cost or value, or both, of the whole or any part of the property of any public utility insofar as the same is material to the exercise of the jurisdiction of the Commission, make revaluations from time to time, and ascertain the cost of all new construction, extensions and additions to the property of every public utility. (1933, c. 307, s. 12; 1963, c. 1165, s. 1.)

§ 62-46. Water gauging stations.

The Commission may require the location, establishment, maintenance and operation of any water gauging station which it finds is needed in the State over and above those required by federal agencies, and the Commission may cooperate with federal and other State agencies as to the location, construction and reports and the results of operation of such station. (1933, c. 307, s. 33; 1963, c. 1165, s. 1.)

§ 62-47. Reports from municipalities operating own utilities.

Every municipality furnishing gas, electricity or telephone service shall make an annual report to the Commission, verified by the oath of the general manager or superintendent thereof, on the same forms as provided for reports of public utilities, giving the same information as required of public utilities. (1933, c. 307, s. 34; 1963, c. 1165, s. 1.)

§ 62-48. Appearance before courts and agencies.

(a) The Commission is authorized and empowered to initiate or appear in such proceedings before federal and State courts and agencies as in its opinion may be necessary to secure for the users of public utility service in this State just and reasonable rates and service; provided, however, that the Commission shall not appear in any State appellate court in support of any order or decision of the Commission entered in a proceeding in which a public utility had the burden of proof.

(b) The Commission may, when appearing before federal courts and agencies on behalf of the using and consuming public in matters relating to the wholesale rates and supply of natural gas, employ, subject to the approval of the Governor, private legal counsel and be reimbursed for any resulting legal fees and costs from past and future refunds received by the North Carolina natural gas distribution companies, and may establish procedures for those natural gas distribution companies to set aside reasonable amounts of those refunds for this purpose. The Commission is also authorized to establish procedures whereby the State may be reimbursed from past and future refunds received by the North Carolina natural gas distribution companies for travel expenses incurred by staff members of the Commission and Public Staff designated to provide assistance to the Commission's private legal counsel in natural gas matters before federal courts and agencies. (1899, c. 164, s. 14; Rev., s. 1110; 1907, c. 469, s. 5; C.S., s. 1075; 1929, c. 235; 1933, c. 134, s. 8;

1941, c. 97; 1963, c. 1165, s. 1; 1977, c. 468, s. 11; 1985, c. 312, s. 1; 1985 (Reg Sess., 1986), c. 1014, s. 233.)

§ 62-49. Publication of utilities laws.

The Commission is authorized and directed to secure publication of all North Carolina laws affecting public utilities, together with the Commission rules and regulations, in an annotated edition, and the Commission may adopt rules for distribution of said publication, and shall publish biennial supplements to said utilities laws containing all amendments and additions thereto, and may republish said laws at such times as may be reasonable and necessary. (1963, c. 1165, s. 1; 1967, c. 1133.)

§ 62-50. Safety standards for gas pipeline facilities.

(a) The Commission may promulgate and adopt safety standards for the operation of natural gas pipeline facilities in North Carolina. These safety standards shall apply to the pipeline facilities of gas utilities and pipeline carriers under franchise from the Utilities Commission and to pipeline facilities of other gas operators, as defined in subsection (g) of this section. The Commission shall require that all gas operators file with the Commission reports of all accidents occurring in connection with the operation of their gas pipeline facilities located in North Carolina. The Commission may require that all gas operators file with the Commission copies of their construction, operation, and maintenance standards and procedures, and any amendments thereto, and such other information as may be necessary to show compliance with the safety standards promulgated by the Commission. Where the Commission has reason to believe that any gas operator is not in compliance with the Commission's safety standards, the Commission may, after notice and hearing, order that gas operator to take such measures as may be necessary to comply with the standards. The Commission may require all gas operators to furnish engineering reports showing that their pipeline facilities are in safe operating condition and are being operated in conformity with the Commission's safety standards.

(b) The Commission is hereby authorized to enter into agreements with the United States department of Transportation and other federal agencies and with other states or public utilities commissions of other states for the regulation of natural gas pipelines located within the State of North Carolina and upon the execution of such cooperative agreements, the Commission is authorized to utilize Commission personnel for inspection, investigation, and regulation of safety standards for interstate and intrastate natural gas pipelines in North Carolina, and to share in the cost of such regulation with other agencies having duties with respect to the regulation of said natural gas pipelines, and to receive funds from the United States Department of Transportation for such regulation. The Commission may use Commission personnel to inspect and investigate all gas incidents, facilities, and records kept pursuant to the provision of 49 Code of Federal Regulations, Parts 191, 192, and 193, and to cooperate with other state and federal agencies in determining the probable cause or cause or causes of gas incidents. Any information obtained during an investigation of a gas incident shall be reduced to writing and a report containing that information shall be filed with the Chief Clerk of the Commission and the report shall be subject to public inspection but the report shall not be admissible in evidence in any civil or criminal proceeding arising from the incident.

(c) The Utilities Commission is hereby authorized to enter into cooperative agreements for inspection of all natural gas pipelines of North Carolina to the end that the Utilities Commission may enter into agreements with the United States Department of Transportation or other federal or state agencies to regulate and inspect the safety standards for all natural gas pipelines in the State of North Carolina, including interstate natural gas pipelines.

(d) Any person who violates any provision of this section, or any regulation of the Utilities Commission issued thereunder, shall be subject to a civil penalty for each violation for each day that the violation continues. The maximum penalty for each day of a violation and for all the days of a continuing violation may not exceed the maximum penalties that would apply if the penalties had been imposed under 49 U.S.C. Appx. § 1679a(a) by the Secretary of the United States Department of Transportation. Penalties assessed under this subsection shall be credited to the General Fund as nontax revenue.

(e) Any action for civil penalty or any claim for said penalty may be compromised by the Utilities Commission and settled for an agreed amount. In determining the amount of the penalty imposed in civil action, or the amount agreed upon in compromise, the amount of the penalty shall be considered in relation to the size of the business of the person charged, the gravity of the violation, and the good faith of the person charged in attempting to achieve compliance, after any prior notification of a violation. The amount of the penalty, when finally determined in a civil action, or the amount agreed upon in compromise, may be deducted from any sums owing by the State to the person charged, or may be collected as in the case of any judgment in a civil action in the State courts.

(f) The General Court of Justice of North Carolina is authorized to issue court orders, restraining orders, injunctions and other processes of the court in actions by the Utilities Commission to enforce the provisions of this Chapter relating to gas pipeline safety, and the Commission is authorized to bring actions in said court, including actions for mandatory injunctions, restraining orders, temporary restraining orders, penalties, damages and such other relief as may be necessary to secure compliance with the provisions of this section and regulations of the Commission duly enacted and adopted hereunder relating to gas pipeline safety. This provision is in addition to other powers of the Commission and the courts in relation to the enforcement of provisions of this Chapter in the courts, and shall not limit the present powers of the Commission in bringing actions in the courts for enforcement of other provisions of this Chapter.

(g) For the purpose of this section, "gas operators" include gas utilities and gas pipeline carriers operating under a franchise from the Utilities Commission, municipal corporations operating municipally owned gas distribution systems, regional natural gas districts organized and operated pursuant to Article 28 of Chapter 160A of the General Statutes, and public housing authorities and any person operating apartment complexes or mobile home parks that distribute or submeter natural gas to their tenants. This section does not confer any other jurisdiction over municipally owned gas distribution systems, regional natural gas districts, public housing authorities or persons operating apartment complexes or mobile home parks. (1967, c. 1134, s. 1; 1969, c. 646; 1971, cc. 549, 1145; 1979, c. 269, s. 1; 1989, c. 481, ss. 1, 2; 1993, c. 189, s. 1; 1997-426, s. 9.)

§ 62-51. To inspect books and records of corporations affiliated with public utilities.

Members of the Commission, Commission staff, and public staff are hereby authorized to inspect the books and records of corporations affiliated with public utilities regulated by the Utilities Commission under the provisions of this Chapter, including parent corporations and subsidiaries of parent corporations.

This authorization shall extend to all reasonably necessary inspection of all books and records of account and agreements and transactions between public utilities doing business in North Carolina and their affiliated corporations where such records relate either directly or indirectly to the provision of intrastate service by the utility. The right to inspect such books and records shall apply both to books and records in the State of North Carolina and such books and records located outside of the State of North Carolina. If any such affiliated corporation shall refuse to permit such inspection of its books and records and its transactions with public utilities doing business in North Carolina, the Utilities Commission is empowered to order the public utility regulated in North Carolina to show cause why it should not secure from its affiliated corporation such books and records for inspection in North Carolina or why their franchise to operate as a public utility in North Carolina should not be cancelled. (1969, c. 764, s. 1; 1977, c. 468, s. 12.)

§ 62-52. Interruption of service.

The Utilities Commission may adopt appropriate rules and regulations which would allow public utilities to temporarily interrupt service when a structure is moved by the owner of such structure (or by a licensed mover authorized and acting on behalf of the owner) over or along public roads or streets and there are public utility facilities in place which would impede the movement of such structure. Such rules and regulations shall require:

(1)   The owner to demonstrate that the public health and safety of the utility's customers and that of the general public will not be affected by the interruption of such service,

(2)   That the inconvenience to said customers and the general public can be fully anticipated and reduced to a minimum,

(3)   The utility cooperate with the owner in furnishing information relative to (1) and (2), and

(4)   An initial application fee be paid the utility toward its cost to be incurred in investigating and planning.

Should the owner and the public utility be unable to agree on a practical procedure and/or the direction to follow in overcoming the impeding facilities in order that the public health and safety of the utility's customers and that of the general public will not be affected, then and in such event the owner may petition the Utilities Commission to require the utility to temporarily interrupt its service to its customers by disconnecting the impeding facilities, provided the owner can demonstrate to the satisfaction of the Commission that the public health and safety of the utility's customers and that of the general public will not be affected by such interruption of service and that the public utility was unreasonable in the procedure, direction and cost proposed to the owner to overcome the impeding facility.

In any event, the owner of said structure shall reimburse the utility its full cost involved in such disconnection and reconnection including but not limited to planning, engineering, notification and administrative costs, labor, material and equipment. Should the impeding facility be overcome other than by disconnection, the owner shall nevertheless reimburse the utility its full cost related thereto. (1981 (Reg. Sess., 1982), c. 1186, s. 1.)

§ 62-53. Electric membership corporation subsidiaries.

In addition to any other authority granted to the Commission in this Chapter, the Commission shall have the authority to regulate electric membership corporations as provided in G.S. 117-18.1. (1999-180, s. 4.)

§ 62-54. Notification of opportunity to object to telephone solicitation.

The Commission shall require each local exchange company and each competing local provider certified to do business in North Carolina to notify all telephone subscribers who subscribe to residential service from that company of the provisions of Article 4 of Chapter 75 of the General Statutes and of the federal laws and regulations allowing consumers to object to receiving telephone solicitations. The notification shall be drafted pursuant to G.S. 75-102(m), shall be distributed at least annually, and shall be distributed by one of the following methods: bill insert or bill message, direct mail, or e-mail when the subscriber has affirmatively selected e-mail as a means of notification. The Commission shall also ensure that this information is printed in a clear, conspicuous manner in the consumer information pages of each telephone directory distributed to residential customers. (2000-161, s. 3; 2003-411, s. 5; 2009-122, s. 2.)

§§ 62-55 through 62-59. Reserved for future codification purposes.

Article 4.

Procedure Before the Commission.

§ 62-60. Commission acting in judicial capacity; administering oaths and hearing evidence; decisions; quorum.

For the purpose of conducting hearings, making decisions and issuing orders, and in formal investigations where a record is made of testimony under oath, the Commission shall be deemed to exercise functions judicial in nature and shall have all the powers and jurisdiction of a court of general jurisdiction as to all subjects over which the Commission has or may hereafter be given jurisdiction by law. The commissioners and members of the Commission's staff designated and assigned as examiners shall have full power to administer oaths and to hear and take evidence. The Commission shall render its decisions upon questions of law and of fact in the same manner as a court of record. A majority of the commissioners shall constitute a quorum, and any order or decision of a majority of the commissioners shall constitute the order or decision of the Commission, except as otherwise provided in this Chapter. (1949, c. 989, s. 1; 1963, c. 1165, s. 1.)

§ 62-60.1. Commission to sit in panels of three.

(a) The Utilities Commission shall sit in panels of three commissioners each unless the chairman by order shall set the proceeding for hearing by the full Commission.

(b) Any order or decision made unanimously by a panel of three commissioners shall constitute the order or decision of the Commission, except as otherwise provided in this Chapter; provided, however, that upon motion of any three commissioners not sitting on the panel, made within 10 days of issuance of such order or decision of the panel, with notice to parties of record, the order or decision of the panel shall thereby be stayed and the full Commission shall review the order or decision of the panel and shall within 30 days of said motion either affirm or modify the order or decision of the panel or remand the matter to the panel for further proceedings; provided that the foregoing shall not limit the right of parties to seek review of such order or decision under G.S. 62-90.

(c)   In the event an order or decision of the panel of three is not made unanimously, such order or decision shall be a recommended order only, subject to review by the full Commission, with all commissioners eligible to participate in the final arguments and decision. Review shall take place in accordance with the provisions of G.S. 62-78 and the Commission shall decide the matter in controversy and make appropriate order or decision thereon within 60 days of the date of the recommended order. If within the filing period specified by the panel no exception has been filed by a party, or if the Commission within the same period has not advised the parties that it will conduct a review upon its own motion, the recommended order or decision shall become the final order or decision of the Commission. Nothing in this section shall amend or repeal the provisions of G.S. 62-134.

(d)   This section shall become effective July 1, 1975, and shall not affect the utilization of or the procedures outlined for utilization of a hearing commissioner or a hearing examiner as provided for elsewhere in Chapter 62. (1975, c. 243, s. 4; 1977, c. 468, s. 13.)

§ 62-61. Witnesses; production of papers; contempt.

The Commission shall have the same power to compel the attendance of witnesses, require the examination of persons and parties, and compel the production of books and papers, and punish for contempt, as by law is conferred upon the superior courts. (1949, c. 989, s. 1; 1963, c. 1165, s. 1.)

§ 62-62. Issuance and service of subpoenas.

All subpoenas for witnesses to appear before the Commission, a division of the Commission or a hearing commissioner or examiner and notice to persons or corporations, shall be issued by the Commission or its chief clerk or a deputy clerk and be directed to any sheriff or other officer authorized by law to serve process issued out of the superior courts, who shall execute the same and make due return thereof as directed therein, under the penalties prescribed by law for a failure to execute and return the process of any court. The Commission shall have the authority to require the applicant for a subpoena for persons and documents to make a reasonable showing that the evidence of such persons or documents will be material and relevant to the issue in the proceeding. (1949, c. 989, s. 1; 1963, c. 1165, s. 1; 1995, c. 379, s. 14(c).)

§ 62-63. Service of process and notices.

The chief clerk, a deputy clerk, or any authorized agent of the Commission may serve any notice issued by it and his return thereof shall be evidence of said service; and it shall be the duty of the sheriffs and all officers authorized by law to serve process issuing out of the superior courts, to serve any process, subpoenas and notices issued by the Commission, and such officers shall be entitled to the same fees as are prescribed by law for serving similar papers issuing from the superior court. Service of notice of all hearings, investigations and proceedings by the Commission may be made upon any person upon whom a summons may be served in accordance with the provisions governing civil actions in the superior courts of this State, and may be made personally by an authorized agent of the Commission or by mailing in a sealed envelope, registered, with postage prepaid, or by certified mail. (1949, c. 989, s. 1; 1957, c. 1152, s. 2; 1963, c. 1165, s. 1.)

§ 62-64. Bonds.

All bonds or undertakings required to be given by any of the provisions of this Chapter shall be payable to the State of North Carolina, and may be sued on as are other undertakings which are payable to the State. (1949, c. 989, s. 1; 1963, c. 1165, s. 1.)

§ 62-65. Rules of evidence; judicial notice.

(a) When acting as a court of record, the Commission shall apply the rules of evidence applicable in civil actions in the superior court, insofar as practicable, but no decision or order of the Commission shall be made or entered in any such proceeding unless the same is supported by competent material and substantial evidence upon consideration of the whole record. Oral evidence shall be taken on oath or affirmation. The rules of privilege shall be effective to the same extent that they are now or hereafter recognized in civil actions in the superior court. The Commission may exclude incompetent, irrelevant, immaterial and unduly repetitious or cumulative evidence. All evidence, including records and documents in the possession of the Commission of which it desires to avail itself, shall be made a part of the record in the case by definite reference thereto at the hearing. Any party introducing any document or record in evidence by reference shall bear the expense of all copies required for the record in the event of an appeal from the Commission's order. Every party to a proceeding shall have the right to call and examine witnesses, to introduce exhibits, to cross-examine opposing witnesses on any matter relevant to the issues, to impeach any witness regardless of which party first called such witness to testify and to rebut the evidence against him. If a party does not testify in his own behalf, he may be called and examined as if under cross-examination.

(b) The Commission may take judicial notice of its decisions, the annual reports of public utilities on file with the Commission, published reports of federal regulatory agencies, the decisions of State and federal courts, State and federal statutes, public information and data published by official State and federal agencies and reputable financial reporting services, generally recognized technical and scientific facts within the Commission's specialized knowledge, and such other facts and evidence as may be judicially noticed by justices and judges of the General Court of Justice. When any Commission decision relies upon such judicial notice of material facts not appearing in evidence, it shall be so stated with particularity in such decision and any party shall, upon petition filed within 10 days after service of the decision, be afforded an opportunity to contest the purported facts noticed or show to the contrary in a rehearing set with proper notice to all parties; but the Commission may notify the parties before or during the hearing of facts judicially noticed, and afford at the hearing a reasonable opportunity to contest the purported facts noticed, or show to the contrary. (1949, c. 989, s. 1; 1959, c. 639, s. 2; 1963, c. 1165, s. 1; 1973, c. 108, s. 21.)

§ 62-66. Depositions.

The Commission or any party to a proceeding may take and use depositions of witnesses in the same manner as provided by law for the taking and use of depositions in civil actions in the superior court. (1949, c. 989, s. 1; 1963, c. 1165, s. 1.)

§ 62-67. Repealed by Session Laws 1981, c. 193, s. 1.

§ 62-68. Use of affidavits.

At any time, 10 or more days prior to a hearing or a continued hearing, any party or the Commission may send by registered or certified mail or deliver to the opposing parties a copy of any affidavit proposed to be used in evidence, together with the notice as herein provided. Unless an opposing party or the Commission at least five days prior to the hearing, if the affidavit and notice are received at least 20 days prior to such hearing, otherwise at any time prior to or during such hearing, sends by registered or certified mail or delivers to the proponent a request to cross-examine the affiant at the hearing, the right to cross-examine such affiant is waived and the affidavit, if introduced in evidence, shall be given the same effect as if the affiant had testified orally. If an opportunity to cross-examine an affiant at the hearing is not afforded after request therefor is made as herein provided, the affidavit shall not be received in evidence. The notice accompanying the affidavit shall set forth the name and address of the affiant and shall contain a statement that the affiant will not be called to testify orally and will not be subject to cross-examination unless the opposing parties or the Commission demand the right of cross-examination by notice mailed or delivered to the proponent at least five days prior to the hearing if the notice and affidavit are received at least 20 days prior to such hearing, otherwise at any time prior to or during such hearing. (1949, c. 989, s. 1; 1957, c. 1152, s. 3; 1963, c. 1165, s. 1.)

§ 62-69. Stipulations and agreements; prehearing conference.

(a) In all contested proceedings the Commission, by prehearing conferences and in such other manner as it may deem expedient and in the public interest, shall encourage the parties and their counsel to make and enter stipulations of record for the following purposes:

(1) Eliminating the necessity of proof of all facts which may be admitted and the authenticity of documentary evidence,

(2) Facilitating the use of exhibits, and

(3) Clarifying the issues of fact and law.

The Commission may make informal disposition of any contested proceeding by stipulation, agreed settlement, consent order or default.

(b) Unless otherwise provided in the Commission's rules of practice and procedure, such prehearing conferences may be ordered by the Commission or requested by any party to a proceeding in substantially the same manner, and with substantially the same subsequent procedure, as provided by law for the conduct of pretrial hearings in the superior court. (1949, c. 989, s. 1; 1963, c. 1165, s. 1.)

§ 62-70. Ex parte communications.

(a) In all matters and proceedings pending on the Commission's formal docket, with adversary parties of record, all communications or contact of any nature whatsoever between any party and the Commission or any of its members, or any hearing examiner assigned to such docket, whether verbal or written, formal or informal, which pertains to the merits of such matter or proceeding, shall be made only with full knowledge of, or notice to, all other parties of record. All parties shall have an opportunity to be informed fully as to the nature of such communication and to be present and heard with respect thereto. In all matters and proceedings which are judicial in nature, it is the specific intent of this section that all members of the Commission shall conduct all trials, hearings and proceedings before them in the manner and in accordance with the judicial standards applicable to judges of the General Court of Justice, as provided in Chapter 7A of the General Statutes, and upon the initiation of any such proceedings, and particularly during the trial or hearing thereof, there shall be no communications or contacts of any nature, including telephone communications, written correspondence, or direct office conferences, between any party or such party's attorney and any member of the Commission or any hearing examiner, without all other parties to such proceeding having full notice and opportunity to be present and heard with respect to any such contact or communication.

Any commissioner who knowingly receives any such communication or contact during such proceeding and who fails promptly to report the same to the Attorney General, or who otherwise violates any of the provisions of this subsection shall be liable to impeachment. Any examiner who knowingly receives any such communication or contact during such proceeding and who fails promptly to report the same to the Attorney General or who otherwise violates any of the provisions of this subsection shall be subject to dismissal from employment for cause.

(b)   In the event any such communication or contact shall be received by the Commission or any commissioner or any hearing examiner assigned to such docket without such knowledge or notice to all other parties, the Commission shall immediately cause a formal record of such violation to be made in its docket and thereafter no ruling or decision shall be made in favor of such violating party until the aggrieved party shall waive such violation or the Commission shall find as a fact that such party was not prejudiced thereby or that any such prejudice, if present, has been removed.

(c)   Any contacts or communications made in violation of this section which are not recorded by the Commission may be recorded by notice to the Commission by any aggrieved party and, unless the Commission shall find that such violation did not in fact occur, such recording shall have the same effect as if done by the Commission.

(d)   In matters not under this section, the Commission may secure information and receive communications ex parte, it being the purpose of this section to protect adversary interests where they exist but not otherwise to restrict unduly the administrative and legislative functions of the Commission.

(e)   This section shall not modify any notice required in the case of pleadings and proceedings which are subject to other requirements of notice to parties of record, whether by statute or by rule of the Commission, and the Commission may adopt reasonable rules to coordinate this section with such other requirements.

(f)   In addition to the foregoing provisions regarding contacts with members of the Commission and hearing examiners, if any party of record, including the assistant attorney general when he is a party, confers with or otherwise contacts any staff personnel employed by the Commission regarding the merits of a pending proceeding, the staff employee shall promptly forward by regular mail a momorandum of the date and general subject matter of such contact to all other parties of record to the proceeding.

(g)   Notwithstanding the foregoing, no communication by a public utility or by the public staff regarding the level of rates specifically proposed to be charged by a public utility shall be made or directed to the Commission, a member of the Commission, or hearing examiner, except in the form of written tariff, petition, application, pleading, written response, written recommendation, recorded conference, intervention, answer, pleading, sworn testimony and related exhibits, oral argument on the record, or brief. Willful violations of the provisions of this section on the part of any public utility shall subject such public utility to the penalties provided in G.S. 62-310(a). Willful violations of the provisions of this section by a member of the public staff shall subject such person to dismissal for cause. (1963, c. 1165, s. 1; 1977, c. 468, s. 14; 1979, c. 332, s. 2.)

§ 62-71. Hearings to be public; record of proceedings.

(a)   All formal hearings before the Commission, a panel of three commissioners, a commissioner or an examiner shall be public, and shall be conducted in accordance with such rules as the Commission may prescribe. A full and complete record shall be kept of all proceedings on any formal hearing, and all testimony shall be taken by a reporter appointed by the Commission. Any party to a proceeding shall be entitled to a copy of the record or any part thereof upon the payment of the reasonable cost thereof as determined by the Commission.

(b)   The Commission in its discretion may approve stenographic or mechanical methods of recording testimony, or a combination of such methods, and a transcript of any such record shall be valid for all purposes, subject to protest and settlement by the Commission.

(c)   The Commission is authorized to provide daily transcripts of testimony in cases of substantial public interest and in other cases where time is an important factor to the parties involved.

(d) The Commission shall have authority to contract with or employ on a temporary basis, when deemed necessary by the chairman of the Commission, court reporters in addition to those employed on a full-time basis by the Commission, for the purpose of recording and transcribing testimony given at hearings before the Commission involving any Class A or B utility. The Commission is authorized to charge the cost of employing such court reporters directly to the involved utility or utilities. (1949, c. 989, s. 1; 1963, c. 1165, s. 1; 1975, c. 243, s. 9; 1981, c. 1022.)

§ 62-72. Commission may make rules of practice and procedure.

Except as otherwise provided in this Chapter, the Commission is authorized to make and promulgate rules of practice and procedure for the Commission hearings. (1949, c. 989, s. 1; 1963, c. 1165, s. 1.)

§ 62-73. Complaints against public utilities.

Complaints may be made by the Commission on its own motion or by any person having an interest, either direct or as a representative of any persons having a direct interest in the subject matter of such complaint by petition or complaint in writing setting forth any act or thing done or omitted to be done by any public utility, including any rule, regulation or rate heretofore established or fixed by or for any public utility in violation of any provision of law or of any order or rule of the Commission, or that any rate, service, classification, rule, regulation or practice is unjust and unreasonable. Upon good cause shown and in compliance with the rules of the Commission, the Commission shall also allow any such person authorized to file a complaint, to intervene in any pending proceeding. The Commission, by rule, may prescribe the form of complaints filed under this section, and may in its discretion order two or more complaints dealing with the same subject matter to be joined in one hearing. Unless the Commission shall determine, upon consideration of the complaint or otherwise, and after notice to the complainant and opportunity to be heard, that no reasonable ground exists for an investigation of such complaint, the Commission shall fix a time and place for hearing, after reasonable notice to the complainant and the utility complained of, which notice shall be not less than 10 days before the time set for such hearing. (1949, c. 989, s. 1; 1963, c. 1165, s. 1.)

§ 62-73.1. Complaints against providers of telephone services.

(a) A local exchange company or competing local provider that is unable to resolve a customer complaint shall (i) provide notice to the consumer of the consumer's right to contact the Public Staff of the Commission and (ii) provide to the consumer, in writing, contact information for the Public Staff, including both a toll-free telephone number and an electronic mail address.

(b) The Public Staff shall keep a record of all complaints received pertaining to the provider, including the nature of each complaint and the resolution thereof. If the Public Staff determines that it cannot reasonably resolve the matter, the matter shall be referred to the Commission. The standard for review by both the Public Staff and the Commission shall be whether the action or inaction of the provider is reasonable and appropriate. (2009-238, s. 5.)

§ 62-74. Complaints by public utilities.

Any public utility shall have the right to complain on any of the grounds upon which complaints are allowed to be filed by other parties, and the same procedure shall be adopted and followed as in other cases, except that the complaint and notice of hearing shall be served by the Commission upon such interested persons as it may designate. (1949, c. 989, s. 1; 1963, c. 1165, s. 1.)

§ 62-75. Burden of proof.

Except as otherwise limited in this Chapter, in all proceedings instituted by the Commission for the purpose of investigating any rate, service, classification, rule, regulation or practice, the burden of proof shall be upon the public utility whose rate, service, classification, rule, regulation or practice is under investigation to show that the same is just and reasonable. In all other proceedings the burden of proof shall be upon the complainant. (1949, c. 989, s. 1; 1963, c. 1165, s. 1; 1985, c. 676, s. 8.)

§ 62-76. Hearings by Commission, panel of three commissioners, single commissioner, or examiner.

(a) Except as otherwise provided in this Chapter, any matter requiring a hearing shall be heard and decided by the Commission or shall be referred to a panel of three commissioners or one of the commissioners or a qualified member of the Commission staff as examiner for hearing, report and recommendation of an appropriate order or decision thereon. Subject to the limitations prescribed in this Article, a panel of three commissioners, hearing commissioner or examiner to whom a hearing has been referred by order of the chairman shall have all the rights, duties, powers and jurisdiction conferred by this Chapter upon the Commission. The chairman, in his discretion, may direct any hearing by the Commission or any panel, commissioner or examiner to be held in such place or places within the State as he may determine to be in the public interest and as will best serve the convenience of interested parties. Before any member of the Commission staff enters upon the performance of duties as an examiner, he shall first take, subscribe to and file with the Commission an oath similar to the oath required of members of the Commission.

(b) Repealed by Session Laws 1975, c. 243, s. 5.

(c) In all cases in which a pending proceeding shall be assigned to a hearing commissioner, such commissioner shall hear and determine the proceedings and submit his recommended order, but, in the event of a petition to the full Commission to review such recommended order, the hearing commissioner shall take no part in such review, either in hearing oral argument or in consideration of the Commission's decision, but his vote shall be counted in such decision to affirm his original order. (1949, c. 989, s. 1; 1959, c. 639, s. 3; 1963, c. 1165, s. 1; 1975, c. 243, ss. 5, 9, 10.)

§ 62-77. Recommended decision of panel of three commissioners, single commissioner or examiner.

Any report, order or decision made or recommended by a panel of three commissioners, commissioner or examiner with respect to any matter referred for hearing shall be in writing and shall set forth separately findings of fact and conclusions of law and shall be filed with the Commission. A copy of such recommended order, report and findings shall be served upon the parties who have appeared in the proceeding. (1949, c. 989, s. 1; 1963, c. 1165, s. 1; 1975, c. 243, s. 9.)

§ 62-78. Proposed findings, briefs, exceptions, orders, expediting cases, and other procedure.

(a)   Prior to each decision or order by the Commission in a proceeding initially heard by it and prior to any recommended decision or order of a panel of three commissioners, commissioner or examiner, the parties shall be afforded an opportunity to submit, within the time prescribed by order entered in the cause, unless further extended by order of the Commission, for the consideration of the Commission, panel, commissioner or examiner, as the case may be, proposed findings of fact and conclusions of law and briefs or, in its discretion, oral arguments in lieu thereof.

(b)   Within the time prescribed by the panel of three commissioners, commissioner, or examiner, the parties shall be afforded an opportunity to file exceptions to the recommended decision or order and a brief in support thereof, provided the time so fixed shall be not less than 15 days from the date of such recommended decision or order. The record shall show the ruling upon each requested finding and conclusion or exception.

(c)   In all proceedings in which a panel of three commissioners, commissioner or examiner has filed a report, recommended decision or order to which exceptions have been filed, the Commission, before making its final decision or order, shall afford the party or parties an opportunity for oral argument. When no exceptions are filed within the time specified to a recommended decision or order, such recommended decision or order shall become the order of the Commission and shall immediately become effective unless the order is stayed or postponed by the Commission; provided, the Commission may, on its own motion, review any such matter and take action thereon as if exceptions thereto had been filed.

(d)   When exceptions are filed, as herein provided, it shall be the duty of the Commission to consider the same and if sufficient reason appears therefor, to grant such review or make such order or hold or authorize such further hearing or proceeding as may be necessary or proper to carry out the purposes of this Chapter. The Commission, after review, upon the whole record, or as supplemented by a further hearing, shall decide the matter in controversy and make appropriate order or decision thereon.

(e) The Commission may expedite the hearing and decision of any case if the public interest so requires by the use of pretrial conferences, daily transcripts of evidence, trial briefs, and prompt oral argument, and by granting priority to the hearing and decision of such case. (1949, c. 989, s. 1; 1959, c. 639, s. 4; 1963, c. 1165, s. 1; 1975, c. 243, ss. 9, 10; c. 867, s. 5.)

§ 62-79. Final orders and decisions; findings; service; compliance.

(a) All final orders and decisions of the Commission shall be sufficient in detail to enable the court on appeal to determine the controverted questions presented in the proceedings and shall include:

(1) Findings and conclusions and the reasons or bases therefor upon all the material issues of fact, law, or discretion presented in the record, and

(2) The appropriate rule, order, sanction, relief or statement of denial thereof.

(b) A copy of every final order or decision under the seal of the Commission shall be served by registered or certified mail upon the person against whom it runs or his attorney and notice thereof shall be given to the other parties to the proceeding or their attorney. Such order shall take effect and become operative when issued unless otherwise designated therein and shall continue in force either for a period which may be designated therein or until changed or revoked by the Commission. If an order cannot, in the judgment of the Commission, be complied with within the time designated therein, the Commission may grant and prescribe such additional time as in its judgment is reasonably necessary to comply with the order, and may, on application and for good cause shown, extend the time for compliance fixed in its order. (1949, c. 989, s. 1; 1957, c. 1152, s. 4; 1959, c. 639, s. 4; 1961, c. 472, s. 1; 1963, c. 1165, s. 1; 1981, c. 193, s. 2.)

§ 62-80. Powers of Commission to rescind, alter or amend prior order or decision.

The Commission may at any time upon notice to the public utility and to the other parties of record affected, and after opportunity to be heard as provided in the case of complaints, rescind, alter or amend any order or decision made by it. Any order rescinding, altering or amending a prior order or decision shall, when served upon the public utility affected, have the same effect as is herein provided for original orders or decisions. (1949, c. 989, s. 1; 1963, c. 1165, s. 1.)

§ 62-81. Special procedure in hearing and deciding rate cases.

(a) All cases or proceedings, declared to be or properly classified as general rate cases under G.S. 62-137, or any proceedings which will substantially affect any utility's overall level of earnings or rate of return, shall be set for trial or hearing by the Commission, which trial or hearing shall be set to commence within six months of the institution or filing thereof, and all such cases or proceedings shall be tried or heard and decided, with the issuance of a final order, by the Commission within nine months of the institution or filing thereof. All such cases or proceedings shall be tried or heard and decided in accordance with the rate-making procedure set forth in G.S. 62-133 and such cases shall be given priority over all other cases or proceedings pending before the Commission. In all such cases the Commission shall make a transcript of the evidence and testimony presented and received by it and shall furnish a copy thereof to any party so requesting by the third business day after the taking of such evidence and testimony.

(b) Any public utility filing or applying for an increase in rates for electric, telephone, natural gas or water service shall notify its customers proposed to be affected by such increase of such filing by regular mail or by newspaper publications, as directed by the Commission, within 30 days of such filing, which notice shall state that the Commission shall set and shall conduct a trial or hearing with respect to such filing or application within six months of said filing date. All other public utilities shall give such notice in such manner as shall be prescribed by the Commission.

(c) In cases or proceedings filed with and pending before the Commission, where the total annual revenue requested, or where the total annual revenue increase requested, is less than three hundred thousand dollars ($300,000), even though all or a substantial portion of the rate structure is being initially established or is under review, the chairman of the Commission may refer the proceeding to a panel of three commissioners or to a hearing commissioner or to a hearing examiner for hearing.

(d) In all proceedings for an increase in rates and all other proceedings declared to be general rate cases under G.S. 62-137, the Commission shall conduct the hearing or portions of the hearing within the area of the State served by the public utility whose rates are under consideration, provided this subsection shall not apply to proceedings held pursuant to G.S. 62-134(e) and 62-133(f).

(e) Notwithstanding the provisions of this section, application by any public utility for permission and authority to adjust its rates and charges based solely upon the cost of fuel used in the generation or production of electric power shall be determined in accordance with the provisions of G.S. 62-134(e).

(f) Notwithstanding the provisions of this section, or other provisions of this Chapter which would otherwise require a hearing, where there is no significant public protest received within 30 days of the publication of notice of a proposed rate change for a water or sewer utility, the Commission may decide the proceeding based on the record without a trial or hearing, provided said utility and all other parties of record have waived their right to any such hearing. Any decision made pursuant to this subsection shall be made in accordance with the provisions of G.S. 62-133 or 62-133.1. (1963, c. 1165, s. 1; 1973, c. 1074; 1975, c. 45; c. 243, ss. 6, 9; c. 867, s. 6; 1977, c. 468, s. 15; 1981, c. 193, s. 3; c. 439.)

§ 62-82. Special procedure on application for certificate for generating facility; appeal from award order.

(a) Notice of Application for Certificate for Generating Facility; Hearing; Briefs and Oral Arguments. - Whenever there is filed with the Commission an application for a certificate of public convenience and necessity for the construction of a facility for the generation of electricity under G.S. 62-110.1, the Commission shall require the applicant to publish a notice thereof once a week for four successive weeks in a newspaper of general circulation in the county where such facility is proposed to be constructed and thereafter the Commission upon complaint shall, or upon its own initiative may, upon reasonable notice, enter upon a hearing to determine whether such certificate shall be awarded. Any such hearing must be commenced by the Commission not later than three months after the filing of such application, and the procedure for rendering decisions therein shall be given priority over all other cases on the Commission's calendar of hearings and decisions, except rate proceedings referred to in G.S. 62-81. Such applications shall be heard as provided in G.S. 62-60.1, and the Commission shall furnish a transcript of evidence and testimony submitted by the end of the second business day after the taking of each day of testimony. The Commission or panel shall require that briefs and oral arguments in such cases be submitted within 30 days after the conclusion of the hearing, and the Commission or panel shall render its decision in such cases within 60 days after submission of such briefs and arguments. If the Commission or panel does not, upon its own initiative, order a hearing and does not receive a complaint within 10 days after the last day of publication of the notice, the Commission or panel shall enter an order awarding the certificate. Notwithstanding this section, applicants for a certificate for solar photovoltaic facilities of 10 kilowatts or less are exempt from the requirement to publish public notice in newspapers.

(b)   Compensation for Damages Sustained by Appeal from Award of Certificate under G.S. 62-110.1; Bond Prerequisite to Appeal. - Any party or parties opposing, and appealing from, an order of the Commission which awards a certificate under G.S. 62-110.1 shall be obligated to recompense the party to whom the certificate is awarded, if such award is affirmed upon appeal, for the damages, if any, which such party sustains by reason of the delay in beginning the construction of the facility which is occasioned by the appeal, such damages to be measured by the increase in the cost of such generating facility (excluding legal fees, court costs, and other expenses incurred in connection with the appeal). No appeal from any order of the Commission which awards any such certificate may be taken by any party opposing such award unless, within the time limit for filing notice of appeal as provided for in G.S. 62-90, such party shall have filed with the Commission a bond with sureties approved by the Commission, or an undertaking approved by the Commission, in such amount as the Commission determines will be reasonably sufficient to discharge the obligation hereinabove imposed upon such appealing party. The Commission may, when there are two or more such appealing parties, permit them to file a joint bond or undertaking. If the award order of the Commission is affirmed on appeal, the Commission shall determine the amount, if any, of damages sustained by the party to whom the certificate was awarded, and shall issue appropriate orders to assure that such damages be paid and, if necessary, that the bond or undertaking be enforced. (1965, c. 287, s. 3; 1975, c. 243, s. 7; 2004-199, s. 23; 2013-410, s. 29.)

§§ 62-83 through 62-89. Reserved for future codification purposes.

Article 5.

Review and Enforcement of Orders.

§ 62-90. Right of appeal; filing of exceptions.

(a) Any party to a proceeding before the Commission may appeal from any final order or decision of the Commission within 30 days after the entry of such final order or decision, or within such time thereafter as may be fixed by the Commission, not to exceed 30 additional days, and by order made within 30 days, if the party aggrieved by such decision or order shall file with the Commission notice of appeal and exceptions which shall set forth specifically the ground or grounds on which the aggrieved party considers said decisions or order to be unlawful, unjust, unreasonable or unwarranted, and including errors alleged to have been committed by the Commission.

All other parties may give notice of cross appeal and set out exceptions which shall set forth specifically the grounds on which the said party considers said decision or order to be unlawful, unjust, unreasonable or unwarranted, and including errors alleged to have been committed by the Commission. Such notice of cross appeal and exceptions shall be filed with the Commission within 20 days after the first notice of appeal and exceptions has been filed, or within such time thereafter as may be fixed by the Commission, not to exceed 20 additional days by order made within 20 days of the first filed notice of appeal and exceptions.

(b) Any party may appeal from all or any portion of any final order or decision of the Commission in the manner herein provided. Copy of the notice of appeal shall be mailed by the appealing party at the time of filing with the Commission, to each party to the proceeding to the addresses as they appear in the files of the Commission in the proceeding. The failure of any party, other than the Commission, to be served with or to receive a copy of the notice of appeal shall not affect the validity or regularity of the appeal.

(c) The Commission may on motion of any party to the proceeding or on its own motion set the exceptions to the final order upon which such appeal is based for further hearing before the Commission.

(d) The appeal shall lie to the appellate division of the General Court of Justice as provided in G.S. 7A-29. The procedure for the appeal shall be as provided by the rules of appellate procedure.

(e), (f) Repealed by Session Laws 1975, c. 391, s. 12.

(g) Repealed by Session Laws 1983, c. 526, s. 5. (1949, c. 989, s. 1; 1955, c. 1207, s. 1; 1959, c. 639, s. 1; 1963, c. 1165, s. 1; 1967, c. 1190, s. 1; 1975, c. 391, s. 12; 1983, c. 526, ss. 4, 5; c. 572.)

§ 62-91. Appeal docketed; title on appeal; priorities on appeal.

Unless otherwise provided by the rules of appellate procedure, the cause on appeal from the Utilities Commission shall be entitled "State of North Carolina ex rel. Utilities Commission (here add any additional parties in support of the Commission Order and their capacity before the Commission), Appellee(s) v. (here insert name of appellant and his capacity before the Commission), Appellant." Appeals from the Utilities Commission pending in the superior courts on September 30, 1967, shall remain on the civil issue docket of such superior court and shall have priority over other civil actions. (1949, c. 989, s. 1; 1963, c. 1165, s. 1; 1967, c. 1190, s. 6; 1975, c. 391, s. 13; 1983, c. 526, s. 6.)

§ 62-92. Parties on appeal.

In any appeal to the appellate division of the General Court of Justice, the complainant in the original complaint before the Commission shall be a party to the record and each of the parties to the proceeding before the Commission shall have a right to appear and participate in said appeal. (1949, c. 989, s. 1; 1963, c. 1165, s. 1; 1967, c. 1190, s. 2; 1983, c. 526, s. 7.)

§ 62-93. No evidence admitted on appeal; remission for further evidence.

No evidence shall be received at the hearing on appeal but if any party shall satisfy the court that evidence has been discovered since the hearing before the Commission that could not have been obtained for use at that hearing by the exercise of reasonable diligence, and will materially affect the merits of the case, the court may, in its discretion, remand the record and proceedings to the Commission with directions to take such subsequently discovered evidence, and after consideration thereof, to make such order as the Commission may deem proper, from which order an appeal shall lie as in the case of any other final order from which an appeal may be taken as provided in G.S. 62-90. (1949, c. 989, s. 1; 1955, c. 1207, s. 2; 1963, c. 1165, s. 1.)

§ 62-94. Record on appeal; extent of review.

(a) On appeal the court shall review the record and the exceptions and assignments of error in accordance with the rules of appellate procedure, and any alleged irregularities in procedures before the Commission, not shown in the record, shall be considered under the rules of appellate procedure.

(b) So far as necessary to the decision and where presented, the court shall decide all relevant questions of law, interpret constitutional and statutory provisions, and determine the meaning and applicability of the terms of any Commission action. The court may affirm or reverse the decision of the Commission, declare the same null and void, or remand the case for further proceedings; or it may reverse or modify the decision if the substantial rights of the appellants have been prejudiced because the Commission's findings, inferences, conclusions or decisions are:

(1) In violation of constitutional provisions, or

(2) In excess of statutory authority or jurisdiction of the Commission, or

(3) Made upon unlawful proceedings, or

(4) Affected by other errors of law, or

(5) Unsupported by competent, material and substantial evidence in view of the entire record as submitted, or

(6) Arbitrary or capricious.

(c) In making the foregoing determinations, the court shall review the whole record or such portions thereof as may be cited by any party and due account shall be taken of the rule of prejudicial error. The appellant shall not be permitted to rely upon any grounds for relief on appeal which were not set forth specifically in his notice of appeal filed with the Commission.

(d) The court shall also compel action of the Commission unlawfully withheld or unlawfully or unreasonably delayed.

(e) Upon any appeal, the rates fixed or any rule, regulation, finding, determination, or order made by the Commission under the provisions of this Chapter shall be prima facie just and reasonable. (1949, c. 989, s. 1; 1955, c. 1207, s. 3; 1963, c. 1165, s. 1; 1969, c. 614; 1975, c. 391, s. 14.)

§ 62-95. Relief pending review on appeal.

Pending judicial review, the Commission is authorized, where it finds that justice so requires, to postpone the effective date of any action taken by it. Upon such conditions as may be required and to the extent necessary to prevent irreparable injury, a judge of the appellate court with jurisdiction over the case on appeal is authorized to issue all necessary and appropriate process to postpone the effective date of any action by the Commission or take such action as may be necessary to preserve status or rights of any of the parties pending conclusion of the proceedings on appeal. The court may require the applicant for such stay to post adequate bond as required by the court. (1949, c. 989, s. 1; 1963, c. 1165, s. 1; 1967, c. 1190, s. 8; 1983, c. 526, s. 8.)

§ 62-96. Appeal to Supreme Court.

Appeals of final orders of the Utilities Commission to the Supreme Court are governed by Article 5 of General Statutes Chapter 7A. In all appeals filed in the

Court of Appeals, any party may file a motion for discretionary review in the Supreme Court pursuant to G.S. 7A-31. If the Commission is the appealing party, it is not required to give any undertaking or make any deposit to assure payment of the cost of the appeal, and the court may advance the cause on its docket. (1949, c. 989, s. 1; 1963, c. 1165, s. 1; 1967, c. 1190, s. 3; 1983, c. 526, s. 9.)

§ 62-97. Judgment on appeal enforced by mandamus.

In all cases in which, upon appeal, an order or decision of the Commission is affirmed, in whole or in part, the appellate court shall include in its decree a mandamus to the appropriate party to put said order in force, or so much thereof as shall be affirmed, or the appellate court may make such other order as it deems appropriate. (1949, c. 989, s. 1; 1963, c. 1165, s. 1.)

§ 62-98. Peremptory mandamus to enforce order, when no appeal.

(a) If no appeal is taken from an order or decision of the Commission within the time prescribed by law and the person to which the order or decision is directed fails to put the same in operation, as therein required, the Commission may apply to a superior court judge who has jurisdiction pursuant to G.S. 7A-47.1 or G.S. 7A-48 in Wake County or in the district or set of districts as defined in G.S. 7A-41.1 in which the business is conducted, upon 10 days' notice, for a peremptory mandamus upon said person for the putting in force of said order or decision; and if said judge shall find that the order of said Commission was valid and within the scope of its powers, he shall issue such peremptory mandamus.

(b) An appeal shall lie to the Court of Appeals in behalf of the Commission, or the defendant, from the refusal or the granting of such peremptory mandamus. The remedy prescribed in this section for enforcement of orders of the Commission is in addition to other remedies prescribed by law. (1949, c. 989, s. 1; 1963, c. 1165, s. 1; 1967, c. 1190, s. 4; 1987 (Reg. Sess., 1988), c. 1037, s. 92.)

§ 62-99. Repealed by Session Laws 1967, c. 1190, s. 5.

Article 5A.

Siting of Transmission Lines.

§ 62-100. Definitions.

As used in this Article:

(1) The term "begin to construct" includes any clearing of land, excavation, or other action that would adversely affect the natural environment of the route of a transmission line; but that term does not include land surveys, boring to ascertain geological conditions, or similar preliminary work undertaken to determine the suitability of proposed routes for a transmission line that results in temporary changes to the land.

(2) The word "county" means any one of the counties listed in G.S. 153A-10.

(3) The word "land" means any real estate or any estate or interest in real estate, including water and riparian rights, regardless of the use to which it is devoted.

(4) The word "lines" means distribution lines and transmission lines collectively.

(5) The word "municipality" means any incorporated community, whether designated as a city, town, or village and any area over which it exercises any of the powers granted by Article 19 of Chapter 160A of the General Statutes.

(6) The term "public utility" means any of the following:

a. A public utility, as defined in G.S. 62-3(23).

b. An electric membership corporation.

c. A joint municipal power agency.

d. A city or county that is engaged in producing, generating, transmitting, delivering, or furnishing electricity for private or public use.

(7) The term "transmission line" means an electric line designed with a capacity of at least 161 kilovolts. (1991, c. 189, s. 1; 2013-232, s. 1.)

§ 62-101. Certificate to construct transmission line.

(a) No public utility or any other person may begin to construct a new transmission line without first obtaining from the Commission a certificate of environmental compatibility and public convenience and necessity. Only a public utility as defined in this Article may obtain a certificate to construct a new transmission line, except an entity may obtain a certificate to construct a new transmission line solely for the purpose of providing interconnection of an electric generation facility.

(b) A transmission line for which a certificate is required shall be constructed, operated, and maintained in conformity with the certificate. A certificate may be amended or transferred with the approval of the Commission.

(c) A certificate is not required for construction of the following lines:

(1) A line designed to carry less than 161 kilovolts;

(2) The replacement or expansion of an existing line with a similar line in substantially the same location, or the rebuilding, upgrading, modifying, modernizing, or reconstructing of an existing line for the purpose of increasing capacity or widening an existing right-of-way;

(3) A transmission line over which the Federal Energy Regulatory Commission has licensing jurisdiction, if the Commission determines that agency has conducted a proceeding substantially equivalent to the proceeding required by this Article;

(4) Any transmission line for which, before March 6, 1989, a public utility or other person has surveyed a proposed route and, based on that route, has acquired rights-of-way for it by voluntary conveyances or has filed condemnation proceedings for acquiring those rights-of-way which, together,

involve twenty-five percent (25%) or more of the total length of the proposed route;

(5) An electric membership corporation owned transmission line for which the construction or upgrading has had a proceeding conducted which the Commission determines is substantially equivalent to the proceeding required by this Article;

(6) Any line owned by a municipality to be constructed wholly within the corporate limits of that municipality.

(d) The Commission may waive the notice and hearing requirements of this Article and issue a certificate or amend an existing certificate under either of the following circumstances:

(1) When the Commission finds that the owners of land to be crossed by the proposed transmission line segment do not object to such a waiver and either:

a. The transmission line will be less than one mile long; or

b. The transmission line is for the purpose of relocating an existing transmission line segment to resolve a highway or other public project conflict; to accommodate a commercial, industrial, or other private development conflict; or to connect an existing transmission line to a substation, to another public utility, or to a public utility customer when any of these is in proximity to the existing transmission line.

(2) If the urgency of providing electric service requires the immediate construction of the transmission line, provided that the Commission shall give notice to those parties listed in G.S. 62-102(b) before issuing a certificate or approving an amendment.

(e) When justified by the public convenience and necessity and a showing that circumstances require immediate action, the Commission may permit an applicant for a certificate to proceed with initial clearing, excavation, and construction before receiving the certificate required by this section. In so proceeding, however, the applicant acts at its own risk, and by granting such permission, the Commission does not commit to ultimately grant a certificate for the transmission line.

(f) Nothing in this section restricts or impairs the Commission's jurisdiction pursuant to G.S. 62-73 to hear or make complaints. (1991, c. 189, s. 1; 2013-232, s. 2.)

§ 62-102. Application for certificate.

(a) An applicant for the certificate described in G.S. 62-101 shall file an application with the Commission containing the following information:

(1) The reasons the transmission line is needed;

(2) A description of the proposed location of the transmission line;

(3) A description of the proposed transmission line;

(4) An environmental report setting forth:

a. The environmental impact of the proposed action;

b. Any proposed mitigating measures that may minimize the environmental impact; and

c. Alternatives to the proposed action.

(5) A list of all necessary approvals that the applicant must obtain before it may begin to construct the transmission line; and

(6) Any other information the Commission requires.

(b) Within 10 days of filing the application, the applicant shall serve a copy of it on each of the following in the manner provided in G.S. 1A-1, Rule 4:

(1) The Public Staff;

(2) The Attorney General;

(3) The Department of Environment and Natural Resources;

(4) The Department of Commerce;

(5) The Department of Transportation;

(6) The Department of Agriculture and Consumer Services;

(7) The Department of Cultural Resources;

(8) Each county through which the applicant proposes to construct the transmission line;

(9) Each municipality through whose jurisdiction the applicant proposes to construct the transmission line; and

(10) Any other party that the Commission orders the applicant to serve.

The copy of the application served on each shall be accompanied by a notice specifying the date on which the application was filed.

(c) Within 10 days of the filing of the application, the applicant shall give public notice to persons residing in each county and municipality in which the transmission line is to be located by publishing a summary of the application in newspapers of general circulation so as to substantially inform those persons of the filing of the application. This notice shall thereafter be published in those newspapers a minimum of three additional times before the time for parties to intervene has expired. The summary shall also be sent to the North Carolina State Clearinghouse. The summary shall be subject to prior approval of the Commission and shall contain at a minimum the following:

(1) A summary of the proposed action;

(2) A description of the location of the proposed transmission line written in a readable style;

(3) The date on which the application was filed; and

(4) The date by which an interested person must intervene.

(d) Inadvertent failure of service on or notice to any municipality, county, governmental agency, or other person described in this section may be cured by an order of the Commission designed to give that person adequate notice to enable effective participation in the proceeding.

(e) An application for an amendment of a certificate shall be in a form approved by and shall contain any information required by the Commission. Notice of such an application shall be in the same manner as for a certificate. (1991, c. 189, s. 1; 1991 (Reg. Sess., 1992), c. 959, s. 18; 1997-261, s. 3; 1997-443, s. 11A.119(a).)

§ 62-103. Parties.

(a) The following persons shall be parties to a certification proceeding under this Article:

(1) The applicant;

(2) The Public Staff.

(b) The following persons may intervene in a certification proceeding under this Article if a petition to intervene is filed with the Commission within 100 days of the filing of the application and the petition is subsequently granted:

(1) Any State department, municipality, or county entitled to notice under G.S. 62-102(b);

(2) Any person whose land will be crossed by the proposed line;

(3) Any other person who can show a substantial interest in the certification proceeding. (1991, c. 189, s. 1.)

§ 62-104. Hearings.

(a) The Commission shall schedule a hearing upon each application filed under this Article not more than 120 days after the filing and shall conclude the proceeding as expeditiously as possible. The Commission may, however, extend this time period for substantial cause.

(b)   If, after proper notice of the application has been given, no significant protests are filed with the Commission, the Commission may cancel the hearing and decide the case on the basis of the filed record.

(c)   The Commission shall issue an order on each application filed under this Article within 60 days of the conclusion of the hearing. The Commission may extend this time period for substantial cause. (1991, c. 189, s. 1.)

§ 62-105. Burden of proof; decision.

(a)   The burden of proof is on the applicant in all cases under this Article, except that any party proposing an alternative location for the proposed transmission line shall have the burden of proof in sustaining its position. The Commission may consider any factors that it finds are relevant and material to its decision. The Commission shall grant a certificate for the construction, operation, and maintenance of the proposed transmission line if it finds:

(1)   That the proposed transmission line is necessary to satisfy the reasonable needs of the public for an adequate and reliable supply of electric energy;

(2)   That, when compared with reasonable alternative courses of action, construction of the transmission line in the proposed location is reasonable, preferred, and in the public interest;

(3)   That the costs associated with the proposed transmission line are reasonable;

(4)   That the impact the proposed transmission line will have on the environment is justified considering the state of available technology, the nature and economics of the various alternatives, and other material considerations; and

(5)   That the environmental compatibility, public convenience, and necessity require the transmission line.

(b)   If the Commission determines that the location of the proposed transmission line should be modified, it may condition its certificate upon modifications it finds necessary to make the findings and determinations set forth in subsection (a) of this section. (1991, c. 189, s. 1.)

§ 62-106. Effect of local ordinances.

Within 30 days after receipt of notice of an application as provided by G.S. 62-102, a municipality or county shall file with the Commission and serve on the applicant the provisions of an ordinance that may affect the construction, operation, or maintenance of the proposed transmission line in the manner provided by the rules of the Commission. If the municipality or county does not serve notice as provided above of any such ordinance provisions, the provisions of such ordinance may not be enforced by the municipality or county. If the applicant proposes not to comply with any part of the ordinance, the applicant may move the Commission for an order preempting that part of the ordinance. Service of the motion on the municipality or county by the applicant shall make the municipality or county a party to the proceeding. If the Commission finds that the greater public interest requires it, the Commission may include in a certificate issued under this Article an order preempting any part of such county or municipal ordinance with respect to the construction, operation or maintenance of the proposed transmission line. (1991, c. 189, s. 1.)

§ 62-107. Rules.

Pursuant to G.S. 62-31, the Commission may adopt rules to carry out the purposes of this Article. In addition, the Commission shall adopt rules requiring public utilities to file periodic reports stating their short-term and long-term plans for construction of transmission lines in this State. (1991, c. 189, s. 1.)

§ 62-108. Reserved for future codification purposes.

§ 62-109. Reserved for future codification purposes.

Article 6.

The Utility Franchise.

§ 62-110. Certificate of convenience and necessity.

(a)   Except as provided for bus companies in Article 12 of this Chapter, no public utility shall hereafter begin the construction or operation of any public utility plant or system or acquire ownership or control thereof, either directly or indirectly, without first obtaining from the Commission a certificate that public convenience and necessity requires, or will require, such construction, acquisition, or operation: Provided, that this section shall not apply to construction into territory contiguous to that already occupied and not receiving similar service from another public utility, nor to construction in the ordinary conduct of business.

(b)   The Commission shall be authorized to issue a certificate to any person applying to the Commission to offer long distance services as a public utility as defined in G.S. 62-3(23)a.6., provided that such person is found to be fit, capable, and financially able to render such service, and that such additional service is required to serve the public interest effectively and adequately; provided further, that in such cases the Commission shall consider the impact on the local exchange customers and only permit such additional service if the Commission finds that it will not jeopardize reasonably affordable local exchange service.

Notwithstanding any other provision of law, the terms, conditions, rates, and interconnections for long distance services offered on a competitive basis shall be regulated by the Commission in accordance with the public interest. In promulgating rules necessary to implement this provision, the Commission shall consider whether uniform or nonuniform application of such rules is consistent with the public interest. Provided further that the Commission shall consider whether the charges for the provision of interconnections should be uniform.

For purposes of this section, long distance services shall include the transmission of messages or other communications between two or more central offices wherein such central offices are not connected on July 1, 1983, by any extended area service, local measured service, or other local calling arrangement.

(c)   The Commission shall be authorized, consistent with the public interest, to adopt procedures for the issuance of a special certificate to any person for the limited purpose of offering telephone service to the public by means of coin, coinless, or key-operated pay telephone instruments. This service may be in addition to or in competition with public telephone services offered by the certificated telephone company in the service area. The access line from the pay instrument to the network may be obtained from the local exchange telephone company in the service area where the pay instrument is located, from any certificated competitive local provider, or any other provider authorized by the Commission. The Commission shall promulgate rules to implement the service authorized by this section, recognizing the competitive nature of the offerings and, notwithstanding any other provision of law, the Commission shall determine the extent to which such services shall be regulated and to the extent necessary to protect the public interest regulate the terms, conditions, and rates for such service and the terms and conditions for interconnection to the local exchange network.

(d)   The Commission shall be authorized, consistent with the public interest and notwithstanding any other provision of law, to adopt procedures for the purpose of allowing shared use and/or resale of any telephone service provided to persons who occupy the same contiguous premises (as such term shall be defined by the Commission); provided, however, that there shall be no "networking" of any services authorized under this subsection whereby two or more premises where such services are provided are connected, and provided further that any certificated local provider or any other provider authorized by the Commission may provide access lines or trunks connecting such authorized service to the telephone network, and that the local service rates permitted or approved by the Commission for local exchange lines or trunks being shared or resold shall be on a measured usage basis where facilities are available or on a message rate basis otherwise. Provided however, the Commission may permit or approve flat rates, measured rates, message rates, or some combination of those rates for shared or resold services whenever the service is offered to patrons of hotels or motels, occupants of timeshare or condominium complexes serving primarily transient occupants, to patrons of hospitals, nursing homes, rest homes, or licensed retirement centers, or to members of clubs or students living in quarters furnished by educational institutions, or to persons temporarily subleasing residential premises. The Commission shall issue rules to implement the service authorized by this subsection, considering the competitive nature of the offerings and, notwithstanding any other provision of law, the Commission shall determine the extent to which such services shall be regulated and, to the extent necessary to protect the public interest, regulate the terms, conditions, and rates charged for such services and the terms and conditions for interconnection to the local exchange network. The Commission shall require any person offering telephone service under this subsection by means of a Private Branch Exchange ("PBX") or key system to secure adequate local exchange trunks from any certificated local provider or any other provider authorized by the Commission so as to assure a quality of service equal to the quality of service generally found acceptable by the Commission. Unless otherwise ordered by the Commission for good cause shown by the company, the right and obligation of the certificated local provider or any other provider authorized by the Commission to provide local service directly to any person located within its certificated service area shall continue to apply to premises where shared or resold telephone service is available, provided however, the Commission shall be authorized to establish the terms and conditions under which such services should be provided.

(e)   Notwithstanding subsection (d) of this section, the Commission may authorize any telephone services provided to a nonprofit college or university, and its affiliated medical centers, which is qualified under Sections 501 and 170 of the United States Internal Revenue Code of 1986 or which is a State-owned institution, to be shared or resold by that institution on both contiguous campus premises owned or leased by the institution and noncontiguous premises owned or leased exclusively by the institution, provided these services are offered to students or guests housed in quarters furnished by the institution, patrons of hospitals or medical centers of the institution, or persons or businesses providing educational, research, professional, consulting, food, or other support services directly to or for the institution, its students, or guests. The services of a certificated local provider or any other provider authorized by the Commission, when provided to said colleges, universities, and affiliated medical centers shall be rated in the same way as those provided for shared service offered to patrons of hospitals, nursing homes, rest homes, licensed retirement centers, members of clubs or students living in quarters furnished by educational institutions as provided for in subsection (d) of this section. The institutions regulated pursuant to this subsection shall not be prohibited from electing optional services from the certificated local provider or any other provider authorized by the Commission which include measured or message rate services. There shall be no "networking" of any services authorized under this subsection whereby two or more different institutions where such services are provided are interconnected. Any certificated local provider or any other provider authorized by the Commission may provide access lines or trunks connecting such authorized services to the telephone network. The Commission shall require such institutions to secure adequate local exchange trunks from the certificated local provider or any other provider authorized by the Commission to assure a quality of service equal to the quality of service generally found acceptable by the Commission. Unless otherwise ordered by the Commission for good cause shown by the certificated local provider or any other provider authorized by the Commission, the right and obligation of that provider to provide local service directly to any person located within its certificated service area shall continue to apply to premises where shared or resold telephone service is available under this subsection, provided however, the Commission shall be authorized to establish the terms and conditions under which such service should be provided. The Commission shall issue rules to implement the services authorized by this subsection.

(f)   Reserved.

(f1)   Except as provided in subsection (f2) of this section, the Commission is authorized, following notice and an opportunity for interested parties to be heard, to issue a certificate to any person applying to provide local exchange or exchange access services as a public utility as defined in G.S. 62-3(23)a.6., without regard to whether local telephone service is already being provided in the territory for which the certificate is sought, provided that the person seeking to provide the service makes a satisfactory showing to the Commission that (i) the person is fit, capable, and financially able to render such service; (ii) the service to be provided will reasonably meet the service standards that the Commission may adopt; (iii) the provision of the service will not adversely impact the availability of reasonably affordable local exchange service; (iv) the person, to the extent it may be required to do so by the Commission, will participate in the support of universally available telephone service at affordable rates; and (v) the provision of the service does not otherwise adversely impact the public interest. In its application for certification, the person seeking to provide the service shall set forth with particularity the proposed geographic territory to be served and the types of local exchange and exchange access services to be provided. Except as provided in G.S. 62-133.5(f), any person receiving a certificate under this section shall, until otherwise determined by the Commission, file and maintain with the Commission a complete list of the local exchange and exchange access services to be provided and the prices charged for those services, and shall be subject to such reporting requirements as the Commission may require.

Any certificate issued by the Commission pursuant to this subsection shall not permit the provision of local exchange or exchange access service until July 1, 1996, unless the Commission shall have approved a price regulation plan pursuant to G.S. 62-133.5(a) for a local exchange company with an effective date prior to July 1, 1996. In the event a price regulation plan becomes effective prior to July 1, 1996, the Commission is authorized to permit the provision of local exchange or exchange access service by a competing local provider in the franchised area of such local exchange company.

The Commission is authorized to adopt rules it finds necessary (i) to provide for the reasonable interconnection of facilities between all providers of telecommunications services; (ii) to determine when necessary the rates for such interconnection; (iii) to provide for the reasonable unbundling of essential facilities where technically and economically feasible; (iv) to provide for the transfer of telephone numbers between providers in a manner that is technically and economically reasonable; (v) to provide for the continued development and encouragement of universally available telephone service at reasonably affordable rates; and (vi) to carry out the provisions of this subsection in a manner consistent with the public interest, which will include a consideration of whether and to what extent resale should be permitted. In adopting rules to establish an appropriate definition of universal service, the Commission shall consider evolving trends in telecommunications services and the need for consumers to have access to high-speed communications networks, the Internet, and other services to the extent that those services provide social benefits to the public at a reasonable cost.

Local exchange companies and competing local providers shall negotiate the rates for local interconnection. In the event that the parties are unable to agree within 90 days of a bona fide request for interconnection on appropriate rates for interconnection, either party may petition the Commission for determination of the appropriate rates for interconnection. The Commission shall determine the appropriate rates for interconnection within 180 days from the filing of the petition.

Except as provided in subsections (f4) and (f5) of this section, each local exchange company shall be the universal service provider (carrier of last resort) in the area in which it is certificated to operate on July 1, 1995. Each local exchange company or telecommunications service provider with carrier of last resort responsibility may satisfy its carrier of last resort obligation by using any available technology. In continuing this State's commitment to universal service, the Commission shall, by December 31, 1996, adopt interim rules that designate the person that should be the universal service provider and to determine whether universal service should be funded through interconnection rates or through some other funding mechanism. At a time determined by the Commission to be in the public interest, the Commission shall conduct an investigation for the purpose of adopting final rules concerning the provision of universal services, and whether universal service should be funded through interconnection rates or through some other funding mechanism, and, consistent with the provisions of subsections (f4) and (f5) of this section, the person that should be the universal service provider. A local exchange company that has elected to be subject to alternative regulation under G.S. 62-133.5(m) does not have any carrier of last resort obligations.

The Commission shall make the determination required pursuant to this subsection in a manner that furthers this State's policy favoring universally available telephone service at reasonable rates.

(f2) The provisions of subsection (f1) of this section shall not be applicable to franchised areas within the State that are being served by local exchange companies with 200,000 access lines or less located within the State, and it is further provided that such local exchange company providing service to 200,000 access lines or less shall not be subject to the regulatory reform procedures outlined under the terms of G.S. 62-133.5(a) or permitted to compete in territory outside of its franchised area for local exchange and exchange access services until such time as the franchised area is opened to competing local providers as provided for in this subsection. Upon the filing of an application by a local exchange company with 200,000 access lines or less for regulation under the provisions of G.S. 62-133.5(a), the Commission shall apply the provisions of that section to such local exchange company, but only upon the condition that the provisions of subsection (f1) of this section are to be applicable to the franchised area and local exchange and exchange access services offered by such a local exchange company.

(f3) The provisions of subsection (f1) of this section shall not be applicable to areas served by telephone membership corporations formed and existing under Article 4 of Chapter 117 of the General Statutes and exempt from regulation as public utilities, pursuant to G.S. 62-3(23)d. and G.S. 117-35. To the extent a telephone membership corporation has carrier of last resort obligations, it may fulfill those obligations using any available technology.

(f4) When any telecommunications service provider: (i) enters into an agreement to provide local exchange service for a subdivision or other area where access to right-of-way for the provision of local exchange service by other telecommunications service providers has not been granted coincident with any other grant of access by the property owner; or (ii) enters into an agreement after July 1, 2008, to provide communications service that otherwise precludes the local exchange company from providing communications service for the subdivision or other area, the local exchange company is not obligated to provide basic local exchange telephone service or any other communications service to customers in the subdivision or other area. In each of the foregoing instances, the telecommunications service provider shall be the provider in the subdivision or other area under the terms of the agreement and applicable law. The local exchange company for the franchise area or territory in which the subdivision or other area is located shall be relieved of any universal service provider obligation for that subdivision or other area. In that case, the local exchange company and all other telecommunications service providers shall retain the option, but not the obligation, to serve customers in the subdivision or other area. The local exchange company shall provide written notification to the appropriate State agency that the local exchange company is no longer the universal service provider for the subdivision or other area. The appropriate State agency shall retain the right to redesignate a local exchange company or telecommunications service provider as the universal service provider in accordance with the provisions of subsection (f5) of this section. Any person that enters into an agreement with a telecommunications service provider to provide local exchange service for a subdivision or other area as described in this subsection shall notify a purchaser of real property within the subdivision or other area of the agreement.

For any circumstance not described in this subsection, a local exchange company may be granted a waiver of its carrier of last resort obligation in a subdivision or other area by the appropriate State agency based upon a showing by the local exchange company of all of the following:

(1)   Providing service in the subdivision or area would be inequitable or unduly burdensome.

(2)   One or more alternative providers of local exchange service exist.

(3)   Granting the waiver is in the public interest.

(f5)   If the appropriate State agency finds, upon hearing, that the telecommunications service provider serving the subdivision or other area pursuant to subsection (f4) of this section, or its successor in interest, is no longer willing or no longer able to provide adequate services to the subdivision or other area, the appropriate State agency may redesignate the local exchange company for the franchise area or territory in which the subdivision or other area is located, or another telecommunications service provider, to be the universal service provider for the subdivision or other area. If the redesignated local exchange company is subject to price regulation or other alternative regulation under G.S. 62-133.5, it may treat the costs incurred in extending its facilities into the subdivision or other area as exogenous to that form of regulation and may, subject to providing written notice to the Commission, adjust its rates to recover these costs on an equitable basis from its customers whose rates are subject to regulation under G.S. 62-133.5. Any such action shall be subject to review by the Commission in a complaint proceeding initiated by any interested party pursuant to G.S. 62-73. If the redesignated local exchange company is not subject to price regulation or other alternative regulation under G.S. 62-133.5, it may recover the costs incurred in extending its facilities into the subdivision or other area in the form of a surcharge, subject to Commission approval, spread equitably among all of its customers in a proceeding under G.S. 62-136(a), without having to file a general rate case proceeding. During the period that a telecommunications service provider is serving as a universal service provider and prior to the redesignation of a local exchange company as the universal service provider as provided for herein, for the purposes of the appropriate State agency's periodic certification to the Federal Communications Commission in matters regarding eligible telecommunications carrier status, a local company's status shall not be deemed to affect its eligibility to be an eligible telecommunications carrier, and the appropriate State agency shall so certify.

(f6) For purposes of subsections (f4) and (f5) of this section, the following definitions are applicable:

(1) "Appropriate State agency" means the Commission for purposes of any subdivision or other area within the franchise area of a local exchange company, and the Rural Electrification Authority for the purposes of any subdivision or other area within the franchise area or territory of a telephone membership corporation.

(1a) "Communications service" means either voice, video, or data service through any technology.

(2) "Local exchange company" means a local exchange company subject to price regulation, or other alternative regulation or rate base regulation by the

Commission or a telephone membership corporation organized under G.S. 117-30.

(3) "Telecommunications service provider" means a competing local provider, or any other person providing local exchange service by means of voice-over-Internet protocol, wireless, power line, satellite, or other nontraditional means, whether or not regulated by the Commission, but the term shall not include local exchange companies or telephone membership corporations.

(g) In addition to the authority to issue a certificate of public convenience and necessity and establish rates otherwise granted in this Chapter, for the purpose of encouraging water conservation, the Commission may, consistent with the public interest, adopt procedures that allow a lessor to charge for the costs of providing water or sewer service to persons who occupy the same contiguous premises. The following provisions shall apply:

(1) All charges for water or sewer service shall be based on the user's metered consumption of water, which shall be determined by metered measurement of all water consumed. The rate charged by the lessor shall not exceed the unit consumption rate charged by the supplier of the service.

(1a) If the contiguous premises were built prior to 1989 and the lessor determines that the measurement of the tenant's total water usage is impractical or not economical, the lessor may allocate the cost for water and sewer service to the tenant using equipment that measures the tenant's hot water usage. In that case, each tenant shall be billed a percentage of the landlord's water and sewer costs for water usage in the dwelling units based upon the hot water used in the tenant's dwelling unit. The percentage of total water usage allocated for each dwelling unit shall be equal to that dwelling unit's individually submetered hot water usage divided by all submetered hot water usage in all dwelling units. The following conditions apply to billing for water and sewer service under this subdivision:

a. A lessor shall not utilize a ratio utility billing system or other allocation billing system that does not rely on individually submetered hot water usage to determine the allocation of water and sewer costs.

b. The lessor shall not include in a tenant's bill the cost of water and sewer service used in common areas or water loss due to leaks in the lessor's water mains. A lessor shall not bill or attempt to collect for excess water usage resulting from a plumbing malfunction or other condition that is not known to the tenant or that has been reported to the lessor.

c.   All equipment used to measure water usage shall comply with guidelines promulgated by the American Water Works Association.

d.   The lessor shall maintain records for a minimum of 12 months that demonstrate how each tenant's allocated costs were calculated for water and sewer service. Upon advanced written notice to the lessor, a tenant may inspect the records during reasonable business hours.

e.   Bills for water and sewer service sent by the lessor to the tenant shall contain all the following information:

1.   The amount of water and sewer services allocated to the tenant during the billing period.

2.   The method used to determine the amount of water and sewer services allocated to the tenant.

3.   Beginning and ending dates for the billing period.

4.   The past-due date, which shall not be less than 25 days after the bill is mailed.

5.   A local or toll-free telephone number and address that the tenant can use to obtain more information about the bill.

(2)   The lessor may charge a reasonable administrative fee for providing water or sewer service not to exceed the maximum administrative fee authorized by the Commission.

(3)   The Commission shall issue rules to define contiguous premises and to implement this subsection. In issuing the rule to define contiguous premises, the Commission shall consider contiguous premises where manufactured homes, as defined in G.S. 143-145(7), or spaces for manufactured homes are rented.

(4)   The Commission shall develop an application that lessors must submit for authority to charge for water or sewer service. The form shall include all of the following:

a. A description of the applicant and the property to be served.

b. A description of the proposed billing method and billing statements.

c. The schedule of rates charged to the applicant by the supplier.

d. The schedule of rates the applicant proposes to charge the applicant's customers.

e. The administrative fee proposed to be charged by the applicant.

f. The name of and contact information for the applicant and its agents.

g. The name of and contact information for the supplying water or sewer system.

h. Any additional information that the Commission may require.

(5) The Commission shall approve or disapprove an application within 30 days of the filing of a completed application with the Commission. If the Commission has not issued an order disapproving a completed application within 30 days, the application shall be deemed approved.

(6) A provider of water or sewer service under this subsection may increase the rate for service so long as the rate does not exceed the unit consumption rate charged by the supplier of the service. A provider of water or sewer service under this subsection may change the administrative fee so long as the administrative fee does not exceed the maximum administrative fee authorized by the Commission. In order to change the rate or administrative fee, the provider shall file a notice of revised schedule of rates and fees with the Commission. The Commission may prescribe the form by which the provider files a notice of a revised schedule of rates and fees under this subsection. The form shall include all of the following:

a. The current schedule of the unit consumption rates charged by the provider.

b. The schedule of rates charged by the supplier to the provider that the provider proposes to pass through to the provider's customers.

c. The schedule of the unit consumption rates proposed to be charged by the provider.

d. The current administrative fee charged by the provider, if applicable.

e. The administrative fee proposed to be charged by the provider.

(7) A notification of revised schedule of rates and fees shall be presumed valid and shall be allowed to become effective upon 14 days notice to the Commission, unless otherwise suspended or disapproved by order issued within 14 days after filing.

(8) Notwithstanding any other provision of this Chapter, the Commission shall determine the extent to which the services shall be regulated and, to the extent necessary to protect the public interest, regulate the terms, conditions, and rates that may be charged for the services. Nothing in this subsection shall be construed to alter the rights, obligations, or remedies of persons providing water or sewer services and their customers under any other provision of law.

(9) A provider of water or sewer service under this subsection shall not be required to file annual reports pursuant to G.S. 62-36 or to furnish a bond pursuant to G.S. 62-110.3.

(h) In addition to the authority to issue a certificate of public convenience and necessity and establish rates otherwise granted in this Chapter, the Commission may, consistent with the public interest, adopt procedures that allow a lessor of a residential building or complex that has individually metered units for electric service in the lessor's name to charge for the actual costs of providing electric service to each tenant when the lessor has a separate lease for each bedroom in the unit. The following provisions shall apply to the charges authorized under this subsection:

(1) The lessor shall equally divide the actual amount of the individual electric service bill for a unit among all the tenants in the unit and shall send one bill to each tenant. The amount charged shall be prorated when a tenant has not leased the unit for the same number of days as the other tenants in the unit during the billing period. Each bill may include an administrative fee up to the amount of the then-current administrative fee authorized by the Commission in Rule 18-6 for water service and, when applicable, a late fee in an amount determined by the Commission. The lessor shall not charge the cost of

electricity from any other unit or common area in a tenant's bill. The lessor may, at the lessor's option, pay any portion of any bill sent to a tenant.

(2) A lessor who charges for electric service under this subsection is solely responsible for the prompt payment of all bills rendered by the electric utility providing service to the residential building or complex and is the customer of the electric utility subject to all rules, regulations, tariffs, riders, and service regulations associated with the provision of electric service to retail customers of the utility.

(3) The lessor shall maintain records for a minimum of 36 months that demonstrate how each tenant's allocated costs were calculated for electric service. A tenant may inspect these records, including the actual per unit public utility billings, during reasonable business hours and may obtain copies of the records for a reasonable copying fee.

(4) Bills for electric service sent by the lessor to the tenant shall contain all of the following information:

a. The bill charged by the electric supplier for the unit as a whole and the amount of charges allocated to the tenant during the billing period.

b. The name of the electric power supplier providing electric service to the unit.

c. Beginning and ending dates for the usage period and, if provided by the electric supplier, the date the meter was read for that usage period.

d. The past-due date, which shall not be less than 25 days after the bill is mailed to the tenant.

e. A local or toll-free telephone number and address that the tenant can use to obtain more information about the bill.

f. The amount of any administrative fee and late fee approved by the Commission and included in the bill.

g. A statement of the tenant's right to address questions about the bill to the lessor and the tenant's right to file a complaint with, or otherwise seek recourse from, the Commission if the tenant cannot resolve an electric service billing dispute with the lessor.

(5) The Commission shall develop an application that a lessor must submit for Commission approval to charge for electric service as provided in this section. The form shall include all of the following:

a. A description of the lessor and the property to be served.

b. A description of the proposed billing method and billing statements.

c. The administrative fee and late payment fee, if any, proposed to be charged by the lessor.

d. The name of and contact information for the lessor and the lessor's agents.

e. The name of and contact information for the supplier of electric service to the lessor's rental property.

f. A copy of the lease forms used by the lessor for tenants who are billed for electric service pursuant to this subsection.

g. Any additional information that the Commission may require.

(6) The Commission shall approve or disapprove an application within 60 days of the filing of a completed application with the Commission. If the Commission has not issued an order disapproving a completed application within 60 days, the application shall be deemed approved.

(7) A lessor who charges for electric service under this subsection shall not be required to file annual reports pursuant to G.S. 62-36.

(8) The Commission shall adopt rules to implement the provisions of this subsection. (1931, c. 455; 1933, c. 134, s. 8; 1941, c. 97; 1963, c. 1165, s. 1; 1983 (Reg. Sess., 1984), c. 1043, s. 2; 1985, c. 676, s. 9; c. 680; 1987, c. 445, s. 1; 1989, c. 451, ss. 1, 2; 1995, c. 27, s. 4; 1995 (Reg. Sess., 1996), c. 753, s. 1; 1997-207, s. 1; 1998-180, ss. 1, 2; 1998-212, s. 15.8B; 1999-112, s. 1; 2001-252, s. 1; 2001-502, s. 1; 2002-14, s. 1; 2003-99, s. 1; 2003-173, s. 1; 2004-143, s. 7; 2005-385, ss. 1, 2; 2009-202, s. 1; 2009-279, s. 1; 2011-52, s. 1; 2011-252, s. 4.)

§ 62-110.1. Certificate for construction of generating facility; analysis of long-range needs for expansion of facilities; ongoing review of construction costs; inclusion of approved construction costs in rates.

(a)   Notwithstanding the proviso in G.S. 62-110, no public utility or other person shall begin the construction of any steam, water, or other facility for the generation of electricity to be directly or indirectly used for the furnishing of public utility service, even though the facility be for furnishing the service already being rendered, without first obtaining from the Commission a certificate that public convenience and necessity requires, or will require, such construction.

(b)   For the purpose of subsections (a) and (d) of this section, "public utility" shall include any electric membership corporation operating within this State, and the term "public utility service" shall include the service rendered by any such electric membership corporation.

(c)   The Commission shall develop, publicize, and keep current an analysis of the long-range needs for expansion of facilities for the generation of electricity in North Carolina, including its estimate of the probable future growth of the use of electricity, the probable needed generating reserves, the extent, size, mix and general location of generating plants and arrangements for pooling power to the extent not regulated by the Federal Energy Regulatory Commission and other arrangements with other utilities and energy suppliers to achieve maximum efficiencies for the benefit of the people of North Carolina, and shall consider such analysis in acting upon any petition by any utility for construction. In developing such analysis, the Commission shall confer and consult with the public utilities in North Carolina, the utilities commissions or comparable agencies of neighboring states, the Federal Energy Regulatory Commission, the Southern Growth Policies Board, and other agencies having relevant information and may participate as it deems useful in any joint boards investigating generating plant sites or the probable need for future generating facilities. In addition to such reports as public utilities may be required by statute or rule of the Commission to file with the Commission, any such utility in North Carolina may submit to the Commission its proposals as to the future needs for electricity to serve the people of the State or the area served by such utility, and insofar as practicable, each such utility and the Attorney General may attend or be represented at any formal conference conducted by the Commission in developing a plan for the future requirements of electricity for North Carolina or this region. In the course of making the analysis and developing the plan, the Commission shall conduct one or more public hearings. Each year, the Commission shall submit to the Governor and to the appropriate committees of the General Assembly a report of its analysis and plan, the progress to date in carrying out such plan, and the program of the Commission for the ensuing year in connection with such plan.

(d)   In acting upon any petition for the construction of any facility for the generation of electricity, the Commission shall take into account the applicant's arrangements with other electric utilities for interchange of power, pooling of plant, purchase of power and other methods for providing reliable, efficient, and economical electric service.

(e)   As a condition for receiving a certificate, the applicant shall file an estimate of construction costs in such detail as the Commission may require. The Commission shall hold a public hearing on each application and no certificate shall be granted unless the Commission has approved the estimated construction costs and made a finding that construction will be consistent with the Commission's plan for expansion of electric generating capacity. A certificate for the construction of a coal or nuclear facility shall be granted only if the applicant demonstrates and the Commission finds that energy efficiency measures; demand-side management; renewable energy resource generation; combined heat and power generation; or any combination thereof, would not establish or maintain a more cost-effective and reliable generation system and that the construction and operation of the facility is in the public interest. In making its determination, the Commission shall consider resource and fuel diversity and reasonably anticipated future operating costs. Once the Commission grants a certificate, no public utility shall cancel construction of a generating unit or facility without approval from the Commission based upon a finding that the construction is no longer in the public interest.

(e1)   Upon the request of the public utility or upon its own motion, the Commission may review the certificate to determine whether changes in the probable future growth of the use of electricity indicate that the public convenience and necessity require modification or revocation of the certificate. If the Commission finds that completion of the generating facility is no longer in the public interest, the Commission may modify or revoke the certificate.

(f)   The public utility shall submit a progress report and any revision in the cost estimate for the construction approved under subsection (e) of this section during each year of construction. Upon the request of the public utility or upon its own motion, the Commission may conduct an ongoing review of construction of the facility as the construction proceeds. If the Commission approves any revised construction cost estimate and finds that incurrence of the cost of that portion of the construction of the facility under review was reasonable and prudent, the certificate shall remain in effect. If the Commission disapproves any part of the revised cost estimate or finds that the incurrence of the cost of that portion of the construction of the facility then under review was unreasonable or imprudent, the Commission may modify or revoke the certificate.

(f1)   The public utility shall recover through rates in a general rate case conducted pursuant to G.S. 62-133 the actual costs it has incurred in constructing a generating facility in reliance on a certificate issued under this section as provided in this subsection, unless new evidence is discovered (i) that could not have been discovered by due diligence at an earlier time and (ii) that reasonably tends to show that a previous determination by the Commission that a material item of cost was just and reasonable and prudently incurred was erroneous. If the Commission determines that evidence has been submitted that meets the requirements of this subsection, the public utility shall have the burden of proof to demonstrate that the material item of cost was in fact just and reasonable and prudently incurred.

(1)   When a facility has been completed, and the construction of the facility has been subject to ongoing review under subsection (f) of this section, the reasonable and prudent costs of construction approved by the Commission during the ongoing review shall be included in the public utility's rate base without further review by the Commission.

(2)   If a facility has not been completed, and the construction of the facility has been subject to ongoing review under subsection (f) of this section, the reasonable and prudent costs of construction approved by the Commission during the ongoing review shall be included in the public utility's rate base without further review by the Commission.

(3)   If a facility is under construction or has been completed and the construction of the facility has not been subject to ongoing review under subsection (f) of this section, the costs of construction shall be included in the public utility's rate base if the Commission finds that the incurrence of these costs is reasonable and prudent.

(f2)   If the construction of a facility is cancelled, including cancellation as a result of modification or revocation of the certificate under subsection (e1) of this section, and the construction of the facility has been subject to ongoing review under subsection (f), absent newly discovered evidence (i) that could not have been discovered by due diligence at an earlier time and (ii) that reasonably tends to show that a previous determination by the Commission that a material item of cost was just and reasonable and prudently incurred was erroneous, the public utility shall recover through rates in a general rate case conducted pursuant to G.S. 62-133 the costs of construction approved by the Commission during the ongoing review that were actually incurred prior to cancellation, amortized over a reasonable time as determined by the Commission. In the general rate case, the Commission shall make any adjustment that may be required because costs of construction previously added to the utility's rate base pursuant to subsection (f1) of this section are removed from the rate base and recovered in accordance with this subsection. Any costs of construction actually incurred, but not previously approved by the Commission, shall be recovered only if they are found by the Commission to be reasonable and prudent. If the Commission determines that evidence has been submitted that meets the requirements of this subsection, the public utility shall have the burden of proof to demonstrate that the material item of cost was just and reasonable and prudently incurred.

(f3)   If the construction of a facility is cancelled, including cancellation as a result of the modification or revocation of the certificate under subsection (e1) of this section, and the construction of the facility has not been subject to ongoing review under subsection (f) of this section, the public utility shall recover through rates in a general rate case conducted pursuant to G.S. 62-133 the costs of construction that were actually incurred prior to the cancellation and are found by the Commission to be reasonable and prudent, amortized over a reasonable time as determined by the Commission. In the general rate case, the Commission shall make any adjustment that may be required because costs of construction previously added to the utility's rate base pursuant to subsection (f1) of this section are removed from the rate base and recovered in accordance with this subsection.

(g)   The certification requirements of this section shall not apply to a nonutility-owned generating facility fueled by renewable energy resources under two megawatts in capacity or to persons who construct an electric generating facility primarily for that person's own use and not for the primary purpose of producing electricity, heat, or steam for sale to or for the public for compensation; provided, however, that such persons shall, nevertheless, be required to report to the Utilities Commission the proposed construction of such a facility before beginning construction thereof.

(h)   Notwithstanding any other subsections of this section to the contrary, the Commission shall render its decision on an application for a certificate within

45 days of the date the application is filed if (i) the public utility that has applied for the certificate is subject to the provisions of subsection (e) of G.S. 143-215.107D; (ii) the application involves a request by the public utility to construct a generating unit that uses natural gas as the primary fuel at a specific coal-fired generating site that the public utility owns or operates on July 1, 2009; (iii) the coal-fired generating units at the site are not operated with flue gas desulfurization devices; (iv) the public utility will permanently cease operations of all of the coal-fired generating units at the site on or before the completion of the generating unit that is the subject of the certificate application; and (v) the installation of the generating unit that uses natural gas as the primary fuel allows the public utility to meet the requirements of subsection (e) of G.S. 143-215.107D. When the public utility applies for a certificate as provided in this subsection, it shall submit to the Commission and the Department of Environment and Natural Resources a revised verified statement required pursuant to subsection (i) of G.S. 62-133.6 and to the Commission an estimate of the costs of construction of the generating unit that uses natural gas as the primary fuel in such detail as the Commission may require. The provisions of G.S. 62-82 and subsection (e) of this section shall not apply to a certificate applied for pursuant to this subsection. The authority granted pursuant to this subsection expires January 1, 2011. (1965, c. 287, s. 2; 1975, c. 780, s. 1; 1979, c. 652, s. 2; 2007-397, s. 6; 2009-390, s. 1(b); 2013-187, s. 2.)

§ 62-110.2. Electric service areas outside of municipalities.

(a) As used in this section, unless the context otherwise requires, the term:

(1) "Premises" means the building, structure, or facility to which electricity is being or is to be furnished; provided, that two or more buildings, structures, or facilities which are located on one tract or contiguous tracts of land and are utilized by one electric consumer for commercial, industrial, institutional, or governmental purposes, shall together constitute one "premises," except that any such building, structure, or facility shall not, together with any other building, structure, or facility, constitute one "premises" if the electric service to it is separately metered and the charges for such service are calculated independently of charges for service to any other building, structure, or facility; and

(2) "Line" means any conductor for the distribution or transmission of electricity, other than

a. In the case of overhead construction, a conductor from the pole nearest the premises of a consumer to such premises, or a conductor from a line tap to such premises, and

b. In the case of underground construction, a conductor from the transformer (or junction point, if there be one) nearest the premises of a consumer to such premises.

(3) "Electric supplier" means any public utility furnishing electric service or any electric membership corporation.

(b) In areas outside of municipalities, electric suppliers shall have rights and be subject to restrictions as follows:

(1) Every electric supplier shall have the right to serve all premises being served by it, or to which any of its facilities for service are attached, on April 20, 1965.

(2) Every electric supplier shall have the right, subject to subdivision (4) of this subsection, to serve all premises initially requiring electric service after April 20, 1965, which are located wholly within 300 feet of such electric supplier's lines as such lines exist on April 20, 1965, except premises which, on said date, are being served by another electric supplier or to which any of another electric supplier's facilities for service are attached.

(3) Every electric supplier shall have the right, subject to subdivision (4) of this subsection, to serve all premises initially requiring electric service after April 20, 1965, which are located wholly within 300 feet of lines that such electric supplier constructs after April 20, 1965, to serve consumers that it has the right to serve, except premises located wholly within a service area assigned to another electric supplier pursuant to subsection (c) hereof.

(4) Any premises initially requiring electric service after April 20, 1965, which are located wholly or partially within 300 feet of the lines of one electric supplier and also wholly or partially within 300 feet of the lines of another electric supplier, as each of such supplier's lines exist on April 20, 1965, or as extended to serve consumers that the supplier has the right to serve, may be served by such one of said electric suppliers which the consumer chooses, and any electric supplier not so chosen by the consumer shall not thereafter furnish service to such premises.

(5) Any premises initially requiring electric service after April 20, 1965, which are not located wholly within 300 feet of the lines of any electric supplier and are not located partially within 300 feet of the lines of two or more electric suppliers may be served by any electric supplier which the consumer chooses, unless such premises are located wholly or partially within an area assigned to an electric supplier pursuant to subsection (c) hereof, and any electric supplier not so chosen by the consumer shall not thereafter furnish service to such premises.

(6) Any premises initially requiring electric service after April 20, 1965, which are located partially within a service area assigned to one electric supplier and partially within a service area assigned to another electric supplier pursuant to subsection (c) hereof, or are located partially within a service area assigned to one electric supplier pursuant to subsection (c) hereof and partially within 300 feet of the lines of another electric supplier, as such lines exist on April 20, 1965, or as extended to serve consumers it has the right to serve, may be served by such one of said electric suppliers which the consumer chooses, and the electric supplier not so chosen shall not thereafter furnish service to such premises.

(7) Any premises initially requiring electric service after April 20, 1965, which are located only partially within a service area assigned to one electric supplier pursuant to subsection (c) hereof and are located wholly outside the service areas assigned to other electric suppliers and are located wholly more than 300 feet from other electric suppliers' lines, may be served by any electric supplier which the consumer chooses, and any electric supplier not so chosen by the consumer shall not thereafter furnish service to such premises.

(8) Every electric supplier shall have the right to serve all premises located wholly within the service area assigned to it pursuant to subsection (c) hereof.

(9) No electric supplier shall furnish temporary electric service for the construction of premises which it would not have the right to serve under this subsection if such premises were already constructed. The construction of lines for, and the furnishing of, temporary service for the construction of premises which any other electric supplier, if chosen by the consumer, would have the right to serve if such premises were already constructed, shall not impair the right of such other electric supplier to furnish service to such premises after the construction thereof, if then chosen by the consumer; nor, unless the consumer chooses to have such premises served by the supplier which furnished the

temporary service, shall the furnishing of such temporary service or the construction of a line therefor impair the right of any other electric supplier to furnish service to any other premises which, without regard to the construction of such temporary service line, it has the right to serve.

(10) No electric supplier shall furnish electric service to any premises in this State outside the limits of any incorporated city or town except as permitted by this section; provided, that nothing in this section shall restrict the right of an electric supplier to furnish electric service to itself or to exchange or interchange electric energy with, purchase electric energy from or sell electric energy to any other electric supplier.

(c) (1) In order to avoid unnecessary duplication of electric facilities, the Commission is authorized and directed to assign, as soon as practicable after January 1, 1966, to electric suppliers all areas, by adequately defined boundaries, that are outside the corporate limits of municipalities and that are more than 300 feet from the lines of all electric suppliers as such lines exist on the dates of the assignments; provided, that the Commission may leave unassigned any area in which the Commission, in its discretion, determines that the existing lines of two or more electric suppliers are in such close proximity that no substantial avoidance of duplication of facilities would be accomplished by assignment of such area. The Commission shall make assignments of areas in accordance with public convenience and necessity, considering, among other things, the location of existing lines and facilities of electric suppliers and the adequacy and dependability of the service of electric suppliers, but not considering rate differentials among electric suppliers.

(2) The Commission, upon agreement of the affected electric suppliers, is authorized to reassign to one electric supplier any area or portion thereof theretofore assigned to another; and the Commission, notwithstanding the lack of such agreement, is authorized to reassign to one electric supplier any area or portion thereof theretofore assigned to another, except premises being served by the other electric supplier or to which any of its facilities for service are attached and except such portions of such area as are within 300 feet of the other electric supplier's lines, upon finding that such reassignment is required by public convenience and necessity. In determining whether public convenience and necessity requires such reassignment, the Commission shall consider, among other things, the adequacy and dependability of the service of the affected electric suppliers, but shall not consider rate differentials between such electric suppliers.

(d)   Notwithstanding the provisions of subsections (b) and (c) of this section:

(1)   Any electric supplier may furnish electric service to any consumer who desires service from such electric supplier at any premises being served by another electric supplier, or at premises which another electric supplier has the right to serve pursuant to other provisions of this section, upon agreement of the affected electric suppliers; and

(2)   The Commission shall have the authority and jurisdiction, after notice to all affected electric suppliers and after hearing, if a hearing is requested by any affected electric supplier or any other interested party, to order any electric supplier which may reasonably do so to furnish electric service to any consumer who desires service from such electric supplier at any premises being served by another electric supplier, or at premises which another electric supplier has the right to serve pursuant to other provisions of this section, and to order such other electric supplier to cease and desist from furnishing electric service to such premises, upon finding that service to such consumer by the electric supplier which is then furnishing service, or which has the right to furnish service, to such premises, is or will be inadequate or undependable, or that the rates, conditions of service or service regulations, applied to such consumer, are unreasonably discriminatory.

(e) The furnishing of electric service in any area which becomes a part of any municipality after April 20, 1965, either by annexation or incorporation, (whether or not such area, or any portion thereof, shall have been assigned pursuant to subsection (c) of this section) shall be subject to the provisions of Part 2, Article 16 of Chapter 160A of the General Statutes, and any provisions of this section inconsistent with said Article shall not be applicable within such area after the effective date of such annexation or incorporation. (1965, c. 287, s. 5; 1989 (Reg. Sess., 1990), c. 1024, s. 14.)

§ 62-110.3. Bond required for water and sewer companies.

(a)   No franchise may be granted to any water or sewer utility company until the applicant furnishes a bond, secured with sufficient surety as approved by the Commission, in an amount not less than ten thousand dollars ($10,000). The bond shall be conditioned upon providing adequate and sufficient service within all the applicant's service areas, including those for which franchises have previously been granted, shall be payable to the Commission, and shall be in a form acceptable to the Commission. In setting the amount of a bond, the Commission shall consider and make appropriate findings as to the following:

(1)   Whether the applicant holds other water or sewer franchises in this State, and if so its record of operation,

(2)   The number of customers the applicant now serves and proposes to serve,

(3)   The likelihood of future expansion needs of the service,

(4)   If the applicant is acquiring an existing company, the age, condition, and type of the equipment, and

(5)   Any other relevant factors, including the design of the system.

Any interest earned on a bond shall be payable to the water or sewer company that posted the bond.

(b)   Notwithstanding the provisions of G.S. 62-110(a) and subsection (a) of this section, no water or sewer utility shall extend service into territory contiguous to that already occupied without first having advised the Commission of such proposed extension. Upon notification, the Commission shall require the utility to furnish an appropriate bond, taking into consideration both the original service area and the proposed extension. This subsection shall apply to all service areas of water and sewer utilities without regard to the date of the issuance of the franchise.

(c)   The utility, the Public Staff, the Attorney General, and any other party may, at any time after the amount of a bond is set, apply to the Commission to raise or lower the amount based on changed circumstances.

(d)   The appointment of an emergency operator, either by the superior court in accordance with G.S. 62-118(b) or by the Commission with the consent of the owner or operator, operates to forfeit the bond required by this section. The court or Commission, as appropriate, shall determine the amount of money needed to alleviate the emergency and shall order that amount of the bond to be paid to the Commission as trustee for the water or sewer system.

(e)   If the person who operated the system before the emergency was declared desires to resume operation of the system upon a finding that the emergency no longer exists, the Commission shall require him to post a new bond, the amount of which may be different from the previous bond. (1987, c. 490, s. 2; 1995, c. 28, s. 1.)

§ 62-110.4. Alternative Operator Services.

The Commission shall not issue a certificate of public convenience and necessity pursuant to G.S. 62-110(b) to any interexchange carrier which the Commission has determined to have the characteristics of an alternative operator service unless the Commission shall have determined that class of interexchange carriers to be in the public interest and shall have promulgated rules to protect the public interest and to require, at a minimum, that any such interexchange carrier assure appropriate disclosure to end-users of its identity, services, rates, charges, and fees. In order to effectuate notice to end-users, the Commission may, notwithstanding any other provision of law, require that any person owning or operating a facility for the use of the travelling or transient public which has contracted with such an interexchange carrier prominently display an end-user notice provided for in the Commission's rules. (1989, c. 366.)

§ 62-110.5. Commission may exempt certain nonprofit and consumer-owned water or sewer utilities.

The Commission may exempt any water or sewer utilities owned by nonprofit membership or consumer-owned corporations from regulation under this Chapter, subject to those conditions the Commission deems appropriate, if:

(1) The members or consumer-owners of the corporation elect the governing board of the corporation pursuant to the corporation's articles of incorporation and bylaws; and

(2) The Commission finds that the organization and the quality of service of the utility are adequate to protect the public interest to the extent that additional regulation is not required by the public convenience and necessity. (1997-437, s. 2.)

§ 62-110.6. Rate recovery for construction costs of out-of-state electric generating facilities.

(a) The Commission shall, upon petition of a public utility, determine the need for and, if need is established, approve an estimate of the construction costs and construction schedule for an electric generating facility in another state that is intended to serve retail customers in this State.

(b) The petition may be filed at any time after an application for a certificate or license for the construction of the facility has been filed in the state in which the facility will be sited. The petition shall contain a showing of need for the facility, an estimate of the construction costs, and the proposed construction schedule for the facility.

(c) The Commission shall conduct a public hearing to consider and determine the need for the facility and the reasonableness of the construction cost estimate and proposed construction schedule. If the Commission finds that the construction will be needed to assure the provision of adequate public utility service within North Carolina, the Commission shall approve a construction cost estimate and a construction schedule for the facility. In making its determinations under this section, the Commission may consider whether the state in which the facility will be sited has issued a certificate or license for construction of the facility and approved a construction cost estimate and construction schedule for the facility. The Commission shall issue its order not later than 180 days after the public utility files its petition.

(d) G.S. 62-110.1(f) shall apply to the construction cost estimate determined by the Commission to be appropriate, and the actual costs the public utility incurs in constructing the facility shall be recoverable through rates in a general rate case pursuant to G.S. 62-133 as provided in G.S. 62-110.1(f1).

(e) If the construction of a facility is cancelled, the public utility shall recover through rates in a general rate case conducted pursuant to G.S. 62-133 the costs of construction that were actually incurred prior to the cancellation and are found by the Commission to be reasonable and prudent, as provided in subsections (f2) and (f3) of G.S. 62-110.1. (2007-397, s. 7.)

§ 62-110.7. Project development cost review for a nuclear facility.

(a) For purposes of this section, "project development costs" mean all capital costs associated with a potential nuclear electric generating facility incurred before (i) issuance of a certificate under G.S. 62-110.1 for a facility located in North Carolina or (ii) issuance of a certificate by the host state for an out-of-state facility to serve North Carolina retail customers, including, without limitation, the costs of evaluation, design, engineering, environmental analysis and permitting, early site permitting, combined operating license permitting, initial site preparation costs, and allowance for funds used during construction associated with such costs.

(b) At any time prior to the filing of an application for a certificate to construct a potential nuclear electric generating facility, either under G.S. 62-110.1 or in another state for a facility to serve North Carolina retail customers, a public utility may request that the Commission review the public utility's decision to incur project development costs. The public utility shall include with its request such information and documentation as is necessary to support approval of the decision to incur proposed project development costs. The Commission shall hold a hearing regarding the request. The Commission shall issue an order within 180 days after the public utility files its request. The Commission shall approve the public utility's decision to incur project development costs if the public utility demonstrates by a preponderance of evidence that the decision to incur project development costs is reasonable and prudent; provided, however, the Commission shall not rule on the reasonableness or prudence of specific project development activities or recoverability of specific items of cost.

(c) All reasonable and prudent project development costs, as determined by the Commission, incurred for the potential nuclear electric generating facility shall be included in the public utility's rate base and shall be fully recoverable through rates in a general rate case proceeding pursuant to G.S. 62-133.

(d) If the public utility is allowed to cancel the project, the Commission shall permit the public utility to recover all reasonable and prudently incurred project development costs in a general rate case proceeding pursuant to G.S. 62-133 amortized over a period equal to the period during which the costs were incurred, or five years, whichever is greater. (2007-397, s. 7.)

§ 62-111. Transfers of franchises; mergers, consolidations and combinations of public utilities.

(a)   No franchise now existing or hereafter issued under the provisions of this Chapter other than a franchise for motor carriers of passengers shall be sold, assigned, pledged or transferred, nor shall control thereof be changed through stock transfer or otherwise, or any rights thereunder leased, nor shall any merger or combination affecting any public utility be made through acquisition or control by stock purchase or otherwise, except after application to and written approval by the Commission, which approval shall be given if justified by the public convenience and necessity. Provided, that the above provisions shall not apply to regular trading in listed securities on recognized markets.

(b)   No certificates issued under the provisions of this Chapter for motor carriers of passengers shall be sold, assigned, pledged, transferred, or control changed through stock transfer or otherwise, or any rights thereunder leased, nor shall any merger or combination affecting any motor carrier of passengers be made through acquisition of control by stock purchases or otherwise, except after application to and written approval by the Commission as in this section provided, provided that the above provisions shall not apply to regular trading in listing securities on recognized markets. The applicant shall give not less than 10 days' written notice of such application by registered mail or by certified mail to all connecting and competing carriers. When the Commission is of the opinion that the transaction is consistent with the purposes of this Chapter the Commission may, in the exercise of its discretion, grant its approval, provided, however, that when such transaction will result in a substantial change in the service and operations of any motor carrier of passengers party to the transaction, or will substantially affect the operations and services of any other motor carrier, the Commission shall not grant its approval except upon notice and hearing as required in G.S. 62-262.1 for bus companies upon an application for an original certificate. In all cases arising under the subsection it shall be the duty of the Commission to require the successor carrier to satisfy the Commission that the operating debts and obligations of the seller, assignor, pledgor, lessor or transferor, including taxes due the State of North Carolina or any political subdivision thereof are paid or the payment thereof is adequately secured. The Commission may attach to its approval of any transaction arising under the section such other conditions as the Commission may determine are necessary to effectuate the purposes of this Article.

(c) No sale of a franchise for a motor carrier of household goods shall be approved by the Commission until the seller shall have filed with the Commission a statement under oath of all debts and claims against the seller, of which such seller has any knowledge or notice, (i) for gross receipts, use or privilege taxes due or to become due the State, as provided in the Revenue Act, (ii) for wages due employees of the seller, other than salaries of officers and in the case of motor carriers, (iii) for unremitted C.O.D. collections due shippers, (iv) for loss of or damage to goods transported, or received for transportation, (v) for overcharges on property transported, and, (vi) for interline accounts due other carriers, together with a bond, if required by the Commission, payable to the State, executed by a surety company authorized to do business in the State, in an amount double the aggregate of all such debts and claims conditioned upon the payment of the same within the amount of such bond as the amounts and validity of such debts and claims are established by agreement of the parties, or by judgment. This subsection shall not be applicable to sales by personal representatives of deceased or incompetent persons, receivers or trustees in bankruptcy under court order.

(d) No person shall obtain a franchise for the purpose of transferring the same to another, and an offer of such transfer within one year after the same was obtained shall be prima facie evidence that such certificate was obtained for the purpose of sale.

(e) The Commission shall approve applications for transfer of motor carrier franchises made under this section upon finding that said sale, assignment, pledge, transfer, change of control, lease, merger, or combination is in the public interest, will not adversely affect the service to the public under said franchise, will not unlawfully affect the service to the public by other public utilities, that the person acquiring said franchise or control thereof is fit, willing and able to perform such service to the public under said franchise, and that service under said franchise has been continuously offered to the public up to the time of filing said application or in lieu thereof that any suspension of service exceeding 30 days has been approved by the Commission as provided in G.S. 62-112(b)(5). Provided, however, the Commission shall approve, without imposing conditions or limitations, applications for the transfer of a bus company franchise made under this section upon finding that the person acquiring the franchise or control of the franchise is fit, willing and able to perform services to the public under that franchise. (1947, c. 1008, s. 22; 1949, c. 1132, s. 20; 1953, c. 1140, s. 3; 1957, c. 1152, s. 10; 1961, c. 472, ss. 6, 7; 1963, c. 1165, s. 1; 1967, c. 1202; 1985, c. 676, ss. 10, 11; 1995, c. 523, s. 2.)

§ 62-112. Effective date, suspension and revocation of franchises; dormant motor carrier franchises.

(a) Franchises shall be effective from the date issued unless otherwise specified therein, and shall remain in effect until terminated under the terms thereof, or until suspended or revoked as herein provided.

(b) Any franchise may be suspended or revoked, in whole or in part, in the discretion of the Commission, upon application of the holder thereof; or, after notice and hearing, may be suspended or revoked, in whole or in part, upon complaint, or upon the Commission's own initiative, for wilful failure to comply with any provision of this Chapter, or with any lawful order, rule, or regulation of the Commission promulgated thereunder, or with any term, condition or limitation of such franchise; provided, however, that any such franchise may be suspended by the Commission upon notice to the holder or lessee thereof without a hearing for any one or more of the following causes:

(1) For failure to provide and keep in force at all times security, bond, insurance or self-insurance for the protection of the public as required in G.S. 62-268 of this Chapter.

(2) For failure to file and keep on file with the Commission applicable tariffs or schedules of rates as required in this Chapter.

(3) For failure to pay any gross receipts, use or privilege taxes due the State of North Carolina within 30 days after demand in writing from the agency of the State authorized by law to collect the same; provided, that this subdivision shall not apply to instances in which there is a bona fide controversy as to tax liability.

(4) For failure for a period of 60 days after execution to pay any final judgment rendered by a court of competent jurisdiction against any holder or lessee of a franchise for any debt or claim specified in G.S. 62-111(b) and (c).

(5) For failure to begin operations as authorized by the Commission within the time specified by order of the Commission, or for suspension of authorized operations for a period of 30 days without the written consent of the Commission, save in the case of involuntary failure or suspension brought about by compulsion upon the franchise holder or lessee.

(c) The failure of a common carrier of passengers or household goods by motor vehicles to perform any transportation for compensation under the authority of its certificate for a period of 30 consecutive days shall be prima facie evidence that said franchise is dormant and the public convenience and necessity is no longer served by such common carrier certificate. Upon finding after notice and hearing that no such service has been performed for a period of 30 days the Commission is authorized to find that the franchise is dormant and to cancel the certificate of such common carrier. The Commission in its discretion may give consideration in such finding to other factors affecting the performance of such service, including seasonal requirements of the passengers or commodities authorized to be transported, the efforts of the carrier to make its services known to the public, the equipment and other facilities maintained by the carrier for performance of such service, and the means by which such carrier holds itself out to perform such service. A proceeding may be brought under this section by the Commission on its own motion or upon the complaint of any shipper or any other carrier. The franchise of a motor carrier may be canceled under the provisions of this section in any proceeding to sell or transfer or otherwise change control of said franchise brought under the provisions of G.S. 62-111, upon finding of dormancy as provided in this section. Any motor carrier who has obtained authority to suspend operations under the provisions of G.S. 62-112(b)(5) and the rules of the Utilities Commission issued thereunder shall not be subject to cancellation of its franchise under this section during the time such suspension of operations is authorized. In determining whether such carrier has made reasonable efforts to perform service under said franchise the Commission may in its discretion give consideration to disabilities of the carrier including death of the owner and physical disabilities.

(d) This section shall be applicable to bus companies. (1947, c. 1008, s. 23; 1949, c. 1132, s. 21; 1963, c. 1165, s. 1; 1967, c. 1201; 1985, c. 676, s. 12; 1995, c. 523, s. 3.)

§ 62-113. Terms and conditions of franchises.

(a) Each franchise shall specify the service to be rendered and the routes over which, the fixed termini, if any, between which, and the intermediate and off-route points, if any, at which, and in case of operations not over specified routes or between fixed termini, the territory within which, a motor carrier or other public utility is authorized to operate: and there shall, at the time of issuance and from time to time thereafter, be attached to the privileges granted by the franchise such reasonable terms, conditions, and limitations as the public convenience and necessity may from time to time require, including terms, conditions, and limitations as to the extension of the route or routes of a carrier, and such terms and conditions as are necessary to carry out, with respect to the operations of a carrier or other public utility, the requirements established by the Commission under this Chapter; provided, however, that no terms, conditions, or limitations shall restrict the right of a motor carrier of household goods only to add to its equipment and facilities over the routes, between the termini, or within the territory specified in the franchises, as the development of the business and the demands of the public shall require. This subsection shall not be applicable to bus companies or their franchises.

(b) Each bus company franchise shall specify the fixed routes over which, and the fixed termini, if any, between which the bus company may operate. A franchise for bus companies engaged in charter operations may provide for fixed routes or statewide operating authority.

(c) Any broadband service provider that provides voice grade communication services within a defined service territory or franchise area, and elects to provide broadband service in areas contiguous to its service territory or franchise area, may provide such voice grade service as an incident to such broadband service to a customer when the incumbent telecommunications or cable provider is not currently providing broadband service to the customer, without violating its service territory restrictions or franchise agreement. (1947, c. 1008, s. 12; 1949, c. 1132, s. 11; 1963, c. 1165, s. 1; 1985, c. 676, s. 13; 1995, c. 523, s. 4; 2009-80, s. 1.)

§ 62-114: Repealed by Session Laws 1995, c. 523, s. 5.

§ 62-115. Issuance of partnership franchises.

No franchise shall be issued under this Article to two or more persons until such persons have executed a partnership agreement, filed a copy of said agreement with the Commission, and indicated to the Commission, in writing, that they have complied with Article 14 of Chapter 66 relating to doing business under an assumed name. (1947, c. 1008, s. 14; 1949, c. 1132, s. 14; 1961, c. 472, s. 5; 1963, c. 1165, s. 1.)

§ 62-116. Issuance of temporary or emergency authority.

(a)   Upon the filing of an application in good faith for a franchise, the Commission may in its discretion, after notice by regular mail to all persons holding franchises authorizing similar services within the same territory and upon a finding that no other adequate existing service is available, pending its final decision on the application, issue to the applicant appropriate temporary authority to operate under such just and reasonable conditions and limitations as the Commission deems necessary or desirable to impose in the public interest; provided, however, that pending such final decision on the application, the applicant shall comply with all the provisions of this Chapter, and with the lawful orders, rules and regulations of the Commission promulgated thereunder, applicable to holders of franchises, and upon failure of an applicant so to do, after reasonable notice from the Commission requiring compliance therewith in the particulars set out in the notice, and after hearing, the application may be dismissed by the Commission without further proceedings, and temporary authority issued to such applicant may be revoked. The authority granted under this section shall not create any presumption nor be considered in the action on the permanent authority application.

(b)   Upon its own initiative, or upon written request by any customer or by any representative of a local or State government agency, and after issuance of notice to the owner and operator and after hearing in accordance with G.S. 1A-1, Rule 65(b), the Commission may grant emergency operating authority to any person to furnish water or sewer utility service to meet an emergency to the extent necessary to relieve the emergency; provided, that the Commission shall find from such request, or from its own knowledge, that a real emergency exists and that the relief authorized is immediate, pressing and necessary in the public interest, and that the person so authorized has the necessary ability and is willing to perform the prescribed emergency service. Upon termination of the emergency, the emergency operating authority so granted shall expire upon order of the Commission. An emergency is defined herein as the imminent danger of losing adequate water or sewer utility service or the actual loss thereof. (1947, c. 1008, s. 10; 1949, c. 1132, s. 9; 1963, c. 1165, s. 1; 1973, c. 1108.)

§ 62-117. Same or similar names prohibited.

No public utility holding or operating under a franchise issued under this Chapter shall adopt or use a name used by any other public utility, or any name so similar to a name of another public utility as to mislead or confuse the public, and the Commission may, upon complaint, or upon its own initiative, in any such case require the public utility to discontinue the use of such name, preference being given to the public utility first adopting and using such name. (1947, c. 1008, s. 15; 1949, c. 1132, s. 15; 1963, c. 1165, s. 1.)

§ 62-118. Abandonment and reduction of service.

(a)   Upon finding that public convenience and necessity are no longer served, or that there is no reasonable probability of a public utility realizing sufficient revenue from a service to meet its expenses, the Commission shall have power, after petition and notice, to authorize by order any public utility to abandon or reduce such service. Upon request from any party having an interest in said utility service, the Commission shall hold a public hearing on such petition, and may on its own motion hold a public hearing on such petition. Provided, however, that abandonment or reduction of service of motor carriers shall not be subject to this section, but shall be authorized only under the provisions of G.S. 62-262(k) and G.S. 62-262.2.

(b)   If any person or corporation furnishing water or sewer utility service under this Chapter shall abandon such service without the prior consent of the Commission, and the Commission subsequently finds that such abandonment of service causes an emergency to exist, the Commission may, unless the owner or operator of the affected system consents, apply in accordance with G.S. 1A-1, Rule 65, to a superior court judge who has jurisdiction pursuant to G.S. 7A-47.1 or 7A-48 in the district or set of districts as defined in G.S. 7A-41.1 in which the person or corporation so operates, for an order restricting the lands, facilities and rights-of-way used in furnishing said water or sewer utility service to continued use in furnishing said service during the period of the emergency. An emergency is defined herein as the imminent danger of losing adequate water or sewer utility service or the actual loss thereof. The court shall have jurisdiction to restrict the lands, facilities, and rights-of-way to continued use in furnishing said water or sewer utility service by appropriate order restraining their being placed to other use, or restraining their being prevented from continued use in furnishing said water or sewer utility service, by any person, corporation, or their representatives. The court may, in its discretion, appoint an emergency operator to assure the continued operation of such water or sewer utility service. The court shall have jurisdiction to require that reasonable compensation be paid to the owner, operator or other party entitled thereto for the use of any lands, facilities, and rights-of-way which are so restricted to continued use for furnishing water or sewer utility service during the period of the emergency, and it may require the emergency operator of said lands, facilities, and rights-of-way to post bond in an amount required by the court. In no event shall such compensation, for each month awarded, exceed the net average monthly income of the utility for the 12-month period immediately preceding the order restricting use.

(c) Whenever the Commission, upon complaint or investigation upon its own motion, finds that the facilities being used to furnish water or sewer utility service are inadequate to such an extent that an emergency (as defined in G.S. 62-118(b) above) exists, and further finds that there is no reasonable probability of the owner or operator of such utility obtaining the capital necessary to improve or replace the facilities from sources other than the customers, the Commission shall have the power, after notice and hearing, to authorize by order that such service be abandoned or reduced to those customers who are unwilling or unable to advance their fair share of the capital necessary for such improvements. The amount of capital to be advanced by each customer shall be subject to approval by the Commission, and shall be advanced under such conditions as will enable each customer to retain a proprietary interest in the system to the extent of the capital so advanced. The remedy prescribed in this subsection is in addition to other remedies prescribed by law. (1933, c. 307, s. 32; 1963, c. 1165, s. 1; 1971, c. 552, s. 1; 1973, c. 1393; 1985, c. 676, s. 14; 1987 (Reg. Sess., 1988), c. 1037, s. 93; 1989 (Reg. Sess., 1990), c. 1024, s. 15.)

Article 6A.

Radio Common Carriers.

§§ 62-119 through 62-125: Repealed by Session Laws 1995, c. 523, s. 31.

§§ 62-126 through 62-129. Reserved for future codification purposes.

Article 7.

Rates of Public Utilities.

§ 62-130. Commission to make rates for public utilities.

(a)   The Commission shall make, fix, establish or allow just and reasonable rates for all public utilities subject to its jurisdiction. A rate is made, fixed, established or allowed when it becomes effective pursuant to the provisions of this Chapter.

(b)   Repealed by Session Laws 1985, c. 676, s. 15.

(c)   The Commission may make, require or approve, after public hearing, for intrastate shipments what are known as milling-in-transit, processing-in-transit, or warehousing-in-transit rates on grain, lumber to be dressed, cotton, peanuts, tobacco, or such other commodities as the Commission may designate.

(d)   The Commission shall from time to time as often as circumstances may require, change and revise or cause to be changed or revised any rates fixed by the Commission, or allowed to be charged by any public utility.

(e)   In all cases where the Commission requires or orders a public utility to refund moneys to its customers which were advanced by or overcollected from its customers, the Commission shall require or order the utility to add to said refund an amount of interest at such rate as the Commission may determine to be just and reasonable; provided, however, that such rate of interest applicable to said refund shall not exceed ten percent (10%) per annum. (1899, c. 164, ss. 2, 7, 14; 1903, c. 683; Rev., ss. 1096, 1099, 1106; 1907, c. 469, s. 4; Ex. Sess. 1908, c. 144, s. 1; 1913, c. 127, s. 2; 1917, c. 194; C.S., ss. 1066, 1071, 3489; Ex. Sess. 1920, c. 51, s. 1; 1925, c. 37; 1929, cc. 82, 91; 1933, c. 134, s. 8; 1941, c. 97; 1953, c. 170; 1963, c. 1165, s. 1; 1981, c. 461, s. 1; 1985, c. 676, s. 15(1).)

§ 62-131. Rates must be just and reasonable; service efficient.

(a) Every rate made, demanded or received by any public utility, or by any two or more public utilities jointly, shall be just and reasonable.

(b) Every public utility shall furnish adequate, efficient and reasonable service. (1933, c. 307, ss. 2, 3; 1963, c. 1165, s. 1.)

§ 62-132. Rates established under this Chapter deemed just and reasonable; remedy for collection of unjust or unreasonable rates.

The rates established under this Chapter by the Commission shall be deemed just and reasonable, and any rate charged by any public utility different from those so established shall be deemed unjust and unreasonable. Provided, however, that upon petition filed by any interested person, and a hearing thereon, if the Commission shall find the rates or charges collected to be other than the rates established by the Commission, and to be unjust, unreasonable, discriminatory or preferential, the Commission may enter an order awarding such petitioner and all other persons in the same class a sum equal to the difference between such unjust, unreasonable, discriminatory or preferential rates or charges and the rates or charges found by the Commission to be just and reasonable, nondiscriminatory and nonpreferential, to the extent that such rates or charges were collected within two years prior to the filing of such petition. (1913, c. 127, s. 3; C.S., s. 1067; 1929, cc. 241, 342; 1933, c. 134, s. 8; 1941, c. 97; 1963, c. 1165, s. 1.)

§ 62-133. How rates fixed.

(a) In fixing the rates for any public utility subject to the provisions of this Chapter, other than bus companies, motor carriers and certain water and sewer utilities, the Commission shall fix such rates as shall be fair both to the public utilities and to the consumer.

(b) In fixing such rates, the Commission shall:

(1) Ascertain the reasonable original cost of the public utility's property used and useful, or to be used and useful within a reasonable time after the test period, in providing the service rendered to the public within the State, less that portion of the cost that has been consumed by previous use recovered by depreciation expense. In addition, construction work in progress may be included in the cost of the public utility's property under any of the following circumstances:

a. To the extent the Commission considers inclusion in the public interest and necessary to the financial stability of the utility in question, reasonable and prudent expenditures for construction work in progress may be included, subject to the provisions of subdivision (4a) of this subsection.

b. For baseload electric generating facilities, reasonable and prudent expenditures shall be included pursuant to subdivisions (2) or (3) of G.S. 62-110.1(f1), whichever applies, subject to the provisions of subdivision (4a) of this subsection.

(1a) Apply the rate of return established under subdivision (4) of this subsection to rights-of-way acquired through agreements with the Department of Transportation pursuant to G.S. 136-19.5(a) if acquisition is consistent with a definite plan to provide service within five years of the date of the agreement and if such right-of-way acquisition will result in benefits to the ratepayers. If a right-of-way is not used within a reasonable time after the expiration of the five-year period, it may be removed from the rate base by the Commission when rates for the public utility are next established under this section.

(2) Estimate such public utility's revenue under the present and proposed rates.

(3) Ascertain such public utility's reasonable operating expenses, including actual investment currently consumed through reasonable actual depreciation.

(4) Fix such rate of return on the cost of the property ascertained pursuant to subdivision (1) of this subsection as will enable the public utility by sound management to produce a fair return for its shareholders, considering changing economic conditions and other factors, including, but not limited to, the inclusion of construction work in progress in the utility's property under sub-subdivision b. of subdivision (1) of this subsection, as they then exist, to maintain its facilities and services in accordance with the reasonable requirements of its customers in the territory covered by its franchise, and to compete in the market for capital

funds on terms that are reasonable and that are fair to its customers and to its existing investors.

(4a)   Require each public utility to discontinue capitalization of the composite carrying cost of capital funds used to finance construction (allowance for funds) on the construction work in progress included in its rate based upon the effective date of the first and each subsequent general rate order issued with respect to it after the effective date of this subsection; allowance for funds may be capitalized with respect to expenditures for construction work in progress not included in the utility's property upon which the rates were fixed. In determining net operating income for return, the Commission shall not include any capitalized allowance for funds used during construction on the construction work in progress included in the utility's rate base.

(5)   Fix such rates to be charged by the public utility as will earn in addition to reasonable operating expenses ascertained pursuant to subdivision (3) of this subsection the rate of return fixed pursuant to subdivisions (4) and (4a) on the cost of the public utility's property ascertained pursuant to subdivisions (1) and (1a) of this subsection.

(c)   The original cost of the public utility's property, including its construction work in progress, shall be determined as of the end of the test period used in the hearing and the probable future revenues and expenses shall be based on the plant and equipment in operation at that time. The test period shall consist of 12 months' historical operating experience prior to the date the rates are proposed to become effective, but the Commission shall consider such relevant, material and competent evidence as may be offered by any party to the proceeding tending to show actual changes in costs, revenues or the cost of the public utility's property used and useful, or to be used and useful within a reasonable time after the test period, in providing the service rendered to the public within this State, including its construction work in progress, which is based upon circumstances and events occurring up to the time the hearing is closed.

(d)   The Commission shall consider all other material facts of record that will enable it to determine what are reasonable and just rates.

(e)   The fixing of a rate of return shall not bar the fixing of a different rate of return in a subsequent proceeding.

(f)   Repealed by Session Laws 1991, c. 598, s. 7.

(g) Reserved.

(h) Repealed by Session Laws 1998-128, s. 4, effective September 4, 1998. (1899, c. 164, s. 2, subsec. 1; Rev., s. 1104; C.S., s. 1068; 1933, c. 134, s. 8; 1941, c. 97; 1963, c. 1165, s. 1; 1971, c. 1092; 1973, c. 956, s. 1; c. 1041, s. 1; 1975, c. 184, s. 2; 1977, c. 691, ss. 2, 3; 1981, c. 476; 1981 (Reg. Sess., 1982), c. 1197, s. 6; 1985, c. 676, s. 15(2); 1989 (Reg. Sess., 1990), c. 962, s. 4; 1991, c. 598, s. 7; 1998-128, s. 4; 2007-397, s. 8.)

§ 62-133.1. Small water and sewer utility rates.

(a) In fixing the rates for any water or sewer utility, the Commission may fix such rates on the ratio of the operating expenses to the operating revenues, such ratio to be determined by the Commission, unless the utility requests that such rates be fixed under G.S. 62-133(b). Nothing in this subsection shall be held to extinguish any remedy or right not inconsistent herewith. This subsection shall be in addition to other provisions of this Chapter which relate to public utilities generally, except that in cases of conflict between such other provisions, this section shall prevail for water and sewer utilities.

(b) A water or sewer utility may enter into uniform contracts with nonusers of its utility service within a specific subdivision or development for the payment by such nonusers to the utility of a fee or charge for placing or maintaining lines or other facilities or otherwise making and keeping such utility's service available to such nonusers; or such a utility may, by contract of assignment, receive the benefits and assume the obligations of uniform contracts entered into between the developers of subdivisions and the purchasers of lots in such subdivisions whereby such developer has contracted to make utility service available to lots in such subdivision and purchasers of such lots have contracted to pay a fee or charge for the availability of such utility service; provided, however, that the maximum nonuser rate shall be as established by contract, except that the contractual charge to nonusers of the utility service can never exceed the lawfully established minimum rate to user customers of the utility service. (1973, c. 956, s. 2.)

§ 62-133.2. Fuel and fuel-related charge adjustments for electric utilities.

(a) The Commission shall permit an electric public utility that generates electric power by fossil fuel or nuclear fuel to charge an increment or decrement as a rider to its rates for changes in the cost of fuel and fuel-related costs used in providing its North Carolina customers with electricity from the cost of fuel and fuel-related costs established in the electric public utility's previous general rate case on the basis of cost per kilowatt hour.

(a1) As used in this section, "cost of fuel and fuel-related costs" means all of the following:

(1) The cost of fuel burned.

(2) The cost of fuel transportation.

(3) The cost of ammonia, lime, limestone, urea, dibasic acid, sorbents, and catalysts consumed in reducing or treating emissions.

(4) The total delivered noncapacity related costs, including all related transmission charges, of all purchases of electric power by the electric public utility, that are subject to economic dispatch or economic curtailment.

(5) The capacity costs associated with all purchases of electric power from qualifying cogeneration facilities and qualifying small power production facilities, as defined in 16 U.S.C. § 796, that are subject to economic dispatch by the electric public utility.

(6) Except for those costs recovered pursuant to G.S. 62-133.8(h), the total delivered costs of all purchases of power from renewable energy facilities and new renewable energy facilities pursuant to G.S. 62-133.8 or to comply with any federal mandate that is similar to the requirements of subsections (b), (c), (d), (e), and (f) of G.S. 62-133.8.

(7) The fuel cost component of other purchased power.

(8) Cost of fuel and fuel-related costs shall be adjusted for any net gains or losses resulting from any sales by the electric public utility of fuel and other fuel-related costs components.

(9) Cost of fuel and fuel-related costs shall be adjusted for any net gains or losses resulting from any sales by the electric public utility of by-products

produced in the generation process to the extent the costs of the inputs leading to that by-product are costs of fuel or fuel-related costs.

(a2) For those costs identified in subdivisions (4), (5), and (6) of subsection (a1) of this section, the annual increase in the aggregate amount of these costs that are recoverable by an electric public utility pursuant to this section shall not exceed two percent (2%) of the electric public utility's total North Carolina retail jurisdictional gross revenues for the preceding calendar year. The costs described in subdivisions (4), (5), and (6) of subsection (a1) of this section shall be recoverable from each class of customers as a separate component of the rider as follows:

(1) For the costs described in subdivision (4) of subsection (a1) of this section, the specific component for each class of customers shall be determined by allocating these costs among customer classes based on the electric public utility's North Carolina energy usage for the prior year, as determined by the Commission, until the Commission determines how these costs shall be allocated in a general rate case for the electric public utility commenced on or after January 1, 2008.

(2) For the costs described in subdivisions (5) and (6) of subsection (a1) of this section, the specific component for each class of customers shall be determined by allocating these costs among customer classes based on the electric public utility's North Carolina peak demand for the prior year, as determined by the Commission, until the Commission determines how these costs shall be allocated in a general rate case for the electric public utility commenced on or after January 1, 2008.

(a3) Notwithstanding subsections (a1) and (a2) of this section, for an electric public utility that has fewer than 150,000 North Carolina retail jurisdictional customers as of December 31, 2006, the costs identified in subdivisions (1), (2), (6), and (7) of subsection (a1) of this section and the fuel cost component, as may be modified by the Commission, of electric power purchases identified in subdivision (4) of subsection (a1) of this section shall be recovered through the increment or decrement rider approved by the Commission pursuant to this section. For the costs identified in subdivision (6) of subsection (a1) of this section that are incurred on or after January 1, 2008, the annual increase in the amount of these costs shall not exceed one percent (1%) of the electric public utility's total North Carolina retail jurisdictional gross revenues for the preceding calendar year. These costs described in subdivision (6) of subsection (a1) of this section shall be recoverable from each class of customers as a separate component of the rider. For the costs described in subdivision (6) of subsection (a1) of this section, the specific component for each class of customers shall be determined by allocating these costs among customer classes based on the electric public utility's North Carolina peak demand for the prior year, as determined by the Commission, until the Commission determines how these costs shall be allocated in a general rate case for the electric public utility commenced on or after January 1, 2008.

(b)   The Commission shall conduct a hearing within 12 months of each electric public utility's last general rate case order to determine whether an increment or decrement rider is required to reflect actual changes in the cost of fuel and fuel-related costs over or under the cost of fuel and fuel-related costs on a kilowatt-hour basis in base rates established in the electric public utility's last preceding general rate case. Additional hearings shall be held on an annual basis but only one hearing for each electric public utility may be held within 12 months of the last general rate case.

(c)   Each electric public utility shall submit to the Commission for the hearing verified annualized information and data in such form and detail as the Commission may require, for an historic 12-month test period, relating to:

(1)   Cost of fuel and fuel-related costs used in each generating facility owned in whole or in part by the utility.

(2)   Fuel procurement practices and fuel inventories for each facility.

(3)   Burned cost of fuel used in each generating facility.

(4)   Plant capacity factor for each generating facility.

(5)   Plant availability factor for each generating plant.

(6)   Generation mix by types of fuel used.

(7)   Sources and fuel cost component of purchased power used.

(8)   Recipients of and revenues received for power sales and times of power sales.

(9)   Test period kilowatt-hour sales for the utility's total system and on the total system separated for North Carolina jurisdictional sales.

(10) Procurement practices and inventories for: fuel burned and for ammonia, lime, limestone, urea, dibasic acid, sorbents, and catalysts consumed in reducing or treating emissions.

(11) The cost incurred at each generating facility of fuel burned and of ammonia, lime, limestone, urea, dibasic acid, sorbents, and catalysts consumed in reducing or treating emissions.

(12) Any net gains or losses resulting from any sales by the electric public utility of fuel or other fuel-related costs components.

(13) Any net gains or losses resulting from any sales by the electric public utility of by-products produced in the generation process to the extent the costs of the inputs leading to that by-product are costs of fuel or fuel-related costs.

(d) The Commission shall provide for notice of a public hearing with reasonable and adequate time for investigation and for all intervenors to prepare for hearing. At the hearing the Commission shall receive evidence from the utility, the Public Staff, and any intervenor desiring to submit evidence, and from the public generally. In reaching its decision, the Commission shall consider all evidence required under subsection (c) of this section as well as any and all other competent evidence that may assist the Commission in reaching its decision including changes in the cost of fuel consumed and fuel-related costs that occur within a reasonable time, as determined by the Commission, after the test period is closed. The Commission shall incorporate in its cost of fuel and fuel-related costs determination under this subsection the experienced over-recovery or under-recovery of reasonable costs of fuel and fuel-related costs prudently incurred during the test period, based upon the prudent standards set pursuant to subsection (d1) of this section, in fixing an increment or decrement rider. Upon request of the electric public utility, the Commission shall also incorporate in this determination the experienced over-recovery or under-recovery of costs of fuel and fuel-related costs through the date that is 30 calendar days prior to the date of the hearing, provided that the reasonableness and prudence of these costs shall be subject to review in the utility's next annual hearing pursuant to this section. The Commission shall use deferral accounting, and consecutive test periods, in complying with this subsection, and the over-recovery or under-recovery portion of the increment or decrement shall be reflected in rates for 12 months, notwithstanding any changes in the base fuel cost in a general rate case. The burden of proof as to the correctness and reasonableness of the charge and as to whether the cost of fuel and fuel-related costs were reasonably and prudently incurred shall be on the utility. The Commission shall allow only that portion, if any, of a requested cost of fuel and fuel-related costs adjustment that is based on adjusted and reasonable cost of fuel and fuel-related costs prudently incurred under efficient management and economic operations. In evaluating whether cost of fuel and fuel-related costs were reasonable and prudently incurred, the Commission shall apply the rule adopted pursuant to subsection (d1) of this section. To the extent that the Commission determines that an increment or decrement to the rates of the utility due to changes in the cost of fuel and fuel-related costs over or under base fuel costs established in the preceding general rate case is just and reasonable, the Commission shall order that the increment or decrement become effective for all sales of electricity and remain in effect until changed in a subsequent general rate case or annual proceeding under this section.

(d1)   Within one year after ratification of this act, for the purposes of setting cost of fuel and fuel-related costs rates, the Commission shall adopt a rule that establishes prudent standards and procedures with which it can appropriately measure management efficiency in minimizing cost of fuel and fuel-related costs.

(e)   If the Commission has not issued an order pursuant to this section within 180 days of a utility's submission of annual data under subsection (c) of this section, the utility may place the requested cost of fuel and fuel-related costs adjustment into effect. If the change in rate is finally determined to be excessive, the utility shall make refund of any excess plus interest to its customers in a manner ordered by the Commission.

(f)   Nothing in this section shall relieve the Commission from its duty to consider the reasonableness of the cost of fuel and fuel-related costs in a general rate case and to set rates reflecting reasonable cost of fuel and fuel-related costs pursuant to G.S. 62-133. Nothing in this section shall invalidate or preempt any condition adopted by the Commission and accepted by the utility in any proceeding that would limit the recovery of costs by any electric public utility under this section.

(g)   On July 1 of every odd-numbered year, the Utilities Commission shall provide a report to the Joint Legislative Commission on Governmental Operations summarizing the proceedings conducted pursuant to this section during the preceding two years. (1981 (Reg. Sess., 1982), c. 1197, s. 1; 1987, c. 677, ss. 1, 5; 1989, c. 15, s. 1; 1991, c. 129, s. 1; 1995, c. 15, ss. 1, 2; 2007-397, s. 5; 2011-291, s. 2.11.)

§ 62-133.3: Repealed by Session Laws 1995, c. 27, s. 5.

§ 62-133.4. Gas cost adjustment for natural gas local distribution companies.

(a)   Rate changes for natural gas local distribution companies occasioned by changes in the cost of natural gas supply and transportation may be determined under this section rather than under G.S. 62-133(b), (c), or (d).

(b)   From time to time, as changes in the cost of natural gas require, each natural gas local distribution company may apply to the Commission for permission to change its rates to track changes in the cost of natural gas supply and transportation. The Commission may, without a hearing, issue an order allowing such rate changes to become effective simultaneously with the effective date of the change in the cost of natural gas or at any other time ordered by the Commission. If the Commission has not issued an order under this subsection within 120 days after the application, the utility may place the requested rate adjustment into effect. If the rate adjustment is finally determined to be excessive or is denied, the utility shall make refund of any excess, plus interest as provided in G.S. 62-130(e), to its customers in a manner ordered by the Commission. Any rate adjustment under this subsection is subject to review under subsection (c) of this section.

(c)   Each natural gas local distribution company shall submit to the Commission information and data for an historical 12-month test period concerning the utility's actual cost of gas, volumes of purchased gas, sales volumes, negotiated sales volumes, and transportation volumes. This information and data shall be filed on an annual basis in the form and detail and at the time required by the Commission. The Commission, upon notice and hearing, shall compare the utility's prudently incurred costs with costs recovered from all the utility's customers that it served during the test period. If those prudently incurred costs are greater or less than the recovered costs, the Commission shall, subject to G.S. 62-158, require the utility to refund any overrecovery by credit to bill or through a decrement in its rates and shall permit the utility to recover any deficiency through an increment in its rates.

(d) Nothing in this section prohibits the Commission from investigating and changing unreasonable rates as authorized by this Chapter, nor does it prohibit the Commission from disallowing the recovery of any gas costs not prudently incurred by a utility.

(e) As used in this section, the word "cost" or "costs" shall be defined by Commission rule or order and may include all costs related to the purchase and transportation of natural gas to the natural gas local distribution company's system. (1991, c. 598, s. 8.)

§ 62-133.5. Alternative regulation, tariffing, and deregulation of telecommunications utilities.

(a) Any local exchange company, subject to the provisions of G.S. 62-110(f1), that is subject to rate of return regulation pursuant to G.S. 62-133 or a form of alternative regulation authorized by subsection (b) of this section may elect to have the rates, terms, and conditions of its services determined pursuant to a form of price regulation, rather than rate of return or other form of earnings regulation. Under this form of price regulation, the Commission shall, among other things, permit the local exchange company to determine and set its own depreciation rates, to rebalance its rates, and to adjust its prices in the aggregate, or to adjust its prices for various aggregated categories of services, based upon changes in generally accepted indices of prices. Upon application, the Commission shall, after notice and an opportunity for interested parties to be heard, approve such price regulation, which may differ between local exchange companies, upon finding that the plan as proposed (i) protects the affordability of basic local exchange service, as such service is defined by the Commission; (ii) reasonably assures the continuation of basic local exchange service that meets reasonable service standards that the Commission may adopt; (iii) will not unreasonably prejudice any class of telephone customers, including telecommunications companies; and (iv) is otherwise consistent with the public interest. Upon approval, and except as provided in subsection (c) of this section, price regulation shall thereafter be the sole form of regulation imposed upon the electing local exchange company, and the Commission shall thenceforth regulate the electing local exchange company's prices, rather than its earnings. The Commission shall issue an order denying or approving the proposed plan for price regulation, with or without modification, not more than 90 days from the filing of the application. However, the Commission may extend the time period for an additional 90 days at the discretion of the Commission. If the Commission approves the application with modifications, the local exchange company subject to such approval may accept the modifications and implement the proposed plan as modified, or may, at its option, (i) withdraw its application and continue to be regulated under the form of regulation that existed immediately prior to the filing of the application; (ii) file another proposed plan for price regulation; or (iii) file an application for a form of alternative regulation under subsection (b) of this section. If the initial price regulation plan is approved with modifications and the local exchange company files another plan pursuant to part (ii) of the previous sentence, the Commission shall issue an order denying or approving the proposed plan for price regulation, with or without modifications, not more than 90 days from that filing by the local exchange company.

(b)   Any local exchange company that is subject to rate of return regulation pursuant to G.S. 62-133 and which elects not to file for price regulation under the provisions of subsection (a) above may file an application with the Commission for forms of alternative regulation, which may differ between companies and may include, but are not limited to, ranges of authorized returns, categories of services, and price indexing. Upon application, the Commission shall approve such alternative regulatory plan upon finding that the plan as proposed (i) protects the affordability of basic local exchange service, as such service is defined by the Commission; (ii) reasonably assures the continuation of basic local exchange service that meets reasonable service standards established by the Commission; (iii) will not unreasonably prejudice any class of telephone customers, including telecommunications companies; and (iv) is otherwise consistent with the public interest. The Commission shall issue an order denying or approving the proposed plan with or without modification, not more than 90 days from the filing of the application. However, the Commission may extend the time period for an additional 90 days at the discretion of the Commission. If the Commission approves the application with modifications, the local exchange company subject to such approval may, at its option, accept the modifications and implement the proposed plan as modified or may, at its option, (i) withdraw its application and continue to be regulated under the form of regulation that existed at the time of filing the application; or (ii) file an application for another form of alternative regulation. If the initial plan is approved with modifications and the local exchange company files another plan pursuant to part (ii) of the previous sentence, the Commission shall issue an order denying or approving the proposed plan, with or without modifications, not more than 90 days from that filing by the local exchange company.

(c) Any local exchange company subject to price regulation under the provisions of subsection (a) of this section may file an application with the Commission to modify such form of price regulation or for other forms of regulation. Any local exchange company subject to a form of alternative regulation under subsection (b) of this section may file an application with the Commission to modify such form of alternative regulation. Upon application, the Commission shall approve such other form of regulation upon finding that the plan as proposed (i) protects the affordability of basic local exchange service, as such service is defined by the Commission; (ii) reasonably assures the continuation of basic local exchange service that meets reasonable service standards established by the Commission; (iii) will not unreasonably prejudice any class of telephone customers, including telecommunications companies; and (iv) is otherwise consistent with the public interest. If the Commission disapproves, in whole or in part, a local exchange company's application to modify its existing form of price regulation, the company may elect to continue to operate under its then existing plan previously approved under this subsection or subsection (a) of this section.

(c1) In determining whether a price regulation plan is otherwise consistent with the public interest, the Commission shall not consider the local exchange company's past or present earnings or rates of return.

(d) Any local exchange company subject to price regulation under the provisions of subsection (a) of this section, or other alternative regulation under subsection (b) of this section, or other form of regulation under subsection (c) of this section shall file tariffs for basic local exchange service and toll switched access services stating the terms and conditions of the services and the applicable rates. However, fees charged by such local exchange companies applicable to charges for returned checks shall not be tariffed or otherwise regulated by the Commission. The filing of any tariff changing the terms and conditions of such services or increasing the rates for such services shall be presumed valid and shall become effective, unless otherwise suspended by the Commission for a term not to exceed 45 days, 14 days after filing. Any tariff reducing rates for basic local exchange service or toll switched access service shall be presumed valid and shall become effective, unless otherwise suspended by the Commission for a term not to exceed 45 days, seven days after filing. Any local exchange company subject to price regulation under the provisions of subsection (a) of this section, or other alternative regulation under subsection (b) of this section, or other form of regulation under subsection (c) of this section may file tariffs for services other than basic local exchange services and toll switched access services. Any tariff changing the terms and conditions of such services or increasing the rates for an existing service or establishing the terms, conditions, or rates for a new service shall be presumed valid and shall become effective, unless otherwise suspended by the Commission for a term not to exceed 45 days, 14 days after filing. Any tariff reducing the rates for such services shall be presumed valid and shall become effective, unless otherwise suspended by the Commission for a term not to exceed 45 days, seven days after filing. In the event of a complaint with regard to a tariff filing under this subsection, the Commission may take such steps as it deems appropriate to assure that such tariff filing is consistent with the plan previously adopted pursuant to subsection (a) of this section, subsection (b) of this section, or subsection (c) of this section.

(e) Any allegation of anticompetitive activity by a competing local provider or a local exchange company shall be raised in a complaint proceeding pursuant to G.S. 62-73.

(f) Notwithstanding the provisions of G.S. 62-140, or any Commission rule or regulations: (i) the Commission shall permit a local exchange company or a competing local provider to offer competitive services with flexible pricing arrangements to business customers pursuant to contract and shall permit other flexible pricing options; and (ii) local exchange companies and competing local providers may provide a promotional offering for any tariffed service or tariffed offering by giving one day's notice to the Commission, but no Commission approval of the notice is required. Promotional offerings of any nontariffed service may be implemented without notice to the Commission or Commission approval. Carriers offering promotions of regulated services that are available for resale must provide a means for interested parties to receive notice of each promotional offering of regulated service, including the duration of the offering, at least one business day prior to the effective date of the promotional offering. Furthermore, local exchange companies and competing local providers may offer special promotions and bundles of new or existing service or products without the obligation to identify or convert existing customers who subscribe to the same or similar services or products. The Commission's complaint authority under G.S. 62-73 and subsection (e) of this section is applicable to any promotion or bundled service offering filed or offered under this subsection.

(g) The following sections of Chapter 62 of the General Statutes shall not apply to local exchange companies subject to price regulation under the terms of subsection (a) of this section or electing companies subject to alternative regulation under the terms of subsection (h) or (m) of this section: G.S. 62-35(c),

62-45, 62-51, 62-81, 62-111, 62-130, 62-131, 62-132, 62-133, 62-134, 62-135, 62-136, 62-137, 62-139, 62-142, and 62-153.

(h) Notwithstanding any other provision of this Chapter, a local exchange company that is subject to rate of return regulation or subject to another form of regulation authorized under this section and whose territory is open to competition from competing local providers may elect to have its rates, terms, and conditions for its services determined pursuant to the plan described in this subsection by filing notice of its intent to do so with the Commission. The election is effective immediately upon filing. A local exchange company shall not be permitted to make the election under this section unless it commits to provide stand-alone basic residential lines to rural customers at rates that are less than or comparable to those rates charged to urban customers for the same service.

(1) Definitions. - The following definitions apply in this subsection:

a. Local exchange company. - The same meaning as provided in G.S. 62-3(16a).

b. Open to competition from competing local providers. - Both of the following apply:

1. G.S. 62-110(f1) applies to the franchised area and to local exchange and exchange access services offered by the local exchange company.

2. The local exchange company is open to interconnection with competing local providers that possess a certificate of public convenience and necessity issued by the Commission. The Commission is authorized to resolve any disputes concerning whether a local exchange company is open to interconnection under this section.

c. Single-line basic residential service. - Single-line residential flat rate basic voice grade local service with touch tone within a traditional local calling area that provides access to available emergency services and directory assistance, the capability to access interconnecting carriers, relay services, access to operator services, and one annual local directory listing (white pages or the equivalent).

d. Stand-alone basic residential line. - Single-line basic residential service that is billed on a billing account that does not also contain another service, feature, or product that is sold by the local exchange company or an affiliate of the local exchange company and is billed on a recurring basis on the local exchange company's bill.

(2) Beginning on the date that the local exchange company's election under this subsection becomes effective, the local exchange company shall continue to offer stand-alone basic residential lines to all customers who choose to subscribe to that service, and the local exchange company may increase rates for those lines annually by a percentage that does not exceed the percentage increase over the prior year in the Gross Domestic Product Price Index as reported by the United States Department of Commerce, Bureau of Economic Analysis, unless otherwise authorized by the Commission. With the sole exception of ensuring the local exchange company's compliance with the preceding sentence, the Commission shall not:

a. Impose any requirements related to the terms, conditions, rates, or availability of any of the local exchange company's stand-alone basic residential lines.

b. Otherwise regulate any of the local exchange company's stand-alone basic residential lines.

(3) Except to the extent provided in subdivision (2) of this subsection, beginning on the date the local exchange company's election under this subsection becomes effective, the Commission shall not do any of the following:

a. Impose any requirements related to the terms, conditions, rates, or availability of any of the local exchange company's retail services.

b. Otherwise regulate any of the local exchange company's retail services.

c. Impose any tariffing requirements on any of the local exchange company's services that were not tariffed as of the date of the election; or impose any constraints on the rates of the local exchange company's services that were subject to full pricing flexibility as of the date of election.

(4) A local exchange company's election under this subsection does not affect the obligations or rights of an incumbent local exchange carrier, as that term is defined by section 251(h) of the Federal Telecommunications Act of 1996 (Act), under sections 251 and 252 of the Act or any Federal Communications Commission regulation relating to sections 251 and 252 of the Act, nor does it affect any authority of the Commission to act in accordance with

federal or State laws or regulations, including those granting authority to set rates, terms, and conditions for access to unbundled network elements and to arbitrate and enforce interconnection agreements.

(5) A local exchange company's election under this subsection does not prevent a consumer from seeking the assistance of the Public Staff of the North Carolina Utilities Commission to resolve a complaint with that local exchange company, as provided in G.S. 62-73.1.

(6) A local exchange company's election under this subsection does not affect the Commission's jurisdiction concerning the following:

a. Enforce federal requirements on the local exchange company's marketing activities. However, the Commission may not adopt, impose, or enforce other requirements on the local exchange company's marketing activities.

b. The telecommunications relay service pursuant to G.S. 62-157.

c. The Life Line or Link Up programs consistent with Federal Communications Commission rules, including, but not limited to, 47 C.F.R. § 54.403(a)(3), as amended from time to time, and relevant orders of the North Carolina Utilities Commission.

d. Universal service funding pursuant to G.S. 62-110(f1).

e. Carrier of last resort obligations pursuant to G.S. 62-110.

f. The authority delegated to it by the Federal Communications Commission to manage the numbering resources involving that local exchange company.

g. Regulatory authority over the rates, terms, and conditions of wholesale services.

(i) A competing local provider authorized by the Commission to do business under the provisions of G.S. 62-110(f1) may also elect to have its rates, terms, and conditions for its services determined pursuant to the plans described in subsection (h) or (m) of this section. However, it is provided further that any provisions of subsection (h) of this section requiring the provision of a specific retail service or impacting the pricing of such service, including stand-alone residence service, shall not apply to competing local providers.

(j) Notwithstanding any other provision of this Chapter, the Commission has jurisdiction over matters concerning switched access and intercarrier compensation of a local exchange company that has elected to operate under price regulation, as well as a local exchange carrier or competing local provider operating under any form of regulation covered under this Article or G.S. 62-110(f1).

(k) To evaluate the affordability and quality of local exchange service provided to consumers in this State, a local exchange company or competing local provider offering basic local residential exchange service that elects to have its rates, terms, and conditions for its services determined pursuant to the plans described in subsection (h) or (m) of this section shall make an annual report to the General Assembly on the state of its company's operations. The report shall be due 30 days after the close of each calendar year and shall cover the period from January 1 through December 31 of the preceding year. The Joint Legislative Commission on Governmental Operations must review the annual reports and decide whether to recommend that the General Assembly take corrective action in response to those reports. The report shall include the following:

(1) An analysis of telecommunications competition by the local exchange company or competing local provider, including access line gain or loss and the impact on consumer choices from the date the local exchange company makes its election to be subject to alternative regulation under the terms of subsection (h) or (m) of this section.

(2) An analysis of service quality based on customer satisfaction studies from the date the local exchange company makes its election to be subject to alternative regulation under the terms of subsection (h) or (m) of this section.

(3) An analysis of the level of local exchange rates from the date the local exchange company makes its election to be subject to alternative regulation under the terms of subsection (h) or (m) of this section.

(l) For a local exchange company that has made an election to be subject to alternative regulation under subsection (m) of this section, the requirement to report annually to the General Assembly under subsection (k) of this section shall no longer apply on and after the third anniversary following the date of the local exchange company's election.

(m) Notwithstanding any other provision of this Chapter, a local exchange company that is subject to rate of return regulation or subject to another form of regulation authorized under this section and who forgoes receipt of any funding from a State funding mechanism, other than interconnection rates, that may be established to support universal service as described in G.S. 62-110(f1) and whose territory is open to competition from competing local providers may elect to have its rates, terms, and conditions for its services determined pursuant to the plan described in this subsection by filing notice of its intent to do so with the Commission. The election is effective immediately upon filing. The terms "local exchange company" and "open to competition from competing local providers" shall have the same meanings as in subsection (h) of this section.

(1) Beginning on the date the local exchange company's election under this subsection becomes effective, the Commission shall not:

a. Impose any requirements related to the terms, conditions, rates, or availability of any of the local exchange company's retail services, regardless of the technology used to provide these services.

b. Otherwise regulate any of the local exchange company's retail services, regardless of the technology used to provide these services.

c. Impose any tariffing requirements on any of the local exchange company's services that were not tariffed as of the date of the election, or impose any constraints on the rates of the local exchange company's services that were subject to full pricing flexibility as of the date of election.

(2) A local exchange company's election under this subsection does not affect the obligations or rights of an incumbent local exchange carrier, as that term is defined by section 251(h) of the Federal Telecommunications Act of 1996 (Act), under sections 251 and 252 of the Act, or any Federal Communications Commission regulation relating to sections 251 and 252 of the Act.

(3) A local exchange company's election under this subsection does not affect the Commission's jurisdiction concerning:

a. Enforcement of federal requirements on the local exchange company's marketing activities as set forth in 47 U.S.C. Part 64. However, the Commission may not adopt, impose, or enforce other requirements on the local exchange company's marketing activities.

b. The telecommunications relay service pursuant to G.S. 62-157.

c. The Life Line or Link Up programs consistent with Federal Communications Commission rules and relevant orders of the North Carolina Utilities Commission.

d. Universal service funding pursuant to G.S. 62-110(f1).

e. The authority delegated to it by the Federal Communications Commission to manage the numbering resources involving that local exchange company.

f. Regulatory authority over the rates, terms, and conditions of wholesale services.

g. The Commission's authority under section 214(e) of the Federal Communications Act of 1934, consistent with Federal Communications Commission rules.

h. The authority of the Commission to act in accordance with federal or State laws or regulations, including those granting authority to set rates, terms, and conditions for access to unbundled network elements and to arbitrate and enforce interconnection agreements.

(4) A local exchange company's election under this subsection does not prevent a consumer from seeking the assistance of the Public Staff of the North Carolina Utilities Commission to resolve a complaint with that local exchange company, as provided in G.S. 62-73.1. (1995, c. 27, s. 6; 2003-91, s. 2; 2007-157, s. 1; 2009-238, ss. 1-4; 2009-570, s. 36; 2010-173, ss. 1-3; 2011-52, s. 3; 2011-291, s. 2.12.)

§ 62-133.6. Environmental compliance costs recovery.

(a) As used in this section:

(1) "Coal-fired generating unit" means a coal-fired generating unit, as defined by 40 Code of Federal Regulations § 96.2 (July 1, 2001 Edition), that is located in this State and has the capacity to generate 25 or more megawatts of electricity.

(2) "Environmental compliance costs" means only those capital costs incurred by an investor-owned public utility to comply with the emissions limitations set out in G.S. 143-215.107D that exceed the costs required to comply with 42 U.S.C. § 7410(a)(2)(D)(i)(I), as implemented by 40 Code of Federal Regulations § 51.121 (July 1, 2001 Edition), related federal regulations, and the associated State or Federal Implementation Plan, or with 42 U.S.C. § 7426, as implemented by 40 Code of Federal Regulations § 52.34 (July 1, 2001 Edition) and related federal regulations. The term "environmental compliance costs" does not include:

a. Costs required to comply with a final order or judgment rendered by a state or federal court under which an investor-owned public utility is found liable for a failure to comply with any federal or state law, rule, or regulation for the protection of the environment or public health.

b. The net increase in costs, above those proposed by the investor-owned public utility as part of its plan to achieve compliance with the emissions limitations set out in G.S. 143-215.107D, that are necessary to comply with a settlement agreement, consent decree, or similar resolution of litigation arising from any alleged failure to comply with any federal or state law, rule, or regulation for the protection of the environment or public health.

c. Any criminal or civil fine or penalty, including court costs imposed or assessed for a violation by an investor-owned public utility of any federal or state law, rule, or regulation for the protection of the environment or public health.

d. The net increase in costs, above those proposed by the investor-owned public utility as part of its plan to achieve the emissions limitations set out in G.S. 143-215.107D, that are necessary to comply with any limitation on emissions of oxides of nitrogen (NOx) or sulfur dioxide (SO2) that are imposed on an individual coal-fired generating unit by the Environmental Management Commission or the Department of Environment and Natural Resources to address any nonattainment of an air quality standard in any area of the State.

(3) "Investor-owned public utility" means an investor-owned public utility, as defined in G.S. 62-3.

(b) The investor-owned public utilities shall be allowed to accelerate the cost recovery of their estimated environmental compliance costs over a seven-year period, beginning January 1, 2003 and ending December 31, 2009. For purposes of this subsection, an investor-owned public utility subject to the provisions of subsections (b) and (d) of G.S. 143-215.107D shall amortize environmental compliance costs in the amount of one billion five hundred million dollars ($1,500,000,000) and an investor-owned public utility subject to the provisions of subsections (c) and (e) of G.S. 143-215.107D shall amortize environmental compliance costs in the amount of eight hundred thirteen million dollars ($813,000,000). During the rate freeze period established in subsection (e) of this section, the investor-owned public utilities shall, at a minimum, recover through amortization seventy percent (70%) of the environmental compliance costs set out in this subsection. The maximum amount for each investor-owned public utility's annual accelerated cost recovery during the rate freeze period shall not exceed one hundred fifty percent (150%) of the annual levelized environmental compliance costs set out in this subsection. The amounts to be amortized pursuant to this subsection are estimates of the environmental compliance costs that may be adjusted as provided in this section. The General Assembly makes no judgment as to whether the actual environmental compliance costs will be greater than, less than, or equal to these estimated amounts. These estimated amounts do not define or limit the scope of the expenditures that may be necessary to comply with the emissions limitations set out in G.S. 143-215.107D.

(c) The investor-owned public utilities shall file their compliance plans, including initial cost estimates, with the Commission and the Department of Environment and Natural Resources not later than 10 days after the date on which this section becomes effective. The Commission shall consult with the Secretary of Environment and Natural Resources and shall consider the advice of the Secretary as to whether an investor-owned public utility's proposed compliance plan is adequate to achieve the emissions limitations set out in G.S. 143-215.107D.

(d) Subject to the provisions of subsection (f) of this section, the Commission shall hold a hearing to review the environmental compliance costs set out in subsection (b) of this section. The Commission may modify and revise those costs as necessary to ensure that they are just, reasonable, and prudent based on the most recent cost information available and determine the annual cost recovery amounts that each investor-owned public utility shall be required to record and recover during calendar years 2008 and 2009. In making its decisions pursuant to this subsection, the Commission shall consult with the Secretary of Environment and Natural Resources to receive advice as to whether the investor-owned public utility's actual and proposed modifications and permitting and construction schedule are adequate to achieve the emissions limitations set out in G.S. 143-215.107D. The Commission shall issue an order pursuant to this subsection no later than December 31, 2007.

(e) Notwithstanding G.S. 62-130(d) and G.S. 62-136(a), the base rates of the investor-owned public utilities shall remain unchanged from the date on which this section becomes effective through December 31, 2007. The Commission may, however, consistent with the public interest:

(1) Allow adjustments to base rates, or deferral of costs or revenues, due to one or more of the following conditions occurring during the rate freeze period:

a. Governmental action resulting in significant cost reductions or requiring major expenditures including, but not limited to, the cost of compliance with any law, regulation, or rule for the protection of the environment or public health, other than environmental compliance costs.

b. Major expenditures to restore or replace property damaged or destroyed by force majeure.

c. A severe threat to the financial stability of the investor-owned public utility resulting from other extraordinary causes beyond the reasonable control of the investor-owned public utility.

d. The investor-owned public utility persistently earns a return substantially in excess of the rate of return established and found reasonable by the Commission in the investor-owned public utility's last general rate case.

(2) Approve any reduction in a rate or rates applicable to a customer or class of customers during the rate freeze period, if requested to do so by an investor-owned public utility that is subject to the emissions limitations set out in G.S. 143-215.107D.

(f) In any general rate case initiated to adjust base rates effective on or after January 1, 2008, the investor-owned public utility shall be allowed to recover its actual environmental compliance costs in accordance with Article 7 of this Chapter less the cumulative amount of accelerated cost recovery recorded pursuant to subsection (b) of this section.

(g) Consistent with the public interest, the Commission is authorized to approve proposals submitted by an investor-owned public utility to implement optional, market-based rates and services, provided the proposal does not increase base rates during the period of time referred to in subsection (e) of this section.

(h) Nothing in this section shall prohibit the Commission from taking any actions otherwise appropriate to enforce investor-owned public utility compliance with applicable statutes or Commission rules or to order any appropriate remedy for such noncompliance allowed by law.

(i) An investor-owned public utility that is subject to the emissions limitations set out in G.S. 143-215.107D shall submit to the Commission and to the Department of Environment and Natural Resources on or before April 1 of each year a verified statement that contains all of the following:

(1) A detailed report on the investor-owned public utility's plans for meeting the emissions limitations set out in G.S. 143-215.107D.

(2) The actual environmental compliance costs incurred by the investor-owned public utility in the previous calendar year, including a description of the construction undertaken and completed during that year.

(3) The amount of the investor-owned public utility's environmental compliance costs amortized in the previous calendar year.

(4) An estimate of the investor-owned public utility's environmental compliance costs and the basis for any revisions of those estimates when compared to the estimates submitted during the previous year.

(5) A description of all permits required in order to comply with the provisions of G.S. 143-215.107D for which the investor-owned public utility has applied and the status of those permits or permit applications.

(6) A description of the construction related to compliance with the provisions of G.S. 143-215.107D that is anticipated during the following year.

(7) A description of the applications for permits required in order to comply with the provisions of G.S. 143-215.107D that are anticipated during the following year.

(8) The results of equipment testing related to compliance with G.S. 143-215.107D.

(9) The number of tons of oxides of nitrogen (NOx) and sulfur dioxide (SO2) emitted during the previous calendar year from the coal-fired generating units that are subject to the emissions limitations set out in G.S. 143-215.107D.

(10) The emissions allowances described in G.S. 143-215.107D(i) that are acquired by the investor-owned public utility that result from compliance with the emissions limitations set out in G.S. 143-215.107D.

(11) Any other information requested by the Commission or the Department of Environment and Natural Resources.

(j) The Secretary shall review the information submitted pursuant to subsection (i) of this section and determine whether the investor-owned public utility's actual and proposed modifications and permitting and construction schedule are adequate to achieve the emissions limitations set out in G.S. 143-215.107D and shall advise the Commission as to the Secretary's findings and recommendations.

(k) Any information, advice, findings, recommendations, or determinations provided by the Secretary pursuant to this section shall not constitute a final agency decision within the meaning of Chapter 150B of the General Statutes and shall not be subject to review under that Chapter. (2002-4, s. 9.)

§ 62-133.7. Customer usage tracking rate adjustment mechanisms for natural gas local distribution company rates.

In setting rates for a natural gas local distribution company in a general rate case proceeding under G.S. 62-133, the Commission may adopt, implement, modify, or eliminate a rate adjustment mechanism for one or more of the company's rate schedules, excluding industrial rate schedules, to track and true-up variations in average per customer usage from levels approved in the general rate case proceeding. The Commission may adopt a rate adjustment mechanism only upon a finding by the Commission that the mechanism is appropriate to track and true-up variations in average per customer usage by rate schedule from levels adopted in the general rate case proceeding and that the mechanism is in the public interest. (2007-227, s. 1.)

§ 62-133.7A. Rate adjustment mechanism for natural gas local distribution company rates.

In setting rates for a natural gas local distribution company in a general rate case proceeding under G.S. 62-133, the Commission may adopt, implement, modify, or eliminate a rate adjustment mechanism to enable the company to recover the prudently incurred capital investment and associated costs of complying with federal gas pipeline safety requirements, including a return based on the company's then authorized return. The Commission shall adopt, implement, modify, or eliminate a rate adjustment mechanism authorized under this section only upon a finding by the Commission that the mechanism is in the public interest. (2013-54, s. 1.)

§ 62-133.8. Renewable Energy and Energy Efficiency Portfolio Standard (REPS).

(a) Definitions. - As used in this section:

(1) "Combined heat and power system" means a system that uses waste heat to produce electricity or useful, measurable thermal or mechanical energy at a retail electric customer's facility.

(2) "Demand-side management" means activities, programs, or initiatives undertaken by an electric power supplier or its customers to shift the timing of electricity use from peak to nonpeak demand periods. "Demand-side management" includes, but is not limited to, load management, electric system equipment and operating controls, direct load control, and interruptible load.

(3) "Electric power supplier" means a public utility, an electric membership corporation, or a municipality that sells electric power to retail electric power customers in the State.

(3a) "Electricity demand reduction" means a measurable reduction in the electricity demand of a retail electric customer that is voluntary, under the real-time control of both the electric power supplier and the retail electric customer, and measured in real time, using two-way communications devices that communicate on the basis of standards.

(4) "Energy efficiency measure" means an equipment, physical, or program change implemented after January 1, 2007, that results in less energy used to perform the same function. "Energy efficiency measure" includes, but is not limited to, energy produced from a combined heat and power system that uses nonrenewable energy resources. "Energy efficiency measure" does not include demand-side management.

(5) "New renewable energy facility" means a renewable energy facility that either:

a. Was placed into service on or after January 1, 2007.

b. Delivers or has delivered electric power to an electric power supplier pursuant to a contract with NC GreenPower Corporation that was entered into prior to January 1, 2007.

c. Is a hydroelectric power facility with a generation capacity of 10 megawatts or less that delivers electric power to an electric power supplier.

(6) "Renewable energy certificate" means a tradable instrument that is equal to one megawatt hour of electricity or equivalent energy supplied by a renewable energy facility, new renewable energy facility, or reduced by implementation of an energy efficiency measure that is used to track and verify compliance with the requirements of this section as determined by the Commission. A "renewable energy certificate" does not include the related emission reductions, including, but not limited to, reductions of sulfur dioxide, oxides of nitrogen, mercury, or carbon dioxide.

(7) "Renewable energy facility" means a facility, other than a hydroelectric power facility with a generation capacity of more than 10 megawatts, that either:

a. Generates electric power by the use of a renewable energy resource.

b. Generates useful, measurable combined heat and power derived from a renewable energy resource.

c. Is a solar thermal energy facility.

(8) "Renewable energy resource" means a solar electric, solar thermal, wind, hydropower, geothermal, or ocean current or wave energy resource; a biomass resource, including agricultural waste, animal waste, wood waste, spent pulping liquors, combustible residues, combustible liquids, combustible gases, energy crops, or landfill methane; waste heat derived from a renewable energy resource and used to produce electricity or useful, measurable thermal energy at a retail electric customer's facility; or hydrogen derived from a renewable energy resource. "Renewable energy resource" does not include peat, a fossil fuel, or nuclear energy resource.

(b) Renewable Energy and Energy Efficiency Standards (REPS) for Electric Public Utilities. -

(1) Each electric public utility in the State shall be subject to a Renewable Energy and Energy Efficiency Portfolio Standard (REPS) according to the following schedule:

Calendar Year	REPS Requirement
2012	3% of 2011 North Carolina retail sales
2015	6% of 2014 North Carolina retail sales
2018	10% of 2017 North Carolina retail sales
2021 and thereafter	12.5% of 2020 North Carolina retail sales

(2) An electric public utility may meet the requirements of this section by any one or more of the following:

a. Generate electric power at a new renewable energy facility.

b. Use a renewable energy resource to generate electric power at a generating facility other than the generation of electric power from waste heat derived from the combustion of fossil fuel.

c. Reduce energy consumption through the implementation of an energy efficiency measure; provided, however, an electric public utility subject to the provisions of this subsection may meet up to twenty-five percent (25%) of the requirements of this section through savings due to implementation of energy efficiency measures. Beginning in calendar year 2021 and each year thereafter, an electric public utility may meet up to forty percent (40%) of the requirements of this section through savings due to implementation of energy efficiency measures.

d. Purchase electric power from a new renewable energy facility. Electric power purchased from a new renewable energy facility located outside the geographic boundaries of the State shall meet the requirements of this section if the electric power is delivered to a public utility that provides electric power to retail electric customers in the State; provided, however, the electric public utility shall not sell the renewable energy certificates created pursuant to this paragraph to another electric public utility.

e. Purchase renewable energy certificates derived from in-State or out-of-state new renewable energy facilities. Certificates derived from out-of-state new renewable energy facilities shall not be used to meet more than twenty-five percent (25%) of the requirements of this section, provided that this limitation shall not apply to an electric public utility with less than 150,000 North Carolina retail jurisdictional customers as of December 31, 2006.

f. Use electric power that is supplied by a new renewable energy facility or saved due to the implementation of an energy efficiency measure that exceeds the requirements of this section for any calendar year as a credit towards the requirements of this section in the following calendar year or sell the associated renewable energy certificates.

g. Electricity demand reduction.

(c) Renewable Energy and Energy Efficiency Standards (REPS) for Electric Membership Corporations and Municipalities. -

(1) Each electric membership corporation or municipality that sells electric power to retail electric power customers in the State shall be subject to a Renewable Energy and Energy Efficiency Portfolio Standard (REPS) according to the following schedule:

Calendar Year	REPS Requirement
2012	3% of 2011 North Carolina retail sales

2015   6% of 2014 North Carolina retail sales

2018 and thereafter   10% of 2017 North Carolina retail sales

(2) An electric membership corporation or municipality may meet the requirements of this section by any one or more of the following:

a. Generate electric power at a new renewable energy facility.

b. Reduce energy consumption through the implementation of demand-side management or energy efficiency measures.

c. Purchase electric power from a renewable energy facility or a hydroelectric power facility, provided that no more than thirty percent (30%) of the requirements of this section may be met with hydroelectric power, including allocations made by the Southeastern Power Administration.

d. Purchase renewable energy certificates derived from in-State or out-of-state renewable energy facilities. An electric power supplier subject to the requirements of this subsection may use certificates derived from out-of-state renewable energy facilities to meet no more than twenty-five percent (25%) of the requirements of this section.

e. Acquire all or part of its electric power through a wholesale purchase power agreement with a wholesale supplier of electric power whose portfolio of supply and demand options meets the requirements of this section.

f. Use electric power that is supplied by a new renewable energy facility or saved due to the implementation of demand-side management or energy efficiency measures that exceeds the requirements of this section for any calendar year as a credit towards the requirements of this section in the following calendar year or sell the associated renewable energy certificates.

g. Electricity demand reduction.

(d) Compliance With REPS Requirement Through Use of Solar Energy Resources. - For calendar year 2018 and for each calendar year thereafter, at least two-tenths of one percent (0.2%) of the total electric power in kilowatt hours sold to retail electric customers in the State, or an equivalent amount of energy, shall be supplied by a combination of new solar electric facilities and new metered solar thermal energy facilities that use one or more of the following applications: solar hot water, solar absorption cooling, solar dehumidification, solar thermally driven refrigeration, and solar industrial process heat. The terms of any contract entered into between an electric power supplier and a new solar electric facility or new metered solar thermal energy facility shall be of sufficient length to stimulate development of solar energy, provided, the Commission shall develop a procedure to determine if an electric power supplier is in compliance with the provisions of this subsection if a new solar electric facility or a new metered solar thermal energy facility fails to meet the terms of its contract with the electric power supplier. As used in this subsection, "new" means a facility that was first placed into service on or after January 1, 2007. The electric power suppliers shall comply with the requirements of this subsection according to the following schedule:

Calendar Year	Requirement for Solar Energy Resources
2010	0.02%
2012	0.07%
2015	0.14%
2018	0.20%

(e) Compliance With REPS Requirement Through Use of Swine Waste Resources. - For calendar year 2018 and for each calendar year thereafter, at least two-tenths of one percent (0.2%) of the total electric power in kilowatt hours sold to retail electric customers in the State shall be supplied, or contracted for supply in each year, by swine waste. The electric power suppliers, in the aggregate, shall comply with the requirements of this subsection according to the following schedule:

Calendar Year	Requirement for Swine Waste Resources
2012	0.07%
2015	0.14%

2018   0.20%

(f)   Compliance With REPS Requirement Through Use of Poultry Waste Resources. - For calendar year 2014 and for each calendar year thereafter, at least 900,000 megawatt hours of the total electric power sold to retail electric customers in the State or an equivalent amount of energy shall be supplied, or contracted for supply in each year, by poultry waste combined with wood shavings, straw, rice hulls, or other bedding material. The electric power suppliers, in the aggregate, shall comply with the requirements of this subsection according to the following schedule:

Calendar Year	Requirement for Poultry Waste Resources
2012	170,000 megawatt hours
2013	700,000 megawatt hours
2014	900,000 megawatt hours

(g)   Control of Emissions. - As used in this subsection, Best Available Control Technology (BACT) means an emissions limitation based on the maximum degree a reduction in the emission of air pollutants that is achievable for a facility, taking into account energy, environmental, and economic impacts and other costs. A biomass combustion process at any new renewable energy facility that delivers electric power to an electric power supplier shall meet BACT. The Environmental Management Commission shall determine on a case-by-case basis the BACT for a facility that would not otherwise be required to comply with BACT pursuant to the Prevention of Significant Deterioration (PSD) emissions program. The Environmental Management Commission may adopt rules to implement this subsection. In adopting rules, the Environmental Management Commission shall take into account cumulative and secondary impacts associated with the concentration of biomass facilities in close proximity to one another. In adopting rules the Environmental Management Commission shall provide for the manner in which a facility that would not otherwise be required to comply with BACT pursuant to the PSD emissions programs shall meet the BACT requirement. This subsection shall not apply to a facility that qualifies as a new renewable energy facility under sub-subdivision b. of subdivision (5) of subsection (a) of this section.

(h) Cost Recovery and Customor Charges. -

(1) For the purposes of this subsection, the term "incremental costs" means all reasonable and prudent costs incurred by an electric power supplier to:

a. Comply with the requirements of subsections (b), (c), (d), (e), and (f) of this section that are in excess of the electric power supplier's avoided costs other than those costs recovered pursuant to G.S. 62-133.9.

b. Fund research that encourages the development of renewable energy, energy efficiency, or improved air quality, provided those costs do not exceed one million dollars ($1,000,000) per year.

c. Comply with any federal mandate that is similar to the requirements of subsections (b), (c), (d), (e), and (f) of this section that exceed the costs that the electric power supplier would have incurred under those subsections in the absence of the federal mandate.

(2) All reasonable and prudent costs incurred by an electric power supplier to comply with any federal mandate that is similar to the requirements of subsections (b), (c), (d), (e), and (f) of this section, including, but not limited to, the avoided costs associated with a federal mandate that exceeds the avoided costs that the electric power supplier would have incurred pursuant to subsections (b), (c), (d), (e), and (f) of this section in the absence of the federal mandate, shall be recovered by the electric power supplier in an annual rider charge assessed in accordance with the schedule set out in subdivision (4) of this subsection increased by the Commission on a pro rata basis to allow for full and complete recovery of all reasonable and prudent costs incurred to comply with the federal mandate.

(3) Except as provided in subdivision (2) of this subsection, the total annual incremental cost to be incurred by an electric power supplier and recovered from the electric power supplier's retail customers shall not exceed an amount equal to the per-account annual charges set out in subdivision (4) of this subsection applied to the electric power supplier's total number of customer accounts determined as of December 31 of the previous calendar year. An electric power supplier shall be conclusively deemed to be in compliance with the requirements of subsections (b), (c), (d), (e), and (f) of this section if the electric power supplier's total annual incremental costs incurred equals an amount equal to the per-account annual charges set out in subdivision (4) of this

subsection applied to the electric power supplier's total number of customer accounts determined as of December 31 of the previous calendar year. The total annual incremental cost recoverable by an electric power supplier from an individual customer shall not exceed the per-account charges set out in subdivision (4) of this subsection except as these charges may be adjusted in subdivision (2) of this subsection.

(4)   An electric power supplier shall be allowed to recover the incremental costs incurred to comply with the requirements of subsections (b), (c), (d), (e), and (f) of this section and fund research as provided in subdivision (1) of this subsection through an annual rider not to exceed the following per-account annual charges:

Customer Class	2008-2011	2012-2014	2015 and thereafter
Residential per account	$10.00	$12.00	$34.00
Commercial per account	$50.00	$150.00	$150.00
Industrial per account	$500.00	$1,000.00	$1,000.00

(5)   The Commission shall adopt rules to establish a procedure for the annual assessment of the per-account charges set out in this subsection to an electric public utility's customers to allow for timely recovery of all reasonable and prudent costs of compliance with the requirements of subsections (b), (c), (d), (e), and (f) of this section and to fund research as provided in subdivision (1) of this subsection. The Commission shall ensure that the costs to be recovered from individual customers on a per-account basis pursuant to subdivisions (2) and (3) of this subsection are in the same proportion as the per-account annual charges for each customer class set out in subdivision (4) of this subsection.

(i)   Adoption of Rules. - The Commission shall adopt rules to implement the provisions of this section. In developing rules, the Commission shall:

(1)   Provide for the monitoring of compliance with and enforcement of the requirements of this section.

(2)   Include a procedure to modify or delay the provisions of subsections (b), (c), (d), (e), and (f) of this section in whole or in part if the Commission

determines that it is in the public interest to do so. The procedure adopted pursuant to this subdivision shall include a requirement that the electric power supplier demonstrate that it made a reasonable effort to meet the requirements set out in this section.

(3) Ensure that energy credited toward compliance with the provisions of this section not be credited toward any other purpose, including another renewable energy portfolio standard or voluntary renewable energy purchase program in this State or any other state.

(4) Establish standards for interconnection of renewable energy facilities and other nonutility-owned generation with a generation capacity of 10 megawatts or less to an electric public utility's distribution system; provided, however, that the Commission shall adopt, if appropriate, federal interconnection standards.

(5) Ensure that the owner and operator of each renewable energy facility that delivers electric power to an electric power supplier is in substantial compliance with all federal and state laws, regulations, and rules for the protection of the environment and conservation of natural resources.

(6) Consider whether it is in the public interest to adopt rules for electric public utilities for net metering of renewable energy facilities with a generation capacity of one megawatt or less.

(7) Develop procedures to track and account for renewable energy certificates, including ownership of renewable energy certificates that are derived from a customer owned renewable energy facility as a result of any action by a customer of an electric power supplier that is independent of a program sponsored by the electric power supplier.

(j) Report. - No later than October 1 of each year, the Commission shall submit a report on the activities taken by the Commission to implement, and by electric power suppliers to comply with, the requirements of this section to the Governor, the Environmental Review Commission, and the Joint Legislative Commission on Governmental Operations. The report shall include any public comments received regarding direct, secondary, and cumulative environmental impacts of the implementation of the requirements of this section. In developing the report, the Commission shall consult with the Department of Environment and Natural Resources.

(k) Tracking of Renewable Energy Certificates. - No later than July 1, 2010, the Commission shall develop, implement, and maintain an Internet Web site for the online tracking of renewable energy certificates in order to verify the compliance of electric power suppliers with the REPS requirements of this section and to facilitate the establishment of a market for the purchase and sale of renewable energy certificates. (2007-397, s. 2(a); 2009-475, s. 14(a); 2011-55, ss. 1, 2, 3; 2011-291, s. 2.13; 2011-309, s. 2; 2011-394, s. 1.)

§ 62-133.9. Cost recovery for demand-side management and energy efficiency measures.

(a) The definitions set out in G.S. 62-133.8 apply to this section. As used in this section, "new," used in connection with demand-side management or energy efficiency measure, means a demand-side management or energy efficiency measure that is adopted and implemented on or after January 1, 2007, including subsequent changes and modifications.

(b) Each electric power supplier shall implement demand-side management and energy efficiency measures and use supply-side resources to establish the least cost mix of demand reduction and generation measures that meet the electricity needs of its customers. An electric membership corporation or municipality that qualifies as an electric power supplier may satisfy the requirements of this section through its purchases from a wholesale supplier of electric power that uses supply-side resources and demand-side management to meet all or a portion of the supply needs of its members and their retail customers, and that, by aggregating and promoting demand-side management and energy efficiency measures for its members, meets the requirements of this section.

(c) Each electric power supplier to which G.S. 62-110.1 applies shall include an assessment of demand-side management and energy efficiency in its resource plans submitted to the Commission and shall submit cost-effective demand-side management and energy efficiency options that require incentives to the Commission for approval.

(d) The Commission shall, upon petition of an electric public utility, approve an annual rider to the electric public utility's rates to recover all reasonable and prudent costs incurred for adoption and implementation of new demand-side management and new energy efficiency measures. Recoverable costs include, but are not limited to, all capital costs, including cost of capital and depreciation expenses, administrative costs, implementation costs, incentive payments to program participants, and operating costs. In determining the amount of any rider, the Commission:

(1) Shall allow electric public utilities to capitalize all or a portion of those costs to the extent that those costs are intended to produce future benefits.

(2) May approve other incentives to electric public utilities for adopting and implementing new demand-side management and energy efficiency measures. Allowable incentives may include:

a. Appropriate rewards based on the sharing of savings achieved by the demand-side management and energy efficiency measures.

b. Appropriate rewards based on capitalization of a percentage of avoided costs achieved by demand-side management and energy efficiency measures.

c. Any other incentives that the Commission determines to be appropriate.

(e) The Commission shall determine the appropriate assignment of costs of new demand-side management and energy efficiency measures for electric public utilities and shall assign the costs of the programs only to the class or classes of customers that directly benefit from the programs.

(f) None of the costs of new demand-side management or energy efficiency measures of an electric power supplier shall be assigned to any industrial customer that notifies the industrial customer's electric power supplier that, at the industrial customer's own expense, the industrial customer has implemented at any time in the past or, in accordance with stated, quantified goals for demand-side management and energy efficiency, will implement alternative demand-side management and energy efficiency measures and that the industrial customer elects not to participate in demand-side management or energy efficiency measures under this section. The electric power supplier that provides electric service to the industrial customer, an industrial customer that receives electric service from the electric power supplier, the Public Staff, or the Commission on its own motion, may initiate a complaint proceeding before the Commission to challenge the validity of the notification of nonparticipation. The procedures set forth in G.S. 62-73, 62-74, and 62-75 shall govern any such complaint. The provisions of this subsection shall also apply to commercial customers with significant annual usage at a threshold level to be established by the Commission.

(g) An electric public utility shall not charge an industrial or commercial customer for the costs of installing demand-side management equipment on the customer's premises if the customer provides, at the customer's expense, equivalent demand-side management equipment.

(h) The Commission shall adopt rules to implement this section.

(i) The Commission shall submit to the Governor and to the Joint Legislative Commission on Governmental Operations a summary of the proceedings conducted pursuant to this section during the preceding two fiscal years on or before September 1 of odd-numbered years. (2007-397, s. 4(a); 2011-291, s. 2.14.)

§ 62-133.10. Retention of fuel and fuel-related cost savings associated with the purchase or construction of a carbon offset facility.

(a) The Commission shall permit an electric public utility that purchases or constructs a carbon offset facility to adjust its fuel and fuel-related costs in G.S. 62-133.2 to retain the North Carolina retail allocation of the system fuel and fuel-related cost savings resulting from the purchase or construction of the facility, not to exceed the annual revenue requirement associated with the allocated North Carolina retail portion of the facility as determined using the cost of service methodology approved by the Commission in the utility's last general rate case.

(b) For purposes of this section, "carbon offset facility" means a facility in this State that meets all of the following:

(1) The facility is purchased or constructed by an electric public utility between July 1, 2009, and July 1, 2014.

(2) The facility uses solar electric, solar thermal, wind, hydropower, geothermal, or ocean current or wave energy to generate electricity or equivalent BTUs.

(3) The electricity or equivalent BTUs produced by the facility will displace electric generation so as to reduce greenhouse gas emissions from existing

fossil fuel fired generating facilities used by the utility to meet the electricity needs of its North Carolina customers.

(c) An electric public utility seeking the adjustment authorized by this section first shall file with the Commission a petition requesting a determination that the facility the utility proposes to purchase or construct is a carbon offset facility. The utility shall include in its petition all of the following information in such form and detail as the Commission may require:

(1) Description and location of the facility.

(2) The benefit of the facility.

(3) A list of all necessary permitting and approvals and their status.

(4) Purchase or construction schedule, with in-service or completion date.

(5) Projected costs to purchase or construct and the annual revenue requirement for the facility.

(6) Projected annual generation output of the facility and information detailing how the generation projections were calculated.

(7) Information demonstrating that the operation of the facility will displace electric generation resulting in a reduction of greenhouse gas emissions from existing fossil fuel fired facilities used by the utility to meet the electricity needs of its North Carolina customers.

(8) The projected fuel and fuel-related cost savings the utility seeks to retain and how the savings were calculated.

(d) Upon the filing of the petition, the Public Staff shall conduct an investigation and shall file a report with the Commission setting forth the results of its investigation and stating whether the facility is a carbon offset facility. The Public Staff's report shall be filed not later than 45 days after the date the petition was filed, unless the Commission grants an extension of time not to exceed 15 days for good cause shown. Other interested persons may file comments in response to the utility's petition and the Public Staff's report not later than 15 days after the Public Staff files its report. The Commission shall enter an order either granting or denying the petition not later than 105 days after the date the petition was filed. A finding by the Commission that the facility is a carbon offset facility shall establish that the utility's decision to purchase or construct the facility is reasonable and prudent.

(e)   Nothing in this section shall be construed to exempt an electric public utility from obtaining all applicable permits and certificates, including a certificate of public convenience and necessity required by G.S. 62-110.1. An electric public utility shall file annual cost and schedule updates with the Commission until the purchase or construction of an approved carbon offset facility is completed.

(f)   Upon placement into service of an approved carbon offset facility, the electric public utility shall, in addition to the information and data provided under G.S. 62-133.2, submit the following in conjunction with its application for a fuel and fuel-related charge adjustment:

(1)   A calculation of the annual revenue requirement associated with the carbon offset facility.

(2)   Information demonstrating the specific items of costs associated with the carbon offset facility's annual revenue requirement are reasonable and prudent.

(3)   The fuel and fuel-related cost savings resulting from operation of the carbon offset facility.

(4)   Actual generation output of the carbon offset facility, including a demonstration and quantification of how this generation displaced electric generation resulting in reduced greenhouse gas emissions from existing fossil fuel fired facilities used by the utility to meet the electricity needs of its North Carolina customers during the test year.

(g)   The Commission shall approve an estimate of the projected fuel and fuel-related cost savings and an annual revenue requirement for an approved facility, as appropriate, in each G.S. 62-133.2 proceeding. The Commission also may approve a true-up procedure for the projected fuel and fuel-related cost savings. In the first G.S. 62-133.2 proceeding conducted after the approved facility is placed in service, the Commission shall determine the reasonable and prudent cost of the facility for ratemaking purposes. The revenue requirement associated with the facility shall include but not be limited to: depreciation; operating and maintenance costs; applicable taxes; and a return on investment, net of accumulated depreciation, accumulated deferred income taxes, and other applicable savings or adjustments. The rate of return on investment shall be based on the then current capital structure, embedded cost of preferred stock, and embedded cost of debt of the public utility net of appropriate income taxes, and the cost of common equity approved in the public utility's then most recent general rate case.

(h) The Commission shall authorize the electric public utility to utilize deferral accounting for the fuel and fuel-related cost savings realized in conjunction with the operation of an approved facility. The Commission shall, by rule or order, approve the terms and conditions of the deferral accounting.

(i) The annual revenue requirement of the approved facility in excess of the annual fuel and fuel-related cost savings shall be deemed recovered through the utility's then current base rates.

(j) The adjustment authorized by this section shall terminate upon the establishment of new rates in the electric public utility's next general rate case following the placement into service and inclusion into base rates of the approved facility. (2009-390, s. 2.)

§ 62-133.11. Rate adjustment for changes in costs based on third-party rates.

(a) The Commission shall permit a water or sewer public utility to adjust its rates approved pursuant to G.S. 62-133 to reflect changes in costs based solely upon changes in the rates imposed by third-party suppliers of purchased water or sewer service, including applicable taxes and fees.

(b) Any water or sewer public utility seeking to adjust its rates pursuant to this section shall file a verified petition in such form and detail as the Commission may require.

(c) The Commission shall issue an order approving, denying, or approving with modifications a rate adjustment requested pursuant to this section within 60 days of the date of filing of a completed petition, unless that time is for good cause extended up to a maximum of 90 days. (2013-106, s. 1.)

§ 62-133.12. Rate adjustment mechanism based on investment in repair, improvement, and replacement of water and sewer facilities.

(a) The Commission may approve a rate adjustment mechanism in a general rate proceeding pursuant to G.S. 62-133 to allow a water or sewer public utility to recover through a system improvement charge the incremental depreciation expense and capital costs associated with the utility's reasonable and prudently incurred investment in eligible water and sewer system improvements. The Commission shall approve a rate adjustment mechanism authorized by this section only upon a finding that the mechanism is in the public interest. The frequency and manner of rate adjustments under the mechanism shall be as prescribed by the Commission.

(b) For purposes of this section, "eligible water system improvements" or "eligible sewer system improvements" shall include only those improvements found necessary by the Commission to enable the water or sewer utility to provide safe, reliable, and efficient service in accordance with applicable water quality and effluent standards.

(c) For purposes of this section, "eligible water system improvements" means:

(1) Distribution system mains, valves, utility service lines (including meter boxes and appurtenances), meters, and hydrants installed as in-kind replacements.

(2) Main extensions installed to eliminate dead ends and to implement solutions to regional water supply in order to comply with primary and, upon specific Commission approval, secondary drinking water standards.

(3) Equipment and infrastructure installed to comply with primary drinking water standards.

(4) Equipment and infrastructure installed at the direction of the Commission to comply with secondary drinking water standards.

(5) Unreimbursed costs of relocating facilities due to highway projects.

(d) For the purposes of this section, "eligible sewer system improvements" means:

(1) Collection main extensions installed to implement solutions to wastewater problems.

(2) Improvements necessary to reduce inflow and infiltration to the collection system to comply with applicable State and federal law and regulations.

(3) Unreimbursed costs of relocating facilities due to highway construction or relocation projects.

(4) Pumps, motors, blowers, and other mechanical equipment installed as in-kind replacements for customers.

(e) The Commission shall provide for audit and reconciliation procedures, including measures for refunds of any over-collections under the system improvement charge with interest pursuant to G.S. 62-130(e).

(f) The Commission may eliminate or modify any rate adjustment mechanism authorized pursuant to this section upon a finding that it is not in the public interest.

(g) Cumulative system improvement charges for a water or sewer utility pursuant to a rate adjustment mechanism approved by the Commission under this section may not exceed five percent (5%) of the total annual service revenues approved by the Commission in the water or sewer utility's last general rate case. (2013-106, s. 2.)

§ 62-134. Change of rates; notice; suspension and investigation.

(a) Unless the Commission otherwise orders, no public utility shall make any changes in any rate which has been duly established under this Chapter, except after 30 days' notice to the Commission, which notice shall plainly state the changes proposed to be made in the rates then in force, and the time when the changed rates will go into effect. The public utility shall also give such notice, which may include notice by publication, of the proposed changes to other interested persons as the Commission in its discretion may direct. All proposed changes shall be shown by filing new schedules, or shall be plainly indicated upon schedules filed and in force at the time and kept open to public inspection. The Commission, for good cause shown in writing, may allow changes in rates without requiring the 30 days' notice, under such conditions as it may prescribe. All such changes shall be immediately indicated upon its schedules by such public utility.

(b)   Whenever there is filed with the Commission by any public utility any schedule stating a new or revised rate or rates, the Commission may, either upon complaint or upon its own initiative, upon reasonable notice, enter upon a hearing concerning the lawfulness of such rate or rates. Pending such hearing and the decision thereon, the Commission, upon filing with such schedule and delivering to the public utility affected thereby a statement in writing of its reasons therefor, may, at any time before they become effective, suspend the operation of such rate or rates, but not for a longer period than 270 days beyond the time when such rate or rates would otherwise go into effect. If the proceeding has not been concluded and an order made within the period of suspension, the proposed change of rate shall go into effect at the end of such period. After hearing, whether completed before or after the rate goes into effect, the Commission may make such order with respect thereto as would be proper in a proceeding instituted after it had become effective.

(c)   At any hearing involving a rate changed or sought to be changed by the public utility, the burden of proof shall be upon the public utility to show that the changed rate is just and reasonable.

(d)   Notwithstanding the provisions of this Article, any public utility engaged solely in distributing electricity to retail customers, which electricity has been purchased at wholesale rates from another public utility, an electric membership corporation or a municipality, may in its discretion, and without the necessity of public hearings as in this section is otherwise provided, elect to adopt the same retail rates to customers charged by the public utility, electric membership corporation or municipality from whom the wholesale power is purchased for the same service, unless the North Carolina Utility Commission finds upon a hearing, either on its own initiative or upon complaint, that the rate of return earned by such utility upon the basis of such rates is unjust and unreasonable. In such a proceeding the burden of proof shall be upon the electrical distribution company.

(e)   Repealed by Session Laws 1981 (Regular Session, 1982), c. 1197, s. 2.

(f)   The Commission may adopt rules prescribing the information and exhibits required to be filed with any applications, or tariff for an increase in utility rates, including but not limited to all of the evidence or proof through the end of the test period which the utility will rely on at any hearing on such increase, and the Commission may suspend such increase until such data, information or exhibits are filed, in addition to the time provided for suspension of such increase in other provisions of this Chapter.

(g)   The provisions of this section shall not be applicable to bus companies or to their rates, fares or tariffs.

(h)   Notwithstanding the requirements of subsections (a) and (b) of this section, the Commission may, in lieu of fixing specific rates or tariffs for competitive services offered by a public utility defined in G.S. 62-3(23)a.6., adopt practices and procedures to permit pricing flexibility, detariffing services, or both. In exercising its authority to permit pricing flexibility, detariffing of services, or both, the Commission shall first determine that the service is competitive. After a determination that the service is competitive, the Commission shall consider the following in deciding whether to permit pricing flexibility, detariffing of services, or both:

(1)   The extent to which competing telecommunications services are available from alternative providers in the relevant geographic or service market;

(2)   The market share, growth in market share, ease of entry, and affiliations of alternative providers;

(3)   The size and number of alternative providers and the ability of such alternative providers to make functionally equivalent or substitute services readily available at competitive rates and on competitive terms and conditions;

(4)   Whether the exercise of Commission authority produces tangible benefits to consumers that exceed those available by reliance on market forces;

(5)   Whether the exercise of Commission authority inhibits the public utility from competing with unregulated providers of functionally equivalent telecommunications services;

(6)   Whether the existence of competition tends to prevent abuses, unjust discrimination or excessive charges for the service or facility offered;

(7)   Whether the public utility would gain an unfair advantage in its competitive activities; and

(8)   Any other relevant factors protecting the public interest.

(i)   On motion of any interested party and for good cause shown, the Commission shall hold hearings prior to adopting any pricing flexibility or detariffing of services permitted under this section. The Commission may also revoke a determination made under this section when the Commission determines, after notice and opportunity to be heard, that the public interest requires that the rates and charges for the service be more fully regulated.

(j)   Notwithstanding the provisions of G.S. 62-140, the Commission may permit public utilities subject to subsection (h) of this section to offer competitive services to business customers upon agreement between the public utility and the customer provided the services are compensatory and cover the costs of providing the service. (1933, c. 307, s. 7; 1939, c. 365, s. 3; 1941, c. 97; 1945, c. 725; 1947, c. 1008, s. 24; 1949, c. 1132, s. 22; 1959, c. 422; 1963, c. 1165, s. 1; 1971, c. 551; 1973, c. 1444; 1975, c. 243, s. 8; c. 510, c. 867, s. 7; 1981 (Reg. Sess., 1982), c. 1197, s. 2; 1985, c. 676, s. 15(3); 1989, c. 112, s. 3.)

§ 62-135. Temporary rates under bond.

(a)   Notwithstanding an order of suspension of an increase in rates, any public utility except a common carrier may, subject to the provisions of subsections (b), (c) and (d) hereof, put such suspended rate or rates into effect upon the expiration of six months after the date when such rate or rates would have become effective, if not so suspended, by notifying the Commission and its consumers of its action in making such increase not less than 10 days prior to the day when it shall be placed in effect; provided, however, that utilities engaged in the distribution of utility commodities bought at wholesale by the utility for distribution to consumers may put such suspended rate or rates, to the extent occasioned by changes in the wholesale rate of such utility commodity, into effect at the expiration of 30 days after the date when such rate or rates would become effective if not so suspended; provided that no rate or rates shall be left in effect longer than one year unless the Commission shall have rendered its decision upon the reasonableness thereof within such period. This section to become effective July 1, 1963.

(b)   No rate or rates placed in effect pursuant to this section shall result in an increase of more than twenty percent (20%) on any single rate classification of the public utility.

(c) No rate or rates shall be placed in effect pursuant to this section until the public utility has filed with the Commission a bond in a reasonable amount approved by the Commission, with sureties approved by the Commission, or an undertaking approved by the Commission, conditioned upon the refund in a manner to be prescribed by order of the Commission, to the persons entitled thereto of the amount of the excess plus interest from the date that such rates were put into effect, if the rate or rates so put into effect are finally determined to be excessive. The amount of said interest shall be determined pursuant to G.S. 62-130(e).

(d) If the rate or rates so put into effect are finally determined to be excessive, the public utility shall make refund of the excess plus interest to its customers within 30 days after such final determination, and the Commission shall set forth in its final order the terms and conditions for such refund. If such refund is not paid in accordance with such order, any persons entitled to such refund may sue therefor, either jointly or severally, and be entitled to recover, in addition to the amount of the refund, all court costs and reasonable attorney fees for the plaintiff, to be fixed by the court. (1933, c. 307, s. 7; 1959, c. 422; 1963, c. 1165, s. 1; 1981, c. 461, s. 2.)

§ 62-136. Investigation of existing rates; changing unreasonable rates; certain refunds to be distributed to customers.

(a) Whenever the Commission, after a hearing had after reasonable notice upon its own motion or upon complaint of anyone directly interested, finds that the existing rates in effect and collected by any public utility are unjust, unreasonable, insufficient or discriminatory, or in violation of any provision of law, the Commission shall determine the just, reasonable, and sufficient and nondiscriminatory rates to be thereafter observed and in force, and shall fix the same by order.

(b) All municipalities in the State are deemed to be directly interested in the rates and service of public utilities operating in such municipalities, and may institute or participate in proceedings before the Commission involving such rates or service. Any municipality may institute proceedings before the Commission to eliminate unfair and unreasonable discrimination in rates or service by any public utility between such complainant or its inhabitants and any other municipality or its inhabitants, and the Commission shall, upon complaint, after hearing afforded to the public utility affected and to all municipalities affected, have authority to remove such discrimination.

(c)   If any refund is made to a distributing company operating as a public utility in North Carolina of charges paid to the company from which the distributing company obtains the energy, service or commodity distributed, the Commission may, in cases where the charges have been included in rates paid by the customers of the distributing company, require said distributing company to distribute said refund plus interest among the distributing company's customers in a manner prescribed by the Commission. The amount of said interest shall be determined pursuant to G.S. 62-130(e). (Ex. Sess. 1913, c. 20, s. 7; C.S., s. 1083; 1933, c. 134, s. 8; c. 307, s. 8; 1937, c. 401; 1941, c. 97; 1963, c. 1165, s. 1; 1981, c. 460, s. 1.)

§ 62-137. Scope of rate case.

In setting a hearing on rates upon its own motion, upon complaint, or upon application of a public utility, the Commission shall declare the scope of the hearing by determining whether it is to be a general rate case, under G.S. 62-133, or whether it is to be a case confined to the reasonableness of a specific single rate, a small part of the rate structure, or some classification of users involving questions which do not require a determination of the entire rate structure and overall rate of return. The procedures established in this section shall not be required when pricing alternatives permitted under G.S. 62-134(h) and (j) are adopted. (1963, c. 1165, s. 1; 1989, c. 112, s. 4.)

§ 62-138. Utilities to file rates, service regulations and service contracts with Commission; publication; certain telephone service prohibited.

(a)   Under such rules as the Commission may prescribe, every public utility, except as permitted under G.S. 62-134(h) and (j):

(1)   Shall file with the Commission all schedules of rates, service regulations and forms of service contracts, used or to be used within the jurisdiction of the Commission; and

(2) Shall keep copies of such schedules, service regulations and contracts open to public inspection. Except, if there is a sufficient likelihood that a public utility defined in G.S. 62-3(23)a.6. may suffer a competitive disadvantage if the rates for a specific competitive service are disclosed, the Commission may waive the public disclosure of the rates. The Commission may revoke the disclosure waiver upon a showing that the competitive disadvantage no longer exists.

(b) Every common carrier of passengers shall file with the Commission, print, and keep open for public inspection schedules showing all rates for the transportation of passengers in intrastate commerce and all services in connection therewith between points on its own routes and between points on its own routes and points on the routes of other such common carriers, and if it establishes joint rates with other common carriers, it shall include in its schedules so filed such joint rates.

(c) Every irregular route common carrier of household goods shall file with the Commission, print, and keep open for public inspection schedules showing all rates for the transportation of household goods in intrastate commerce between points within the area of its authorized operation, and if it establishes joint rates with other common carriers, it shall include in its schedules so filed such joint rates between points within the area of its own authorized operation and points on the line or route of such other common carriers.

(c1) Any person who, though exempt from Commission regulation under Public Law 103-305, agrees to joint line rates or routes as authorized by Public Law 103-305 may file with the Commission, print, and keep open for public inspection schedules showing all such joint rates for the transportation of property in intrastate commerce, and all connected services, between all points the person serves.

(d) The schedules required by this section shall be published, filed, and posted in such form and manner and shall contain such information as the Commission may prescribe; and the Commission is authorized to reject any schedule filed with it which is not in compliance with this section. Any schedule so rejected by the Commission shall be void and its use shall be unlawful.

(e) No public utility, unless otherwise provided by this Chapter, shall engage in service to the public unless its rates for such service have been filed and published in accordance with the provisions of this section.

(f) Under such rules as the Commission may prescribe, every electric membership corporation operating within this State shall file with the Commission, for information purposes, all rates, schedules of rates, charges, service regulations, and forms of service contracts, used or to be used within the State, and shall keep copies of such schedules, rates, charges, service regulations, and contracts open to public inspection.

(g) No public utility may offer or maintain telephone service to any subscriber to such service who has in use or proposes to place in use equipment which will enable said subscriber to observe or monitor telephone calls directed to or placed by said subscriber unless said subscriber shall agree that such equipment shall be used in conformity with the standards for the use of such equipment adopted by the Commission. (1899, c. 164, s. 7; Rev., s. 1109; 1907, c. 217, s. 5; C.S., s. 1074; 1933, c. 134, s. 8; c. 307, s. 4; 1941, c. 97; 1947, c. 1008, s. 25; 1949, c. 1132, s. 23; 1959, c. 209; 1963, c. 1165, s. 1; 1965, c. 287, s. 7; 1977, c. 799; 1989, c. 112, s. 5; 1995, c. 523, s. 6.)

§ 62-139. Rates varying from schedule prohibited; refunding overcharge; penalty.

(a) No public utility shall directly or indirectly, by any device whatsoever, charge, demand, collect or receive from any person a greater or less compensation for any service rendered or to be rendered by such public utility than that prescribed by the Commission, nor shall any person receive or accept any service from a public utility for a compensation greater or less than that prescribed by the Commission.

(b) Any public utility in the State which shall willfully charge a rate for any public utility service in excess of that prescribed by the Commission, and which shall omit to refund the same within 30 days after written notice and demand of the person overcharged, unless relieved by the Commission for good cause shown, shall be liable to him for double the amount of such overcharge, plus a penalty of ten dollars ($10.00) per day for each day's delay after 30 days from such notice or date of denial or relief by the Commission, whichever is later. Such overcharge and penalty shall be recoverable in any court of competent jurisdiction. (1903, c. 590, ss. 1, 2; Rev., ss. 2642, 2643, 2644; Ex. Sess. 1913, c. 20, ss. 5, 12; C.S., ss. 1082, 1086, 3514; 1933, c. 134, s. 8; c. 307, s. 5; 1941, c. 97; 1963, c. 1165, s. 1; 1989, c. 112, s. 6.)

§ 62-140. Discrimination prohibited.

(a) No public utility shall, as to rates or services, make or grant any unreasonable preference or advantage to any person or subject any person to any unreasonable prejudice or disadvantage. No public utility shall establish or maintain any unreasonable difference as to rates or services either as between localities or as between classes of service. The Commission may determine any questions of fact arising under this section; provided that it shall not be an unreasonable preference or advantage or constitute discrimination against any person, firm or corporation or general rate payer for telephone utilities to contract with motels, hotels and hospitals to pay reasonable commissions in connection with the handling of intrastate toll calls charged to a guest or patient and collected by the motel, hotel or hospital; provided further, that payment of such commissions shall be in accordance with uniform tariffs which shall be subject to the approval of the Commission. Provided further, that it shall not be considered an unreasonable preference or advantage for the Commission to order, if it finds the public interest so requires, a reduction in local telephone rates for low-income residential consumers meeting a means test established by the Commission in order to match any reduction in the interstate subscriber line charge authorized by the Federal Communications Commission. If the State repeals any State funding mechanism for a reduction in the local telephone rates for low-income residential consumers, the Commission shall take appropriate action to eliminate any requirement for the reduced rate funded by the repealed State funding mechanism. For the purposes of this section, a State funding mechanism for a reduction in the local telephone rates includes a tax credit allowed for the public utility to recover the reduction in rates.

Nothing in this section prohibits the Commission from establishing different rates for natural gas service to counties that are substantially unserved, to the extent that those rates reflect the cost of providing service to the unserved counties and upon a finding by the Commission that natural gas service would not otherwise become available to the counties.

(b) The Commission shall make reasonable and just rules and regulations:

(1) To prevent discrimination in the rates or services of public utilities.

(2) To prevent the giving, paying or receiving of any rebate or bonus, directly or indirectly, or misleading or deceiving the public in any manner as to rates charged for the services of public utilities.

(c) No public utility shall offer or pay any compensation or consideration or furnish any equipment to secure the installation or adoption of the use of such utility service except upon filing of a schedule of such compensation or consideration or equipment to be furnished and approved thereof by the Commission, and offering such compensation, consideration or equipment to all persons within the same classification using or applying for such public utility service; provided, in considering the reasonableness of any such schedule filed by a public utility the Commission shall consider, among other things, evidence of consideration or compensation paid by any competitor, regulated or nonregulated, of the public utility to secure the installation or adoption of the use of such competitor's service. Provided, further, that nothing herein shall prohibit a public utility from carrying out any contractual commitment in existence at the time of the enactment hereof, so long as such program does not extend beyond December 31, 1963. For the purpose of this subsection, "public utility" shall include any electric membership corporation operating within this State, and the terms "utility service" and "public utility service" shall include the service rendered by any such electric membership corporation. (1899, c. 164, s. 2, subsecs. 3, 5; Rev., s. 1095; 1913, c. 127, s. 6; C.S., s. 1054; 1933, c. 134, s. 8; c. 307, s. 6; 1941, c. 97; 1963, c. 1165, s. 1; 1965, c. 287, s. 8; 1977, 2nd Sess., c. 1146; 1985, c. 694, s. 1; 1997-426, s. 1; 2013-363, s. 11.1.)

§ 62-141. Long and short hauls.

(a) Except when expressly permitted by the Commission, it shall be unlawful for any common carrier to charge or receive any greater compensation in the aggregate for the transportation of like kind of household goods under substantially similar circumstances and conditions for a shorter than for a longer distance over the same line or route in the same direction, the shorter being included within the longer distance; but this shall not be construed as authorizing any common carrier within the terms of this Chapter to charge and receive as great compensation for a shorter as for a longer distance.

(b) Upon application to the Commission, common carriers may in special cases be authorized to charge less for longer than for shorter distances for the transportation of household goods; and the Commission may from time to time prescribe the extent to which such designated common carrier may be relieved from the operation of this section.

(c)   The provisions of this section shall not be applicable to bus companies or to their rates, charges or tariffs. (1899, c. 164, s. 14; Rev., s. 1107; Ex. Sess. 1913, c. 20, s. 9; 1915, c. 17, s. 1; C.C., s. 1072; 1933, c. 134, s. 8; 1941, c. 97; 1963, c. 1165, s. 1; 1985, c. 676, s. 15(4); 1995, c. 523, s. 7.)

§ 62-142. Contracts as to rates.

All contracts and agreements between public utilities as to rates shall be submitted to the Commission for inspection that it may be seen whether or not they are a violation of law or the rules and regulations of the Commission, and all arrangements and agreements whatever as to the division of earnings of any kind by competing public utilities shall be submitted to the Commission for inspection and approval insofar as they affect the rules and regulations made by the Commission to secure to all persons doing business with such utilities just and reasonable rates. The Commission may make such rules and regulations, as to such contracts and agreements as the public interest may require. (1899, c. 164, s. 6; Rev., s. 1108; C.S., s. 1073; 1933, c. 134, s. 8; 1941, c. 97; 1963, c. 1165, s. 1.)

§ 62-143. Schedule of rates to be evidence.

The schedule of rates fixed by statute or under this Article, in suits brought against any public utility involving the rates of a public utility or unjust discrimination in relation thereto, shall be taken in all courts as prima facie evidence that the rates therein fixed are just and reasonable. Any such schedule when certified by a clerk of the Commission as a true copy of a schedule on file with the Commission shall be received in all courts as prima facie evidence of such schedule without further proof, and, if the clerk certifies that said schedule has been approved by the Commission, as prima facie evidence of such approval. (1899, c. 164, s. 7; Rev., s. 1112; C.S., s. 1077; 1933, c. 134, s. 8; 1941, c. 97; 1963, c. 1165, s. 1.)

§ 62-144. Free transportation.

(a)   All common carriers under the supervision of the Commission shall furnish free transportation to the members of the Commission, and, upon written authority of the Commission, such carriers shall also furnish free transportation to such persons as the Commission may designate in its employ or in the employ of the Department of Motor Vehicles for the inspection of equipment and supervision of safe operating conditions and of traffic upon the highways of the State.

(b)   Except as provided in subsection (a), no common carrier shall, directly or indirectly, issue, give, tender, or honor any free fares except to its bona fide officers, agents, commission agents, employees and retired employees, and members of their immediate families: Provided, that common carriers under this Article may exchange free transportation within the limits of this section and may accept as a passenger a totally blind person accompanied by a guide at the usual and ordinary fare charged to one person under such reasonable regulations as may have been established by the carrier and approved by the Commission.

(c)   Any person except those permitted by law accepting free transportation shall be guilty of a Class 1 misdemeanor.

(d)   Nothing in this section shall prohibit the carriage, storage or handling of household goods free or at reduced rates for the United States, State or municipal governments, or for charitable or educational purposes, or the use of passes for journeys wholly within this State which have been or may be issued for interstate journeys under the authority of the United States Interstate Commerce Commission. (1899, c. 164, s. 22; c. 642; 1901, c. 652; c. 679, s. 2; 1905, c. 312; Rev., s. 1105; Ex. Sess. 1908, c. 144, s. 4; 1911, cc. 49, 148; 1913, c. 100; 1915, c. 215; 1917, cc. 56, 160; C.S., ss. 1069, 1070, 3492; 1933, c. 134, s. 8; 1941, c. 97; 1949, c. 1132, s. 27; 1953, c. 1279; 1963, c. 1165, s. 1; 1993, c. 539, s. 477; 1994, Ex. Sess., c. 24, s. 14(c); 1995, c. 523, s. 8.)

§ 62-145. Rates between points connected by more than one route.

When there is more than one route between given points in North Carolina, and freight is routed or directed by the shipper or consignee to be transported over a shorter route, and it is in fact shipped by a longer route between such points, the rate fixed by law or by the Commission for the shorter route shall be the maximum rate which may be charged, and it shall be unlawful to charge more for transporting such freight over the longer route than the lawful charge for the shorter route. (Ex. Sess. 1913, c. 20, s. 11; C.S., s. 1085; 1933, c. 134, s. 8; 1941, c. 97; 1963, c. 1165, s. 1.)

Vision Books Order Form

Fax Orders:	1-980-299-5965
Phone Orders:	1-704-808-0770
E-mail Orders:	www.visionbooks.org
Mail Orders:	Vision Books, LLC P.O. Box 42406 Charlotte, NC 28215

Shipp To:
Name_____
Address_____
City_____State_____Zip_____
Phone_____Fax_____
Email_____@_____

Bill To: We can bill a third party on your behalf.
Name_____
Address_____
City_____State_____Zip_____
Phone   (   )   Fax_____
Email_____@_____

Pamphlet Number ($15.00 Each)	Qty	Total Cost
_____	_____	_____
_____	_____	_____
_____	_____	_____
_____	_____	_____
_____	_____	_____
_____	_____	_____
_____	_____	_____
_____	_____	_____
<u>Full Volume Set 1-92</u>	<u>92 Pamphlets</u>	<u>1,380.00</u>

Free Shipping Shipping & Handling on Full Volume Orders
Add $1.00 Shipping & Handling per pamphlet $_____

Total Cost $_____

Thank you for your order, Management!

DID YOU ENJOY THIS BOOK?

Vision Books, LLC would like to hear from you! If you or someone you know has been fasely imprisoned, we would like to hear your story. If the 'North Carolina Criminal Law and Procedure' has had an effect in your life or if you have suggestions, we would like to hear from you. Send your letters to:

Vision Books, LLC
Attn: Staff Writers
P.O. Box 42406
Charlotte, NC 28215
Email: staff@visionbooks.org

Order Additional Copies:

Fax Orders:	1-980-299-5965
Phone Orders:	1-704-898-0770
E-mail Orders:	www.visionbooks.org
Mail Orders:	Vision Books, LLC P.O. Box 42406 Charlotte, NC 28215

www.ingramcontent.com/pod-product-compliance
Lightning Source LLC
Chambersburg PA
CBHW051627170526
45167CB00001B/95